More than Men and Make-up

Empowering you to achieve
success and happiness

BY SEVEN SUPHI

CAPSTONE

Copyright © 2006 by Seven Suphi

First published 2006 by

Capstone Publishing Limited (a Wiley Company)
The Atrium
Southern Gate
Chichester
West Sussex
PO19 8SQ
www.wileyeurope.com

Email (for orders and customer service enquires): cs-books@wiley.co.uk

Other Wiley Editorial Offices
John Wiley & Sons Inc., 111 River Street, Hoboken, NJ 07030, USA
Jossey-Bass, 989 Market Street, San Francisco, CA 94103-1741, USA
Wiley-VCH Verlag GmbH, Boschstr. 12, D-69469 Weinheim, Germany
John Wiley & Sons Australia Ltd, 42 McDougall Street, Milton, Queensland 4064, Australia
John Wiley & Sons (Asia) Pte Ltd, 2 Clementi Loop #02-01, Jin Xing Distripark, Singapore 129809
John Wiley & Sons Canada Ltd, 22 Worcester Road, Etobicoke, Ontario, Canada M9W 1L1
Wiley also publishes its books in a variety of electronic formats. Some content that appears in print may not be available in electronic books.

British Library Cataloging in Publication Data

A catalogue record for this book is available from the British Library

ISBN 13: 978-1-84112-734-7
ISBN 10: 1-84112-734-5

Typeset in Swiss 721 BT 9.5/14pt by Sparks (www.sparks.co.uk)

Printed and bound in Great Britain by TJ International Ltd, Padstow, Cornwall

This book is printed on acid-free paper responsibly manufactured from sustainable forestry in which at least two trees are planted for each one used for paper production.

Substantial discounts on bulk quantities of Capstone Books are available to corporations, professional associations and other organizations. For details telephone John Wiley & Sons on (+44) 1243–770441, fax (+44) 1243 770571 or email corporatedevelopment@wiley.co.uk

About the Author

SEVEN SUPHI is a High Performance Coach and CEO of Odyssey Solutions Ltd. Seven is a member of the International Coach Federation, a Master Practitioner of NLP and of TimeLine Therapy, a Master Hypnotist and a Reiki level 2 practitioner. She is also a first class honours graduate. Prior to becoming a coach she was an employee of Coopers & Lybrand. She has over thirteen years of corporate experience including coaching, management consultancy and sales. She is committed to one-on-one coaching, working with couples and with teams to help them gain clarity and achieve the outcomes they desire quickly and effectively. She has worked with people in companies including Accenture, IBM, PwC, Oracle, Standard Chartered, HSBC, Amex, LexisNexis and Hummingbird. She also coaches with Seventy Thirty, the exclusive matchmaking and lifestyle company for affluent and successful people. Seven has appeared on national TV and radio, including This Morning, CNN, LBC radio and also in national press, such as *Marie Claire*, *Glamour*, *Saturday Telegraph Magazine* and *The Times*.

Contents

Acknowledgements   *viii*

0.0 *Introduction*   *xi*

0.1 *Getting the Most from this Book*   *xv*

Part 1 Helping You Create the Life You Want   **1**

1.0 Introduction to Part 1   2

1.1 Core Techniques   5

    1.1.1 Relaxation   6

    1.1.2 Circle of Life   8

    1.1.3 Cause or Effect   12

    1.1.4 Reframe: bad to great   15

    1.1.5 Motivation   18

    1.1.6 Perception and reality   21

    1.1.7 Feedback   23

1.2 Know and Accept Yourself   26

    1.2.1 Who am I?   28

    1.2.2 Accept yourself   32

    1.2.3 Values   36

    1.2.4 Beliefs   39

    1.2.5 Behaviours   43

1.3 Know What You Want   46

    1.3.1 Know what you want   48

    1.3.2 Outcome   50

    1.3.3 Life Purpose   53

    1.3.4 Goals   60

1.4 Enjoy the Journey   65

    1.4.1 Enjoy the journey   67

    1.4.2 Eliminate blocks   68

    1.4.3 More confidence and fun each day   81

    1.4.4 Circle of Empowerment   82

    1.4.5 Perception Enhancer   86

    1.4.6 Daily habit   91

1.5   Conclusion to Part 1   94

Part 2: Dealing with Specific Life Challenges   95

2.0 Introduction to Part 2   96

2.1 Relationships   98

    2.1.1 The secret of finding the *right* man   99

    2.1.2 Keeping your man, or not!   108

    2.1.3 Is your man cheating on you?   114

    2.1.4 Starting to date again   121

2.2 Work   127

    2.2.1 Gaining respect at work   128

    2.2.2 Discovering if you're in the right job/career 138

    2.2.3 Making the most of redundancy   147

    2.2.4 Starting work with a boost   151

2.3 Family   161

    2.3.1 Making the most of your time with a new baby 162

    2.3.2 Getting the most out of being a stay-at-home mum 167

    2.3.3 Maximizing your relationship with your kids   173

    2.3.4 Dealing with infertility   179

    2.3.5 Juggling kids, partner, home and work effectively 185

2.4 Finding a Path in Life   191
    2.4.1 Discovering the something that's missing in your life   193
    2.4.2 Re-evaluating your life   199
2.5 Self-esteem   209
    2.5.1 Boosting your confidence   210
    2.5.2 Discovering the attractive and wonderful you   216
    2.5.3 Reversing feelings of self-hatred   222
    2.5.4 Making life less difficult   229
2.6 Health   237
    2.6.1 Losing weight naturally and keeping it off   238
    2.6.2 Giving up smoking   248
    2.6.3 Dealing with PMT   259
    2.6.4 Beating the difficulties of menopause   265
    2.6.5 Eliminating anxiety, worry and stress   271
2.7 Coping with Life Changes   278
    2.7.1 Making the most of a big birthday   279
    2.7.2 Coping with the kids leaving home   283
    2.7.3 Retiring with flair   289
    2.7.4 Coping with losing a loved one   295
2.8 Conclusion to Part 2   301
3.0 More than Men and Make-up – Conclusion   303
Appendices   307
Bibliography   323

Acknowledgements

Writing this book has been an amazing journey, and many people have helped in different ways through its many stages. I thank you all for your support.

Firstly I would like to thank my clients, friends and colleagues who were involved in the research for this book. As I have used fictitious names and altered personal stories I cannot name each of you individually, but I truly appreciate the time, effort and openness you have contributed – you have all helped to make the book what it is today. Thank you.

Like many people I had always believed I would write a book, but if it were not for my cousin Güny (Günsel Suphi) this book wouldn't be here now. It was how Güny lived and her untimely death that spurred me onto writing this when I did – I wish you were still here, and that we could share these adventures together. May your body rest in peace and your spirit fly amongst the farthest corners of the universe enlightening everything that falls upon your path.

Thanks to Sally Smith my editor, for seeing the potential in me and my first book, which you have guided into what it is today. Thank you also for teaming me up with Jill Jeffries, my assistant editor, who has worked diligently to beautifully transform my words by moving a few around and adding very little, making the text more fluid and enticing whilst retaining its meaning and essence. You have a wonderful gift and it has been a real pleasure working with you – thank you.

Also a big thank you to Kate Stanley, Felicity Roberts, and Grace O'Byrne for the marketing, publicity, and production of this book – your expertise is very much appreciated.

I must also say a special thanks to Mike Southon for introducing me to Sally – a true entrepreneur and a man with a great heart and spirit for life – thank you for this introduction as well as the countless others. Equally thanks to Tony Heywood who has helped in connecting me to many key people, one of whom was Mike. Another person who was instrumental in shaping my thoughts was Chris O'Hanlon – thank you very much for your insights, energy and kindness.

I am delighted that Abner Stein agreed to be my agent; thanks to Caspian Dennis for guiding me through the intricacies of publishing, and to Tessa Ingham for helping with the legalities of it – your help and support has been invaluable.

There is one person who has supported and helped me from the book's conception to its current conclusion. You have given me editorial, business and personal advice and your help has been instrumental in discovering many different solutions including The Glide Method. You have reviewed this book more times than any other person. My dear friend Dave Shuker – thank you for your friendship, love and intellect. You have helped me to grow and blossom in ways I had not expected, and I'd equally like to thank you for the opportunity and privilege of contributing to your life. May we continue to help each other grow.

There are four other dear friends I would also like to thank for countless deep conversations and specifically for reviewing this book – it's not an easy task and I appreciate your insights, advice and additional contributions: Bella Savani who connected me with many key people; Sajad Hussain who offered many insights into the effectiveness of the exercises; Liz Shuker whose openness, support and literary insights improved many parts of the book and Mary Ely whose expertise and countless quotes were all gratefully received.

Family and friends are incredibly important to me and though there are too many of you to list here I would like to thank you all for your understanding, support and love. Specifically I would like to thank my sister, Sinem Suphi, whose energy, courage and great sense of style has been an inspiration to many including me – if it were not for you I would not have started my business many years ago, without which there wouldn't be any content with which to even contemplate this book. Thank you dear sister for being you and for reviewing my work – we may disagree at times yet the bond that keeps us together is the one and only true bond – love.

Mum and Dad: this book is dedicated to you because of your unconditional love and undying support throughout my life, including throughout the compilation of this book – thank you for the countless delicious meals, errands and kind words – thank you for it all and above all for nurturing me to grow into the person I am today – I love you both unconditionally, always.

Introduction

Take a moment to think about what you would most like to change in your life. Is it something around your career? Your family? Your relationship with your partner? What is it you really want for yourself?

We live at a time where our old ways of living are increasingly ineffective; the way we naturally learn and evolve is far too slow for the rate of change and pace of life today. To ensure you give yourself the best chance of happiness and success it's important that you empower yourself as much as possible. That's what this book aims to do – to help you utilize the full power of your mind: your conscious logical mind and your intuition, your 'sixth sense' – and as a consequence you'll be able to understand yourself at a far deeper level and empower yourself with the most significant asset you have – you.

This book makes available to everyone techniques that, up until now, only the privileged few have experienced. It's designed to consolidate the things I have learned as a personal coach over many years and present them in a way that will be of most use to you. It's a tool to help you explore yourself and those around you so that you can empower yourself and create the life you want – it enables you to take control of fate and helps you design your own destiny.

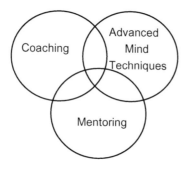

Over the past ten years the concept of personal coaching has been evolving rapidly. Although some standardization is emerging, there is still a lot of confusion in this area, so it's important to be absolutely clear about the type of advanced coaching used in this book. I call it 'High Performance Coaching' and it covers three areas of expertise: Pure Coaching, where the main skills are the questioning and listening abilities of the coach; Advanced Mind Techniques, which are things like Neuro-Linguistic Programming, Hypnosis, the Glide Method and other techniques that utilize the logical and emotional minds; and Mentoring, when someone gives advice based on their own experience in a similar situation. The scope of expertise in this book is the overlap between these three areas, as shown in the diagram above. The techniques that I introduce in this book will work for everyone who wishes to use them. They tap in to the deepest stores of your own wisdom and help you to help yourself. They have been used by many people over many years, with great success.

The book is divided into two parts. Part 1 is full of highly effective techniques to help you create the life you want. It can be read on its own for a complete life coaching make-over. Part 2 looks specifically at different challenges you may face in your life and suggests ways of dealing with them using some of the techniques described in Part 1.

More Than Men and Make-up will introduce you to many powerful techniques that can help you address the root causes of some of the biggest challenges and problems women face in life. It's designed to help you address them in a way that's unique for you, and enables you to do so speedily and practically.

So consider again what you would most like to change in your life and make that your objective as you read through the book.

I wish you an adventurous, fun and enlightening journey – one where you discover more about yourself, and others, than you ever thought possible. Above all, I hope that this book will help you to become more empowered, happy and successful.

Seven Suphi
London, 2006

Getting the Most from this Book

This book is divided into two parts.

Part 1 – Effective solutions:

- explanations of why the techniques are important, and how they work; and
- exercises that apply the techniques to your unique situation so that you can find the best outcome for yourself.

Part 2 – Common challenges women face in life:

- examples of specific problems others have faced;
- a suggested path through the exercises in Part 1 to help you through the issues; and
- details of how the process has helped others.

To really make the most of *More Than Men and Make-Up*, you should have a clear objective in mind. I recommend that you initially read through Part 1 and familiarize yourself with the concepts and techniques of coaching. This is a very useful journey to go through in its own right as it will help you gain insight into your life, your aims, beliefs and priorities, and give you a lot of the groundwork for later chapters. The modules in Part 2 are there for you as and when you wish to work through them. You can use the book in the way that suits you best, at whatever stage you are at in your life.

The exercises are meant to be easy and quick – some will only take a few minutes to complete, others may require longer. Take as much time as you like. Create some space in your life to work on you, to focus on the challenges that you face. You can be sure the time will be well spent.

Many people like to do these exercises on their own, focusing all of their energy on their personal area of interest. Others prefer to do the exercises with a friend, a 'buddy', so they can support and encourage each other as the exercises bring up new discoveries. Either way is equally valid – just do what suits you best.

PRINCIPLES OF SUCCESS AND HAPPINESS

While reading this book, there are three fundamental principles that I would like you to keep in mind.

- Be true to yourself.
- Take 100% responsibility.
- Go to the root causes.

These principles will enable you to take best advantage of the concepts and exercises in the book. They will help bring you empowerment, and the success, happiness and fulfilment that empowerment brings. It's important to be consciously aware of the principles, because if you find yourself in a situation where you don't know which way to turn (maybe your logic is pointing you in one direction, and your emotions in another) then one or all three will act as a shining light, guiding you.

1 – Be true to yourself

Whatever we do, and wherever we are on our journey, is just fine. We all have our own unique path. Sometimes we do very well and things fall into place for us, whilst at other times our lives are challenging and difficult, with many obstacles and setbacks.

What's important is that we are congruent –'true to ourselves' – throughout these times, so that we're not complacent when things go well, or disillusioned and disheartened when they don't. Being true to yourself is as easy as it is tricky, however. To look at the real you with honesty you don't have to go far, and yet it can be very difficult. We create so many illusions of reality that it can be hard to let go of them. Once we start to let go of them, though, we quickly realize how wonderfully liberating and empowering it is.

When we choose to be true to ourselves, to live our values, and to fulfil our life's purpose, everything is simplified. By staying true to ourselves, our path and our life's journey unfold one step at a time.

Not knowing which way to turn is an indication that you need to give the challenge more attention, perhaps gathering more information, and looking at that area of your life very carefully so that you can be absolutely sure you are doing the right thing for you at that time.

Writing this book was one of those instances in my life where my gut said one thing and logic another – I stayed true to myself and evaluated my options and in the end decided to go for it. I learnt so much more than I could have possibly imagined that it's amazing to me now that I ever considered not doing it. Generally that's exactly what living life 'true to oneself' is like – far simpler, happier, more exciting and fulfilling than you would have believed possible.

So be true to yourself and let your life's true path unfold beyond your expectations.

2 – Take 100% responsibility

All too often, when things go wrong, people fail to take responsibility for their part in the problem, even going so far as to point the finger directly at someone else.

Taking responsibility in an environment when others don't is as challenging as it is rewarding. It's challenging to act against an atmosphere of fault-finding and blaming, and equally it's empowering, because by taking responsibility you give yourself far more opportunity to learn and grow. Your energy and attention, instead of being spent on denial and falsifications, which is draining and disempowering, are focused instead on growth and empowerment, which substantially enriches your life.

With single, day-to-day events it may not appear to matter, but when you start to look at the effect of those small events as they stack up over weeks, months and years, you begin to see the positive, cumulative effect of taking responsibility – our ability to achieve is drastically increased.

Even at times when you really don't feel you are in any way responsible, it's worth considering the question 'If I were to take full responsibility for this, what would I learn that might be of some use for me in the future?' For example, say you discover your long-term partner has been cheating on you. If you take the view that he's nothing but a liar and a cheat, you'd be right, but besides making you feel better for a short while it wouldn't get you anywhere. More than likely it would make you feel like a victim and might even eat away at you and affect future relationships. By asking yourself the question 'If I were to take full responsibility for this, what would I learn that might be of some use for me in the future?' and taking on that responsibility, you can get to the cause of the problem. By looking openly at the situation you can learn what you need to learn and because of this be able to let go of the past and truly start to move forward and enjoy your future journey, baggage-free and with more knowledge.

Maybe you'll realize that you chose to go out with him, perhaps even ignoring the warning signs from your sixth sense, and you'll be able to walk away with the empowering lessons that you should listen to and respect your sixth sense and that you need to look again at how you select a partner.

In any given situation we always have a choice over how we react – by choosing to take responsibility we give ourselves more opportunity to learn and grow.

Consider an event in your past that you felt bad about and ask yourself the question 'If I were to take full responsibility for this, what would I learn that might be of some use for me in the future?' and give yourself a few minutes of contemplation time to come up with your personal insights.

3 – Go to the root cause

Imagine opening your fridge and finding that an unpleasant smell lurks within. You wouldn't just put a fridge freshener in there and hope the smell goes away, you'd follow your nose, literally, to find the culprit and dispose of it, cleaning any area that may have been affected. Maybe *then* you'd use a fridge freshener, but only as a 'nice to have', not as the solution to the problem.

Using the fridge freshener as a quick fix would only have covered up the problem temporarily, allowing the culprit to fester, grow and become stronger.

Deluding ourselves when we unconsciously know there is something wrong works in exactly the same way, leaving the real cause of the problem to fester until it gets to a point where it's obvious to everyone. There is only one effective way to solve any problem – find the root cause and deal with it.

To use this book effectively, follow these three principles and, either with a buddy or on your own, go through Part 1 first, then go through those sections in Part 2 that are most appropriate for you. Work through them with an attitude of curiosity and fun that will enable you to enjoy the discoveries about yourself and others. Be as curious as Einstein:

'I have no special talent. I am only passionately curious.'
Albert Einstein

Helping You Create the Life You Want

Introduction to Part 1

In Part 1 you'll find the techniques to help you to create the kind of life you want. They can be used alone, or in conjunction with Part 2 for dealing with specific challenges in your life.

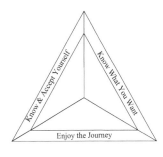

Part 1 comprises four distinct areas. The first area – *Core Techniques* – can be used at any time, in just about any situation, to give you greater flexibility and choice. The other three areas form the sides to our balanced triangle: *Know and Accept Yourself* is full of skills you can use to truly understand yourself and others, and accept what you find; *Know What You Want* is about understanding the importance of knowing what you want, and in discovering what that may be; finally, *Enjoy the Journey* is full of techniques designed to make life that bit easier for you and to maximize your effectiveness and happiness.

In any journey we undertake there is a recipe for a successful outcome – if you want to get from A to B you need to know where you are now, confirm that B is where you want to get to, and know what method you'll use to get there. With those points covered you can then focus on enjoying the journey.

BALANCE IS KEY

Balancing the three elements of *Know and Accept Yourself*, *Know What*

You Want and *Enjoy The Journey* is essential for leading a happy and fulfilled life. If you focused only on knowing and accepting yourself, you'd be a very self-absorbed person who couldn't achieve much. This can happen when we are deeply emotional about something and can make us lose perspective on the big picture.

Or imagine if you mainly focused on what you want – your outcome, your purpose, and your goals. Depending on your character, you could either end up in a fantasy world full of dreams, in the pits of despair for not getting what you want, or, if you are incredibly driven, you might achieve great success but be left wondering what happened to your life while you were being so focused. Men often follow this pattern in life. Some are very good at focusing on a goal no matter what. Then, having achieved it, they discover later in life that it's an empty victory and a mid-life crisis kicks in.

 Finally, if you spent all your time just enjoying the journey you would have a good time whilst you were doing it but you'd be likely to end up with a sense of loss that you hadn't achieved anything and wondering if there isn't more to life than pure enjoyment.

Many of us have experienced one or all of these extremes at certain times in our lives – it's a part of growing up and maturing. But it's worth remembering that each element is as important as the other, and that they need to be kept in balance in our lives or we tend to lose our way.

As you go through the modules in Part 1 you'll see references to this triangle – they are there to highlight how that particular module can benefit you within the overall picture so that you are absolutely clear at every stage.

Core Techniques

Module	Title	Page	Exercise time (mins)
1.1.1	Relaxation	9	30
1.1.2	Circle of Life	11	30
1.1.3	Cause or Effect	15	15
1.1.4	Reframe: bad to great	18	20
1.1.5	Motivation	21	30
1.1.6	Perception and reality	24	10
1.1.7	Feedback	26	15

(It will take approximately 2 hours and 30 minutes to complete all the exercises.)

1.1.1 RELAXATION

'Every now and then go away, have a little relaxation, for when you come back to your work your judgement will be surer. Go some distance away because then the work appears smaller and more of it can be taken in at a glance and a lack of harmony and proportion is more readily seen.'

Leonardo Da Vinci

Relaxation is crucial in utilizing the power of your mind and enabling you to make your discoveries quickly and effortlessly – plus of course it feels pleasurable – so it's imperative that we cover this skill first.

You need to be centred and curious, able to let yourself go completely and trust yourself to learn the most from your experiences. The exercise below is designed to help you achieve this. Some find it easier and quicker to achieve than others, but all can get there – it's just a matter of time.

Exercise – Relax

Aim: To be able to go into a state of deep relaxation while staying aware enough to follow the exercises.

Duration: 30 minutes

What you need:

- an open mind
- an attitude of curiosity and fun
- a safe, quiet environment, free of distractions and disruptions

Important point: Focus within.

1   Sit in a naturally comfortable position for you that allows the blood to flow freely around your body. Let each muscle relax and feel your body becoming heavy. You are aiming for the very relaxed state that you are normally in when you are about to fall asleep.

2   Remember a time in your past, a specific time, where you felt a deep sense of relaxation and calm. As you remember this time, in your mind's eye, go back and experience it again as if it's now: What do you see around you? How do you feel? (Let the feeling wash all over you now.) What do you hear? Smell? **Relax** your body now in exactly the same way, live the experience again as if it were now, and every time you see the word '**Relax**', multiply that feeling and become even more deeply relaxed.

3   As you are sitting there, be aware of your body – your limbs, torso, face – be aware of how your body feels inside and out. Relax your muscles even further and focus. Increase the relaxation throughout your body starting from your toes, your whole feet, up to your ankles, calves, knees, thighs, bum, waist, whole torso. Focus in on your shoulders, relaxing them even more, then your arms and hands (you may be feeling a nice tingling sensation and that's absolutely fine – it's an indication you are getting more relaxed, another indication is that your limbs feel heavy and rather lethargic, like you can barely move or stay awake). Then move the relaxation to your neck, head and face, notice your muscles just relaxing, pay particular attention to the areas around your eyes and mouth, ensuring all are completely relaxed now.

4   Notice your breathing, and with each exhalation relax all your muscles even further. Starting again from your toes, through your whole feet, your ankles, calves, knees, thighs, bum, waist, torso. Focus again on your shoulders, relaxing them even more, then your arms, hands and finally your neck, head and face.

5   Go back to point 3 and repeat the exercise two more times, each time deepening the relaxation further. (Once you have done that and are fully relaxed, then go to point 6.)

6   Every time you see the following text relax your body to this deep level by taking yourself back to this comfortable, relaxed place – you'll see it often throughout the book:

'**Relax –** Sit comfortably and be aware of your body. Feel each muscle in relaxing, and your body becoming heavier with each exhalation.'

With practice you'll be able to reach this state quite quickly.

1.1.2 CIRCLE OF LIFE

'All things appear and disappear because of the concurrence of causes and conditions. Nothing ever exists entirely alone; everything is in relation to everything else.'

Buddha

The Circle of Life is a wonderful tool that helps you gain a different perspective about your life. It looks at eight main areas of life: Partner; Family; Friends; Wealth; Career (it may or may not be paid work, though it often is); Spirituality (how centred and in touch you are within yourself); Fitness; Health.

These areas encompass your whole life. Some people like to rename them or change them around a little, especially to put Health and Fitness together and add Hobbies as another segment. It's completely up to you, but for your first time its recommended that you keep to what is here unless you have a very strong desire to do otherwise, because it has been found to work for most people.

Exercise – Spider's Web
Aim: To get a snapshot of where you are in the eight areas of your life, and to see how balanced your life is.

Duration: 30 minutes

What you need:

- an open mind
- an attitude of curiosity and fun
- a safe, quiet environment, free of distractions and disruptions
- one sheet of paper

Important point: Be relaxed to get the most from the exercise.

Relax – Sit comfortably and be aware of your body. Feel each muscle relaxing, and your body becoming heavier with each exhalation.

1 Look at each of the areas in the Circle of Life diagram above and ask yourself:

'Out of a maximum of ten, what score would I give myself for where I am currently, based on how happy and satisfied I am with my behaviour and achievements in each of the different areas of my life?'

By plotting your scores you will end up with a spider's web, something like this:

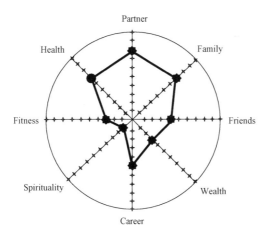

Try it out for yourself with the empty one below:

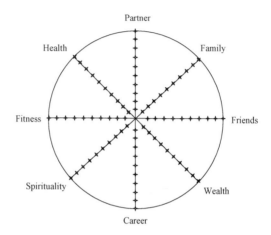

2   Look objectively at your spider's web:
   a   What patterns do you see?
   b   Where are there inconsistencies?
   c   What are you pleased with?
   d   In which areas would you like to increase your score?
   e   Consider how one area of your life may influence another (positively or negatively).

A good balance is more likely to bring harmony into your life but these things are all very personal. One way to look at it is to consider yourself as an individual and your life as a whole, and work out the most effective balance for you based on your purpose, values, beliefs, behaviours and goals (we'll cover more on these topics later). For now, though, let's consider the earlier example:

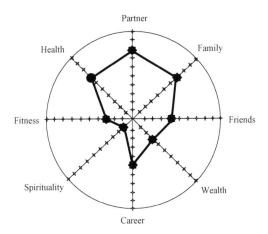

At first glance it would appear that Fitness, Spirituality, Friends and Wealth are the areas that require attention now. However, it may be that Partner fluctuates from 8 to 0 on a periodic basis, and if having a partner is really important to you then it may be more effective for you to focus on that first.

Most of you will instinctively know which areas would benefit from your attention, but for those of you who are unclear or are curious to gather more information, create a spider's web for the past 5–10 years. This should give you a good indication of where to start.

Apart from the Spider's Web, the Circle of Life is also the basis of two important template charts you'll need in later exercises. The Guidance Chart (Appendix A) gives you a bird's-eye view of your progress as you tick off each section in the chart as you work through it. It includes an area in the middle to write down your Life's Purpose. The One Area Chart (Appendix B) enables you to record a summary of your values, beliefs, behaviours, goals and blocks for one specific area of your life.

1.1.3 CAUSE OR EFFECT

'If I always appear prepared, it is because before entering an undertaking, I have meditated long and have foreseen what might occur. It is not genius which reveals to me suddenly and secretly what I should do in circumstances unexpected by others; it is thought and preparation.'

Napoleon Bonaparte

Cause or Effect is a very simple theory that, just by understanding it, gives you greater choice, flexibility and empowerment. The concept is that in any given situation you are either *at cause* or *at effect*, empowered or disempowered. There is no middle ground with this and you choose which side you're on.

To be *at cause* is to take 100% responsibility for yourself and everything that happens to you; it enables you to be absolutely in control of your experiences, choosing your responses and your reality. To be *at effect* is to think and feel that someone or something other than yourself influences and controls you, and your response/life is determined by this outside factor. By being *at effect* you are to all intents and purposes a 'victim' and need to be rescued.

Cause or Effect type of thinking/behaving

At Cause – SOLUTION focused	At Effect – PROBLEM focused
• What do I need to get what I want?	• Justifying your actions
• What's important here?	• Dwelling on how bad the situation is
• What's the best possible outcome here?	• Focusing on negative feelings and dwelling on other similar past events
• Who can help with this?	• Finding someone to punish
• Focusing how on how good you will feel when solved	

Imagine a relationship with someone you love but who treats you badly – a man who doesn't keep to his word, can be manipulative and is sometimes a bit of a bully. If you are *at cause* you are likely to take responsibility for your situation and decide on what you are willing to tolerate or not for 'love'. You ultimately know you have the choice over whether to stay or leave and you'll take action that furthers what you want. If you are *at effect*, however, you may complain to your friends about him but feel you have no choice as to what to do and stay in the situation, stuck and unable to move. Things in your life cause you to be unhappy and you feel you have no power to stop them.

Being *at cause* is empowering, opens up possibilities and opportunities, and feels positive. Sometimes it can feel good to wallow for a bit but the important thing is to be aware that we have a choice, that we can chose to perceive our glass as half full or half empty. (See page 24 for more on this topic.)

In any given situation you have various degrees of control and influence, ranging from complete personal control to none at all (i.e. over what time the sun rises). Sometimes you can be in a middle-ground area, with no direct control but with the power to influence, such as with friends and family, or to a lesser extent, friends of friends and contacts.

Understanding the influence we have over a given situation gives us wisdom and empowers us.

Exercise
Aim: To help you understand whether you are *at cause* or *at effect* in any given situation and to help you move to *cause* if you so wish.
Duration: 15 minutes
What you need:
- an open mind
- an attitude of curiosity and fun
- a safe, quiet environment, free of distractions and disruptions

Important points:

- Be relaxed to get the most from the exercise.
- Have a situation you are slightly unhappy with in mind to use in the exercise.

Relax – Sit comfortably and be aware of your body. Feel each muscle relaxing, and your body becoming heavier with each exhalation.

1 Consider the *at cause*, solution-focused thinking and the *at effect*, problem-focused thinking detailed on page 15 and ask yourself 'Are my thoughts and behaviours those of someone who's *at cause* or *at effect*?' (Please note: if you are having trouble identifying what the answer is then consider if you feel like a victim or as though someone is victimizing you. If so, you're definitely *at effect*.)

2 Consider the question 'Do I have real control over this situation?' If the answer is yes, consider what's stopping you from getting what you want. If the answer is no, ask yourself the following questions:

  a What do I need to do to get what I want?

  b What's really important here?

  c What's the best possible outcome?

  d Experience how good you'll feel when you get what you want.

3 Think about the degree of influence you might have. Do you know anyone who has control over the outcome?

  a Consider the best way to influence them – ask yourself what's in it for them.

  b Decide what's the best time to approach them and how that approach should be made.

4 Do you know anyone else who has influence over this situation?

  a Consider the best way of influencing them – ask yourself what's in it for them.

  b Decide what's the best time to approach them and how that approach should be made.

5 If you have no control *and* no influence, consider what you can do to improve your situation. How can you look at this situation so that

it empowers you and puts you *at cause*? Make a list of all your options now.

6   Notice how your perspective of the situation has shifted just by being aware that you have a choice. In any given situation you can now choose to be *at cause* or *at effect*.

1.1.4 REFRAME: BAD TO GREAT

'The person with the most flexibility rules the world.'

Anonymous

Reframing is looking at a situation from a different perspective, preferably one that gives you more options.

Imagine that a woman comes up to you and is verbally abusive. Your natural reaction might be to retaliate, but by considering the possibility that she might have mistaken you for someone else, be drunk, ill, or perhaps has just had a major upset in her life, you empower yourself with a choice about how best to respond.

Instantly the full impact of the quote above becomes clear – by being more flexible in your perception and behaviour you put yourself in full control, and thus become the ruler of your world, and reality.

Another simple and fun example of a reframe is:

A man walks into a bar.

'Ouch!'

If you are going through a tough time, asking yourself the question 'What can I learn from this, so I have a different experience next time?' will reframe your situation from one where you are having a tough time (being *at effect*) to one where you are empowered and are learning a great lesson for the future (being *at cause*). Another favourite of mine is to ask 'How can I look at this in a way that makes it funny?'

Many of us have a habit of framing things in very unhelpful ways. It's an interesting perspective that has been researched and accepted in psychology – take the quote below:

> 'There is also evidence that women are more likely than men to cope with stress by blaming themselves for their plights and to attribute their achievements to external factors.'
>
> (Bavison & Neale, 1994)

In other words, we are more likely to blame ourselves when things go wrong and less likely to take credit for our successes, whilst men are likely to blame something external to themselves when things go wrong and take full credit when they go well.

It's therefore a very powerful reframe just to switch these two perspectives around. Obviously if we were to always take credit for our successes and blame external factors when things go wrong we would see this as disempowering and conceited, but it's important to experience this perspective even just once. Give it a go with two specific events from your past, one that went well and one that didn't, and experience how they differ.

Exercise

Aim: To help you to reframe a past negative experience to something of value.

Duration: 20 minutes

What you need:

- an open mind
- an attitude of curiosity and fun
- a safe, quiet environment, free of distractions and disruptions
- a sheet of paper

Important point: Be relaxed to get the most from the exercise.

Relax – Sit comfortably and be aware of your body. Feel each muscle relaxing, and your body becoming heavier with each exhalation.

Consider the situation

Consider a time in your past where you had a hurtful experience. Write down on a piece of paper how you feel and what you think about this experience. Ask yourself the following:

1 What did I learn from this experience?
2 If this experience had not happened what would I have missed out on?
3 How am I limiting myself by my current perspective?
4 What would (someone you know who is very different from you) think about this experience?
5 Can this experience be perceived in a fun way?
6 In what way has this experience benefited my life now?
7 How will I view this experience in ten years' time? In twenty years' time?
8 How have these questions helped shift my perspective?

It's a powerful little technique that improves and grows with practice until you ultimately rule your world.

The solution I suggest to my clients, and use myself, is to take 100% responsibility for everything that goes on in and around your life, good and bad. When good things happen highlight and celebrate them, and if something unwanted happens, look for the learning and the good in it.

Three famous and powerful reframes are:

'No one can hurt you without your consent.'

Eleanor Roosevelt

'They cannot take away our self-respect if we do not give it to them.'

Gandhi

'A person who never made a mistake never tried anything new.'

Albert Einstein

1.1.5 MOTIVATION

'Always bear in mind that your own resolution to succeed is more important than any one thing.'

Abraham Lincoln

Your internal drive to take action is motivation, and that's what fuels you to get what you want. Imagine a time in your past where you were truly motivated and nothing was going to stop you. This drive would have either been towards something very pleasurable, such as money or recognition (towards motivation), or away from something you really didn't want, like losing your job, losing a relationship, or fear of being alone (away from motivation).

Often, a bit of both is involved, e.g. wanting to lose weight so that you are be able to get into your thin wardrobe *and* fear of being fat.

Motivation is a skill

Many people believe that you either have motivation or you don't; that it's something that happens, and that it can't be learned or controlled. The truth of the matter is that getting ourselves, or others, motivated is a skill. It's just that some people pick it up unconsciously, whereas for the rest of us it has to be learnt, with conscious effort. Whatever the degree of effort involved, motivation is a powerful skill to have.

Interestingly, most people find it easy to pick up once they realize it's just a technique and, as with every skill, to master it fully, time and practice are needed. Just as with learning to drive a car, we learn the concepts but applying them in practice has its own challenges and rewards. However, before long we are driving without consciously thinking about it.

Exercise – Motivation check

Aim: To help you to uncover your level of commitment for achieving what you want and give you tangible, personal and powerful drivers to get there.

(It's a wonderful technique that is deceptively powerful and it's possible that you may find you are actually not as interested in something as you had initially thought – that's fine too, as it will save you from wasting your time pursuing it.)

Duration: 30 minutes

What you need:

- an open mind
- an attitude of curiosity and fun
- a safe, quiet environment, free of distractions and disruptions
- (if you are doing this on your own) recording equipment – you may wish to record this passage then play it back to yourself)

Important points:

- Be relaxed to get the most from the exercise.
- Really get into the scenarios, as though you are there.

Relax – Sit comfortably and be aware of your body. Feel each muscle relaxing, and your body becoming heavier with each exhalation.

Scenario 1

Imagine the thing you want to achieve. Then imagine you no longer wish to achieve it, and you carry on with your life as you have done in the past.

Now go five years out into your future. What will have happened? Take a few minutes to consider what your situation will be if you take no action. What are you doing? What are you thinking? What are you feeling? What's going on around you? What do you hear? What do you see? How has life changed? How does it affect your family? How does it affect your friends? How does it affect your job/career? How does it affect your health? Really delve into what it would be like, experience it as if you are there now. Even if you want to shy away from it, just stay with it for the experience.

Now go ten years out into your future and consider it all again. When you know exactly what it would be like – STOP, take a deep breath and wipe your mind clear. The easiest way of doing this is to see brilliant white in your mind's eye and shake/wriggle your body. (If you start laughing, that's all the better!).

Scenario 2
Now, imagine a different scenario – that you are fully motivated and that you achieve what you want.

Go five years out into the future and see how your life is different. Take a few minutes to consider it now. What are you doing? What are you thinking? What are you feeling? What's going on around you? What do you hear? What do you see? How has life changed? How does it affect your family? How does it affect your friends? How does it affect your job/career? How does it affect your health?

Now go ten years out into the future and consider how achieving what you want will mean to your life then. Again, really explore what it would be like, experience it as if you are there now, really live and feel what it's like. It's good to dwell on this, to have your whole body soak up what it would mean, and how great it would feel.

Final choice
Which scenario is more important to you? What is it you really want? If it's Scenario 1, then appreciate that you have the clarity now and will not be wasting your time trying to achieve something you don't want. If it's Scenario 2, then you will have dramatically increased your 'away from' and 'towards' motivation helping you to get what you truly want. Ultimately, know that every day you are making choices between such scenarios – the minutes, hours and days all add up into weeks, months and years. Build the life you choose to have.

1.1.6 PERCEPTION AND REALITY

'We don't see things as they are; we see them as we are.'

Anais Nin

What Anais Nin means by this is that we perceive the world through the 'lens' of our conditioning – our values, beliefs and past behaviours.

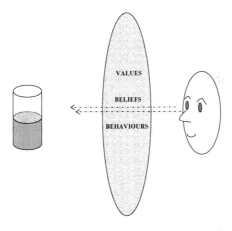

A glass half filled with water can be perceived to be half empty, half full, or not there at all – according to the lens through which we 'see' it. This perception changes as we change internally, though, because we in effect change the filters through which we see the world according to our life experiences, our values, beliefs and past behaviours. So, by changing a belief that, for example, 'I can't paint' to 'I can paint', you are changing the lens through which you see the world and your perception shifts from, in this case, an inability to paint to being able to paint, perhaps with just a need to improve your technique.

We have all had experiences where we supposed one thing at the time, but then, by looking at the situation from a different perspective (by gaining more information), we shifted our perception by 180 degrees. If a glass is 50 per cent full, what's the value to us of perceiving it as half empty when it is just as accurate to perceive it as half full?

Imagine you are annoyed at your partner because he spends long hours at his office and isn't pulling his weight at home. You may feel frustrated, alone, unappreciated and feel the burden of having to 'carry' him. We can see how easy it would be to change these negative feelings on discovering that he is stressed because he fears losing his job and letting you down.

To get as true a picture as possible the trick is to watch out for inconsistencies, to always be curious about how things fit together and support each other, and ultimately to know that 'reality' can be, and generally is, distorted by our perception of it.

Exercise

Aim: Playing with reality so that you empower yourself and have a more enjoyable life.

Duration: 10 minutes

What you need:

- an open mind
- an attitude of curiosity and fun
- a safe, quiet environment, free of distractions and disruptions

Important point: Be relaxed to get the most from the exercise.

Relax – Sit comfortably and be aware of your body. Feel each muscle relaxing, and your body becoming heavier with each exhalation.

1   Think about whether you like the 'glass half full' perspective and, if you do, commit to perceiving your life in this way from now on.

2   Consider something in your life that you thought to be 'negative' and ask yourself:

a   How can this situation be viewed from the 'glass half full' perspective?

b   What are the things I've learned, or gained because of this thing? (Make a list and dwell on it for a minute or two.)

3   Play out in your mind a future event where you catch yourself focusing on a negative, and as you do so you notice it and do the following straight away:

   a   Congratulate yourself for noticing.

   b   Make a list of all that you are thinking and feeling.

   c   Look objectively and ensure you amend the list so that it's coming from a half full perspective.

   d   Notice how that makes a difference to your perspective of yourself, your energy levels, how you feel and what you are able to achieve.

4   Consider how this 'glass half full' perspective alone can transform your life – in five, even ten, years' time.

1.1.7 FEEDBACK

'I haven't failed. I've identified 10,000 ways this doesn't work'
Thomas Alva Edison, after his failed attempts to make the
electric light bulb produce illumination

Feedback is an absolutely fundamental concept to ensure you get what you want. It's a simple shift in perspective on how you deal with an outcome, especially one that's different to the one you intended, and will enable you to get your outcome in the future.

You'll have times in your past when you didn't get what you wanted, where you had set your heart on something and then 'failed' – or at least that's what you may have thought and felt about it. It's a common perspective in our society and one which stifles and disempowers us – getting us to focus on other times when we also didn't get what we wanted.

When you were a baby learning to walk, how many times did you fall over before you succeeded? What did you instinctively do to ensure you achieved your objective? Imagine persevering at something until you get it, in the same way that you did then, certain that the only possible failure is to give up, and that until you succeed you are just learning how not to do something until you discover the right way. Imagine how that perspective could change your energy levels and your approach to life.

The picture below is a visual representation of the full scope of self-empowerment – how you can choose to feed back what you learn from any situation, whether you get the outcome you wanted or not, and can use this information to redefine your outcome or refine how you try and achieve it. It's worth remembering Einstein's definition of insanity and ensuring you truly take on your insights and change your behaviour:

> *'Insanity: doing the same thing over and over again and expecting different results.'*

Albert Einstein

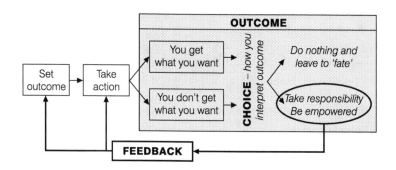

Exercise

Aim: To help you to use the feedback model effectively in any situation you desire.

Duration: 15 minutes

What you need:

- an open mind
- an attitude of curiosity and fun
- a safe, quiet environment, free of distractions and disruptions

Important point: Be relaxed to get the most from the exercise.

Relax – Sit comfortably and be aware of your body. Feel each muscle relaxing, and your body becoming heavier with each exhalation.

1   Consider a specific situation you would like to use the feedback model with and ask yourself the following questions:

   a   Did you get what you wanted?

   b   What worked really well?

   c   What could be improved?

   d   Overall how did it go and what are your insights for next time?

2   Imagine how your life would have been different if you had consistently used this model in the past.

3   Picture using it in the future to positively affect your life in five, or even ten, years' time.

Know and Accept Yourself

Module	Title	Page	Exercise time (mins)
1.2.1	Who am I?	32	30
1.2.2	Accept yourself	36	10
1.2.3	Values	39	20
1.2.4	Beliefs	43	30
1.2.5	Behaviours	47	30

(It will take approximately 2 hours to complete all the exercises for one area of your life. If you wish to work through all the areas of your life then multiply the exercise time for Values, Beliefs and Behaviours by the number of areas you wish to work on.)

1.2.1 WHO AM I?

'Gnothi seauton' ('Know thyself')
Carved into the lintel at the Temple of Apollo, the Delphic oracle

Enjoy the Journey

Most of us recognize that knowing and accepting ourselves is important for a good state of mind, and we tend to believe that we already do it. To an extent it's true, but it isn't the whole story. This is a very powerful module for getting to know and accept yourself more fully because it works at the root level of who you are, in a holistic way.

The challenge – what stops us from really getting to know ourselves?

Once we believe we know something we tend to stop investigating and being curious about it, unfortunately this tendency leads to ignorance about ourselves – life moves on and we are left behind, stagnating.

So, our challenge is to stay curious, to see what we will discover next, and to let that curiosity build our knowledge of ourselves.

Who are you?

Contemplating who you are is a very big concept. Are you your thoughts? Your feelings? Your deeds? Your body? Your soul? And, as if that's not hard enough, you then have the challenge of where you are. Your physical body is clear to see but where does your identity, your character, the 'me' reside? Is it in your mind, your body or some other place outside of your physical body?

Because these are incredibly deep and fascinating concepts you can easily get caught up in them and lose focus on what you are really trying to achieve – an understanding of yourself that is empowering, easy to understand and that works. Therefore, we are going to take a very practical and simple approach, one that's compiled from a number of different perspectives and concepts, and most importantly an approach that has been proven to produce great results – *Basic structure of a person* provides an outlined, holistic image of who we are.

Basic structure of a person

Consider the picture below as a basic structure of a person:

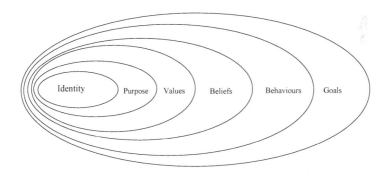

Identity | Purpose | Values | Beliefs | Behaviours | Goals

Identity

At the centre, our core, is our identity – who we really are. Although we have a sense of what our identity is we tend to find it extremely hard to put our finger on it and describe it, other than to say 'It's me!' This is because there is a paradox – our identity is as finite as it is infinite.

If you think about knowing who you are, where you physically are, and how you feel, these are all finite, specific concepts – you have a sense of self and it's of you, here, absolutely here, reading this book. If, however, you consider your capacity to adapt, how you can change and grow, you will realize that you have infinite possibilities of choice and development.

Even our physical body is continuously changing. Dr Deepak Chopra's research shows how frequently different parts of our body regenerate themselves – a whole new layer of skin every month, a new stomach lining every four days, even our entire bodies every few years. We are all both finite and infinite at the same time.

Our finiteness gives us a sense of safety, a knowing, and our infiniteness a sense of excitement and exploration.

One of the biggest and most common mistakes we make is to associate our identity with something that is external to us. It's a major mistake because by doing so we're giving up our right to control who we are, and how we perceive ourselves, because we have handed over the control to an external factor. Unfortunately we tend to do it a lot in our relationships (with partners, children, friends or even work colleagues), our jobs and we often also associate behaviour with identity.

It's so ingrained in our society that it's a part of our language. When you ask someone 'What do you do?' the response is nearly always 'I am a ...'. This is especially prevalent for those people who are specialists in their field such as doctors, lecturers, accountants, dancers, plumbers, surgeons ... Somehow what they do for a living is tied up with their identity, with who they are.

Equally with relationships, we tend to associate our identity with the people we spend time with. We see who they are and how they behave as a reflection of our core, our identity. It's very easy to lose our sense of self and identity if we are not careful about how we build our foundations.

Purpose

Next to our identity is our purpose, our reason for being – what we want to achieve in our lifetime. Unlike our identity, which is rather intangible, this is the first step towards something more concrete. Our purpose is like a powerful adhesive that adds strength to our foundation because it generally affects every aspect of our lives and provides us with a stronger sense of self, of identity.

Values, beliefs, behaviours and goals

Next up is our values, those things that are important to us. We each have our own unique set of values, things like freedom, integrity, love, happiness, money, growth and power. Our values are one level closer to being tangible indicators of who we are. They are also very important because they drive the last three areas – what we believe, how we behave and the goals we set. Interestingly, even though how we behave and the goals we set are the furthest away from our identity, most people define themselves by either one or both of these areas, so that what they are doing, or aiming to do, and how they behave completely defines them.

If we consider ourselves within this simple model of who we are, and how our identity, purpose, values, beliefs and behaviours fit together, we are able to learn a lot more about ourselves. Equally, because of its structure we are more likely to accept what we learn.

Exercise

Aim: To give you an idea of where you believe your identity lies.

Duration: 30 minutes

What you need:

- an open mind
- an attitude of curiosity and fun
- a safe, quiet environment, free of distractions and disruptions
- one sheet of paper

Important point: Be relaxed to get the most from the exercise.

Relax – Sit comfortably and be aware of your body. Feel each muscle relaxing, and your body becoming heavier with each exhalation.

1   Write a page or two, freehand, of what ever comes to mind when you consider 'Who am I?'

2   Consider the following statements and note which have a strong emotional charge to them.
- I am (your purpose).
- I am my values.
- I am my beliefs.
- I am what I do and where and with whom I do it.
- I am what I have.
- I am what I intend to do.
- I am a (your job/career).
- I am a mother.
- I am a daughter.
- I am a sister.
- I am an auntie.
- I am a godmother.

3   Consider what you say to people about yourself when you introduce yourself to them – what do you focus your energy and time on?

4   Look at all the information you have and consider where you have considered your identity to be in the past.

5   Where do you think/feel your identity is now?

1.2.2 ACCEPT YOURSELF

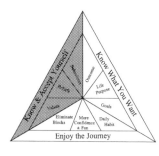

'He who knows others is wise; he who knows himself is enlightened.'

Lao-Tzu

Numerous psychological studies (e.g. Lerner, 1980) have shown that when bad things happen to other people, we tend to believe it's because they are in some way 'bad' people. The most significant of these studies is the just world hypothesis – that 'I am a just person living in a just world and people get what they deserve'. Interestingly, we also apply a similar principle to ourselves: many of us have a habit of blaming ourselves when something bad happens and giving credit to luck, or to someone else, when something good happens (see page 19 for more on this).

Although many of us may think that we accept ourselves, the truth is often that we spend most of our lives giving ourselves a hard time. We say things to ourselves like 'How could I have done that?', 'That was so stupid', 'I am not good enough for that', 'I can't do that'. These are just indications – flags – that we lack acceptance of ourselves and need to take a second look. Once we gain clarity on who we are and adapt our behaviour so that it is in line with our true self, then acceptance follows naturally.

The courage and wisdom to accept ourselves

Many of us find it difficult to truly accept ourselves and we are very quick to criticize and damn ourselves. The effect varies from person to person – some will be more motivated to prove that they can do it despite their own criticisms, and others will just accept the condemnation and limit themselves because of it, but both will carry on living with a burden because of it.

When we start to delve into the question of who we are, we are suddenly faced with things that we like and dislike about ourselves. We may have already been aware of some of them, and others may be a surprise. It takes a lot of courage, determination and/or wisdom to be able to take on board what comes up and to deal with it accordingly.

If we consider again the 'off' smell in the fridge, the answer is simple and straightforward – find the cause and deal with it. But somehow as we grow up we generally stop applying this approach in our lives and the answer becomes difficult for us to acquire. We can become so keen to make everything 'OK' that we skip over the facts and create delusions.

Imagine you met your dream partner, believing after only a few months that they're the person for you, but at the same time you have a little nagging feeling inside that everything isn't entirely right. Most people would ignore that feeling and enjoy the relationship and at first, this may seem fine, but sooner or later the feeling will grow and evidence will start to present itself. Depending on how much you really want that partner you will delude yourself to a greater or lesser degree and try to make everything 'OK'. Some even take their delusions into their marriage!

The reason it takes a lot of courage, determination and wisdom to take on board what comes up and to deal with it accordingly is because when we discover things that we don't like it always has a big negative emotional charge. To be able to face that and accept it is truly courageous. The wisdom comes from knowing that by looking at the facts, finding the root cause and dealing with it straight away, you save yourself a lot of time, effort and negative emotion – it's very much a 'stitch in time saves nine' situation.

If we go back to the picture of the *basic structure of a person* (page 33) we can start to see how its organization makes it easier for us to face our reality. The structure gives us a deeper level of wisdom and also gives us the courage needed to face ourselves. Take, for example, a behaviour, something that you do or did that you dislike – being snappy and rude when you are irritated, for example. In the past you may have felt really awful after such an outburst, thinking yourself to be a bad, mean, or even evil person for having behaved that way, and immediately connecting the behaviour with your identity, even though deep inside you knew that it wasn't really you at all and that you are basically a good person.

By enabling us to separate our behaviour, beliefs and values from each other and from our identity we are able to look at a given situation with more objectivity and distance – we can observe what's going on and then decide what action to take. So if we look at the irritable, rude behaviour and note when it happens, what the triggers are, consider if it's appropriate, if we would like to change it, how we would want to behave instead, we allow ourselves endless options. And all because of a slight shift in perspective – perceiving behaviour as separate from identity.

Exercise

Aim: To discover your level of acceptance of yourself and to increase it. By being aware of their level of acceptance many people find they naturally accept themselves more. This book is designed so that, as you go through it, your awareness and acceptance grows even more.

Duration: 30 minutes

What you need:

- an open mind
- an attitude of curiosity and fun
- a safe, quiet environment, free of distractions and disruptions
- one sheet of paper

Important point: Be relaxed to get the most from the exercise.

Relax – Sit comfortably and be aware of your body. Feel each muscle relaxing, and your body becoming heavier with each exhalation.

1 Write a page or two, freehand, on whatever comes to mind when you consider 'Do I accept myself as I am?'

2 Consider all the things you have learnt about yourself and all the discoveries you will make in the future and ask yourself again 'Do I accept myself as I am?'

3 Be aware of your level of acceptance as you go about your daily life – do you give yourself a hard time or do you accept that you are where you are and that you are on your own unique journey?

1.2.3 VALUES

'Believe nothing, no matter where you read it, or who said it, no matter if I have said it, unless it agrees with your own reason and your own common sense.'

Buddha

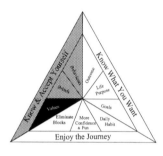

Values are the things that are important to us, things like integrity, honesty, love, fun, fairness or freedom, and we generally have 5 top values for each area of our life with 8–12 more acting as supporting values. Interestingly we've already acquired most of our values by the age of seven, our imprint stage when we are basically a sponge for information, but we adopt them almost randomly from the significant people around us – our parents, family and friends. (Massey, 1979.)

By the time we are adults our values can be such an intuitive part of us that we barely acknowledge or question them, but being aware of our values is hugely important in getting to know ourselves because they are such a significant driver in determining how we live our lives. We are unconsciously driven to follow and satisfy our values and they have the power to make our life seem easy or difficult – If our values are aligned with our goals we tend to experience easy results, but if they're not it can be a very difficult and challenging journey.

So here we are, walking around, largely oblivious to the powerful drivers that we randomly adopted at an age when we were not equipped to choose them! It's no wonder we sometimes struggle to make sense of things.

By understanding our values we are much better able to understand ourselves, our behaviour and our reactions, and to start to exercise a choice about who we want to be. We can adopt values that are useful and let go of ineffective ones, thereby taking control and actively choosing our future rather than leaving it to chance. Equally, just by knowing our values, we are better equipped to make quick and effective decisions because our knowledge acts as a framework against which we can evaluate our decisions.

For example, if you have integrity as a top value you are driven to be honest and generally you will be. If you *do* lie you'll feel one or more negative emotions such as guilt, anger, fear or sadness, because your behaviour is conflicting with your integrity value. These feelings are a flag to say 'Something's not right! You need to look at this!' Most people don't pay much attention to these flags although generally they are negative enough to deter them from repeating that behaviour again.

The values exercise below is designed to help you delve inside yourself and discover your values, both useful and not so useful, so you can start gaining an awareness of them – the first and most important step for building a strong foundation for yourself.

Exercise – Discovering your values
Aim: To discover your most powerful values for each area of your life: Partner, Family, Friends, Wealth, Career, Fitness, Health and Spirituality.
Duration: 20 minutes per area
What you need:
- a sheet of paper
- One Area Chart (Appendix B)
- Guidance Chart (Appendix A)

Important points:
- Be completely relaxed.
- Write down the first thing that comes to mind after the question is asked.
- Do each area of your life at one sitting.

Relax – Sit comfortably and be aware of your body. Feel each muscle relaxing, and your body becoming heavier with each exhalation.

Once you are relaxed read though the simple questions below one by one and answer them with the first thing that pops into your mind. Sometimes you might get stuck, or it can be hard to tell what the answer is, so if you need more clarity, **relax** a little more, repeat the question, and listen for the answer. When you get it, write it down straight away. DON'T try to make sense of it or dwell on it, just move on quickly, asking the questions and writing down the first answer that pops into your mind.

1   Consider the area of your life you wish to get your values for, and ask yourself 'What's important to me about (the area of life you chose)?' For example, if the area that you are working on is Family then you would ask 'What's important to me about family?' The answers will generally be one-word concepts, intangibles like growth, freedom, etc. Write them down on the piece of paper.

Repeat this question until you have all the answers you can think of. Then **relax** your whole body a little further still and ask the question one more time – there are always a few more deep-rooted answers that pop up then. (Most people have between 8–12 values for each area of their lives.)

2   Take your list of values and prioritize them. To do this ask yourself 'If I could only have one value for this area of my life which one would I choose?' Choose one and write it down. Then consider 'If I could have just one more, but only one more, which one would I choose?' Select it and write it down. Carry on through your list of values until you have them all prioritized.

3   In your One Area Chart (Appendix B – you may wish to redraw it onto a larger piece of paper) note down your first five values because these are likely to be the most powerful.

For most of you, discovering your values will be relatively straight-forward, but others may find it a little more difficult. The most common difficulties can be overcome by:

a   relaxing more;

b   opening your mind and focusing further; and

c prioritizing two that seem to be at the same level, by asking your-self 'If I have A and not B is that OK?' Then ask 'If I have B and not A is that OK?' That should give a definite order. On very rare occasions there can be two at the same level. If so, note down both at that level with a dash between them: Value X – Value Y.
Some people are able to do all the areas of their lives in two hours (that's 15 minutes per area) – the more you do, the quicker you get.

4 After working through the exercise for each area of your life you should have a rough sheet of paper with all your workings, a final list, and your top five values written on to your One Area Chart for each area. If any appear to be a block (you'll know because it will have a negative emotional charge to it or it will be a disempowering value), then put it down in your blocks area of the values section – follow your sixth sense, **relax** and gently guide yourself to your answers.

5 Once you have completed the exercise tick off the appropriate sec-tion in the Guidance Chart (Appendix A), go for a short break and congratulate yourself.

Conclusion: Contemplate your discoveries – consider how these values have manifested themselves in your actions in the past, you may also start to see where one area of your life is supporting or hindering an-other. Share your values and discoveries and thoughts with your buddy if you are working with one.

1.2.4 BELIEFS

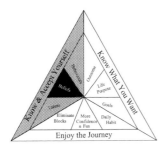

'Whether you think you can or you think you can't, you are probably right.'

Attributed to Henry Ford

Our beliefs are the things we believe to be absolutely true. We have many thousands of beliefs and, as with our values, we adopted most of them in the imprint stage of our development, between 0–7 years of age, from our significant others. (Massey, 1979.)

Even though our beliefs are driven by our values they are still important in their own right because they help shape our actions and how we interpret behaviour and events. We can more fully understand the structure of our beliefs and the power they have over our lives if we consider how they are formed.

Imagine your next-door neighbour comes around, desperately needing your help. It's something you can do relatively effortlessly and it fits with your values, so you agree. At around the time you agree you will have put a meaning to your behaviour in your own mind – for example, 'I helped a neighbour out, which means that I am a nice person'. If you did not have a prior belief that you were a nice person then this would be the start of a new belief. It can be symbolized by a one-legged table – the top being the belief 'I am a nice person' and the leg being the behaviour that created it.

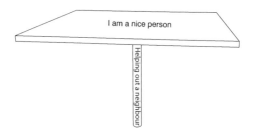

I am a nice person

Helping out a neighbour

Soon you will notice other behaviours that start to build more legs on the table, making the belief stronger and stronger and, before you know it, what was initially just one thought has formed into a solid belief that is driving your behaviours – because you believe that you are a nice person you then tend to do other things in line with that belief.

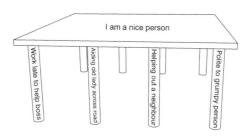

Whilst the belief is forming, other events and behaviours may alter it, but once it's formed it's a very powerful thing. This strengthening of beliefs over time is one of the reasons people tend to become more set in their ways as they get older – they simply have many table legs to support their beliefs.

Once a belief is formed it also acts as a filter through which we perceive our reality. For example, if the person holding the belief 'I am a nice person' behaves in a way that is contrary to this belief they will struggle to accept it and may delude themselves that their behaviour is due to drink, stress, or some other external factor, and become more and more set in their ways rather than just stopping the contrary behaviour because it doesn't fit in with their idea of who they are.

If a belief is not fully formed, however, behaviour conflicting with a person's self-image will cause a lot of internal conflict because there will be two opposing beliefs forming from different behaviours. It would be like building an 'I am a nice person' table at the same time as an 'I am a bad person' table.

When something happens to us it's not the actual event but what we say to ourselves and how we behave that matters (driven initially by our values, then by both our beliefs and past behaviours). From our reactions to events we form our beliefs (or strengthen existing ones) and then our beliefs shape our reality.

Some beliefs are empowering and useful to have, such as 'I can achieve anything I want' or 'I'm good with people', but there are others that are disempowering and limiting, such as 'I'm not good enough' or 'I couldn't do that'. In the beliefs exercise below you will be able to uncover both types. Some you will already be conscious of and others may be a surprise for you; by staying open-minded to the possibilities you will have a very interesting and enlightening exploration.

Exercise – Discovering your beliefs

Aim: To discover your main beliefs for each area of your life.

Duration: 30 minutes per area

What you need:

- several sheets of paper
- One Area Chart (Appendix B)
- Guidance Chart (Appendix A)

Important points:

- Be completely relaxed.
- Write whatever comes to mind.
- Do each area of your life at one sitting.

Relax – Sit comfortably and be aware of your body. Feel each muscle relaxing, and your body becoming heavier with each exhalation.

1 Write on the top line of a sheet of paper '(the area of your life) is…' then turn the sheet over and write on the other side '(the area of your life) is not…'. So, if you were looking at wealth, for example, you'd have written 'Wealth is …' and 'Wealth is not …'.

2 Ask yourself 'Do I know the area by any other name?' (In the case of wealth, you'd perhaps have 'money'.) If you do, take another sheet of paper and write down 'Money is…' and on the other side of the same sheet write 'Money is not…'. Repeat the question until there are no other words left. For some areas there may be just one term and for others there may be two or three.

3 Once you have your titled pages **relax** even more.

4   Taking one sheet of paper at a time:

   a Read the top line.

   b Write down everything that comes to mind, completely switching off any criticisms or corrections – the faster you write the better. If you get stuck just **relax** even more, focus on the top line and write down what comes to mind.

   c Complete all the sheets with as many lines of beliefs as possible.

5   Take a break.

6   Look at your answers. What was expected? What is a discovery? What's the ratio of positive, supportive beliefs to negative ones?

7   Update your One Area Chart. Put your positive answers for the area sections (e.g. 'Wealth is …') into your beliefs area – if any of these are negative then put them into the blocks area of the beliefs section. Then look at the other side (e.g. 'Wealth is not…') and enter any that you intuitively feel are blocks into the blocks area.

Conclusion: The basics of discovering your beliefs are relatively simple; the challenge lies in finding the main beliefs that impact on your life. Another good way to do this is to look at the effect they have on your behaviours.

1.2.5 BEHAVIOURS

'Behaviour is the mirror in which everyone shows their image.'

Goethe

Behaviours are our actions and reactions – the things we do. People attach a lot of importance to them and we are therefore conditioned to pay attention to them; it's ingrained in our society and our language – 'actions speak louder than words'. We judge ourselves and others through our behaviour and as a result our self-esteem can easily become tied up with how we behave.

Whilst it's true that our behaviours have a great influence on how our beliefs are formed, that's only while we are unconscious of the process. Once we are consciously aware of how our beliefs form, our perspective starts to shift and we can take control over what we believe. Behaviours start to lose their importance because we can see that they are at the symptom level, the manifestation of our values, beliefs and blocks, and as such they can be used as good indicators of what's going on – flags for possible internal conflicts and problems – just as a runny nose is a symptom of an underlying problem such as an allergy, emotional upset, or a cold.

Something at a behavioural level always has a deeper-level cause. For example, a weight problem is nearly always the behavioural-level symptom of a deeper problem and we should be wary of judging too quickly or too harshly. We even do it to ourselves and judge our own behaviour harshly – failing at something and judging that we are no good at it, or even taking it to the identity level by saying *we* are no good.

Interestingly, once people are aware that behaviours are merely symptoms, the importance of those behaviours diminishes – we stop judging ourselves and others by what we do and start to recognize how behaviours can influence our perception. The exercise below is designed to help you discover your behaviour patterns.

Exercise – Discovering your behaviours

Aim: To discover your behaviour patterns for each area of your life.
Duration: 30 minutes per area
What you need:
- a sheet of paper
- One Area Chart (Appendix B)
- Discovering Your Behaviours (Appendix C)

Important point: Be completely relaxed.

Relax – Sit comfortably and be aware of your body. Feel each muscle relaxing, and your body becoming heavier with each exhalation.

1   In the context of the area of your life you are working on, consider what happened for each of the age ranges mentioned below. If nothing comes up just skip it and go to the next age bracket. Write down all the things that come to mind. Ask yourself: 'In the context of (area of life) what significant things happened, and what were my behaviours, between the ages of 0–7, 7–13, 13–18, 18–21, 21–26, 26–30, 30–35, 35–40 …?'

There is a table you can use in Appendix C just for this. Let the answers just flow out in whatever form they wish. The quality of your English doesn't matter, what matters is for you to write down the first thing that comes into your mind. Complete all the age ranges.

2   Stop and have a two-minute break once you have completed all age brackets.

3   Looking at your answers from an objective point of view, with a fresh pair of eyes, consider:

a   What are the patterns?

b   What stands out?

c   What's consistent and inconsistent with your values?

d   What's consistent and inconsistent with your beliefs?

e   What behaviours do you like and which would you like to change?

Summarize the behaviours you like and ones you'd like to change.

4   Update your One Area Chart – List the things you like in the general area for behaviours and the things you would like to change in the blocks area.

Conclusion: Think about your discoveries. For those behaviours that are important to you, consider the key drivers directing/motivating them – what values and beliefs are behind them? This is a very powerful way to get to know yourself even better. Share your discoveries and thoughts with your buddy if you are working with one.

Know What You Want

Module	Title	Page	Exercise time (mins)
1.3.1	Know what you want	54	–
1.3.2	Outcome	56	20
1.3.3	Life Purpose	59	80
1.3.4	Goals	65	30

(It will take approximately 2 hours and 10 minutes to complete all the exercises for one area of your life. If you wish to work through all the areas of your life then multiply the exercise time for Goals by the number of areas you wish to work on.)

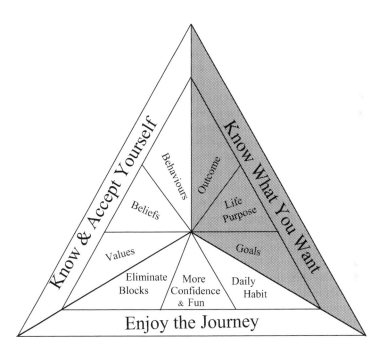

1.3.1 KNOW WHAT YOU WANT

'The future belongs to those who believe in the beauty of their dreams.'

Attributed to Eleanor Roosevelt

Why it's important to know what you want

Enjoy the Journey

A myth persists about a 'famous' goals study conducted on Yale University's graduating seniors in 1953. The story goes that students were asked if they had any written goals for their future – only 3% of the participants had. Many years later it was supposedly discovered that the 3% with goals had accumulated more financial wealth than the other 97% combined. Many motivational speakers and personal effectiveness consultants, including Brian Tracy, Anthony Robbins and Zig Ziglar, have referred to this case, despite it being a myth, because it illustrates the fundamental effectiveness of setting goals and the astounding results that can be achieved by doing so. Goal setters are far more likely to be successful than those who drift along expecting luck or fate to take care of them.

Most of us know this all too well. For example, if we want to get a loaf of bread we go straight to the baker's and that's it. But if we're not sure if we want bread, vegetables, or maybe even fruit, then it's going to take a lot longer and we may end up with something we didn't really want or need, all because we did not think it through.

Generally, we're clear on what we want in our daily activities but we tend to lose that clarity when we look at our lives from a wider perspective. What do we want from our lives? What do we want to accomplish? Wouldn't it be great to be as sure about what you want from life as you are about what to eat for dinner? Imagine how it would affect you – how clear, confident and effective you would be.

As an example, if you don't know the type of person you want to go out with you are more likely to accept an offer of a date that's driven by the other person and not by you. This lack of clarity means you can be out-manoeuvred by others who know what they want, or worse, don't know what they want either – the blind leading the blind! If you know what you want you can concentrate your time and effort in that direction and get it.

Other benefits of knowing what you want

Once you know where you want to get to on your personal journey, you are on your path to happiness and fulfilment, and there are many other benefits.

First of all, this knowledge gives you more choice – by knowing what you want you're able to change and adapt it to suit your changing life style without any ambiguity or the possibility of things being forgotten or brushed under the carpet – there is absolute clarity.

Equally, having made the choice in the first place you're more likely to make choices in the future. All humans are the same in that the more we do something the more likely we are to repeat it, but unfortunately the opposite is also true – the less you choose the less choice you have.

When you know what you want, your passion, drive and energy go up dramatically. Do you remember a time when you were completely fired up, all guns blazing, and there was no stopping you? Perhaps when you were a child and you were about to open your Christmas or birthday present, or as a teenager getting ready for a first date? That really excited, purposeful, happy and curious feeling. That's the feeling – the drive you have when you know what you want out of life. Generally, life becomes more fun, and any knock-backs, however large they may be, become minor obstacles because you're focused and committed to what you want.

Finally, by working at this level and truly discovering what you want from your life, you're addressing your needs at the root level, and because of this the benefits will be long-lasting.

The Outcome, Life Purpose and Goals modules below are designed to help you uncover what you really want so that you're more likely to be happy and successful, as well as having far more choice, increased passion, drive and energy.

1.3.2 OUTCOME

'Look and you will find it – what is unsought will go undetected.'

Sophocles

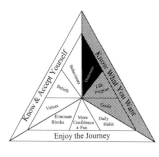

An Outcome is the conclusion, the answer to 'What is it you want?', and because of this, depending on the situation, a Life Purpose ('What is it I want from life?') and Goal ('What is it I want from this area of my life?') can both be considered as Outcomes. Sometimes, though, an Outcome can be far less than that. It can be what you want from anything you do – a business meeting, date, holiday, even a chat with a friend.

This module introduces you to a simple technique that can be applied to almost anything. When it's put into practice it's incredibly powerful, so instead of drifting along and seeing how things work out you can save yourself a lot of time, effort and, in some cases, a substantial amount of money by going through it.

In effect all you are doing is consciously deciding what you want, having that be your focus, and letting your unconscious mind fetch it for you. The exercise below is an effective process for setting an Outcome and, at the very least, just by answering these simple questions – 'What's my Outcome here?', 'What do I want from this event/interaction?' – you will transform your experience of what happens.

Ultimately, by going through the whole Outcome Model you'll have a far greater insight about what you really want and it'll also flush out any secondary gains (i.e. unconscious benefits to you for not getting what you want), which will have to be uncovered and addressed before any other work is done. Secondary gains are in effect blocks that you need to get rid of; but for now, if you have them just jot them down and when you go through the Blocks module you can work through them. It may seem strange that you could be unconsciously sabotaging yourself so that you don't achieve what you want, but actually its quite common and it's important to be aware of it.

Exercise

Aim: To clarify what it is you want *and* if you are ready to get it.
Duration: 20 minutes
What you need:

- an open mind
- an attitude of curiosity and fun
- a safe, quiet environment, free of distractions and disruptions

Important points:

- Be relaxed to get the most from the exercise.
- Write the first thing that comes into your mind when you read/hear the question.

Relax – Sit comfortably and be aware of your body. Feel each muscle relaxing, and your body becoming heavier with each exhalation.

1   What is it you really want? (Be specific and state it in a positive way.)
2   Consider where you are now – really *connect* with it. What's your current situation? What do you see, hear and feel around you right now in relation to the outcome you want?
3   When you get your outcome, what will you see, hear and feel around you? Imagine you have it now and visualize yourself living that life; see yourself in the picture of what it would be like. (Do it as if you have it now, make it as attractive and as compelling as possible, make sure you see yourself in the picture, and put it out into a specific point in the future.)

4   Consider your outcome. How will you know when you have it? What will you need to see, hear, feel and do to know you have it?

5   What will this outcome enable you to do?

6   Is the outcome only for you? If not, who else is it for? Where, when, how and with whom do you want it?

7   Consider your outcome. What resources do you need to be able to achieve it (e.g. skills, empowering emotions, strategies/processes)?

8   Of these resources, which do you already have and which do you need in order to achieve your outcome? (Consider if you have done something like this before? Do you know someone else who has that you can learn from?)

9   Act as if you have achieved your outcome. (As they say in business, 'Perform/dress to the level above and you will get promoted'.)

10   **Relax** even more – be aware of your body. Feel each muscle relaxing, and your body becoming heavier with each exhalation.

11   Consider your outcome. What will you gain if you get it?

12   Consider your outcome. What will you lose if you get it?

13   Consider your outcome. What will happen if you get it?

14   Consider your outcome. What will happen if you don't get it?

15   Consider your outcome. What won't happen if you get it?

16   Consider your outcome. What won't happen if you don't get it?

17   Take a break, then come back and look at your answers. Ensure that:

    a   your Outcome is stated in the positive, is specific and achievable;

    b   there are no inconsistencies in your answers – if there is, it's a symptom of a block that will need to be worked through (see page 75 to understand more about Blocks and page 85 to get rid of them);

    c   the Outcome is what you really want (some people realize after going through this exercise that they didn't really want what they thought they wanted!); and d   you are ready to have it – the answers to questions 11–16 are a good indicator if there is any secondary gain stopping you from getting what you want. Look at them carefully and ensure you are ready to get your Outcome.

Conclusion: this is a very powerful process and the time spent working through it is well invested. It has proved itself to be highly useful in saving time and money and even those who had the right Outcome and were clear of blocks find it a great motivator because it enhances your reason for wanting your Outcome and makes it more tangible. Even so, sometimes you'll be short of time and unable to go through this exercise so, at a minimum, taking a minute and asking yourself these two simple questions will transform your experience: 'What's my Outcome here?', 'What do I want from this event/interaction?'

1.3.3 LIFE PURPOSE

'Man – a being in search of meaning'

Plato

Why have a Life Purpose?

Enjoy the Journey

Our Life Purpose is our reason for being – what we want to achieve in our lifetime. Many of us have a sense that our life has a meaning, that there has to be more to it all than just existing – and we don't yet know what it is.

This is because humans are meaning-making machines – we can't help it, it's the way we're made. It's why we ascribe meaning to people's actions, comments, or even the lack of them. We've probably all had the experience of being attracted to someone and then they walk by and say 'Hello' or look at us and immediately we start wondering what it means: 'Is he looking at someone behind me?', 'Is he being polite?', 'Does he fancy me?'. We look for meaning with everything in our lives, and the ultimate is discovering the meaning to our whole life – our life's purpose. It's so fundamental because it acts like a powerful adhesive that adds strength to our foundation, providing us with a stronger sense of self, of identity. It's the ultimate self-discovery.

Once we give our life meaning it's as if we open a door to another world, full of endless opportunities, fun and growth. It was always there, we just didn't know to open the door. Our Life Purpose is the single most powerful driver we have because it impacts on every aspect of our lives, giving a clarity and simplicity that enables us to focus and persevere. By living our daily lives in the context of our purpose we become capable of achieving a great deal, are highly motivated, and are passionate about our lives. Once you know your purpose, the confusion and detail of life just disappear.

What stops us from discovering our Life Purpose?

At some point many will have had glimpses of their Life Purpose, yet somehow the sensible call of reality forced the dream to one side. Often, people blame a lack of money, but this excuse is used just as much by wealthy people! There are always good and sensible reasons for sidelining a glimpse of a dream before it has even been formed and carrying on with 'real life'.

You may recall times in your past where you thought 'Wouldn't it be lovely if I did … for a living?', 'If only I could be a …', then quickly ignored it as just a fancy and logic prevailed with thoughts such as having already built a career that took a lot of time and money, or that you don't have the skills or the money to do it – or something to that effect.

For many people, recognizing their Life Purpose is so easy that it's difficult to see – like not seeing the wood for the trees. Your Life Purpose is the thing that gives you immense amounts of joy, the activity that you would do for free because it's so pleasurable and fulfilling for you and is the occupation that makes you completely lose track of time. For some it's creating things with their hands, or their minds, or solving complicated problems; for others it's to raise a family and have a happy, healthy life … the list is endless in breadth and depth. It's the thing you would *choose* to do if you had all the money in the world.

Discovering our Life Purpose

If you have ever been reading in an unlit room towards the end of the day when it's getting dark and have been so engrossed with what you were reading that you hadn't paid it much attention, then you'll know the 'Ah' moment of someone walking in and putting the light on – your eyes relax and, although nothing has really changed, the sudden flick of a switch illuminates everything, and you wonder how you could have failed to notice the darkness before.

Discovering your Life Purpose is just like that, only the light can never be put out. Once you know your purpose you can never not know it. The challenge is in persevering until you discover it. Some are fortunate, they discover it at the first attempt, but for many of us it's as if our purpose is hiding behind a cloud and only by actively working to discover it can the cloud start to dissolve to give us glimmers of the truth.

It can take anything from a couple of hours to numerous sessions to get through the cloud; the amount of time needed depends on where you are with your life and if you are ready (consciously and unconsciously) to discover your Life Purpose and to move forward with it. It may not even be absolute or specific – each person has a purpose unique to them – what's important is to start to discover it.

For example, my Life Purpose is: 'To creatively empower people to achieve success, happiness and fulfilment'. That may sound absolute and specific enough; however, if we look at it closely it's still quite vague – which 'people'; 'creatively' how…? I still have some cloud left to dissolve. Even so, I am happy and content that my life is progressing in line with my purpose and I am confident that, as I go through my journey, it will get clearer and clearer, as it has done already. I have clients who have a far clearer Life Purpose than I do and that's great – that's their journey and I am on mine, just as you are on yours.

To be fulfilled it doesn't matter where you are on the journey; what's important is to be on it in an open and honest way, and to observe and listen to what comes next. The exercises below will assist you with dissolving your cloud and beginning to gain clarity around your purpose.

Exercise – Discovering your Life Purpose

(Please note: There are three parts to this exercise – in total it will take about 1 hour and 20 minutes and it's best to do all of them at one sitting. Depending on your character profile, some parts will be easier to complete than others, just go with it and enjoy what comes up.)

Part A – Possibilities

Aim: To give you a top-down view of what your Life Purpose might be.
Duration: 15 minutes
What you need:
- several sheets of paper

Important points:
- Be relaxed to get the most from the exercise.
- Write the first answer that comes into your mind; let them flow out.

Relax – Sit comfortably and be aware of your body. Feel each muscle relaxing, and your body becoming heavier with each exhalation.

Write down whatever pops into mind when you read these questions:

1   Imagine having an infinite amount of money, time and resources. What would you choose to do with your time?

2   Imagine you had £100,000,000 in your current account tomorrow. What would you do with your life?

3   Imagine you had one wish for your life, and that one wish is absolutely guaranteed to happen. What would you wish for?

4   Go out, way out into the future – 20, 30, 40 … years – to a time when you're living a purposeful life, where you're healthy, happy, content

and fulfilled. Go there now and experience it as if it's happening now. See, feel, hear, smell, taste as if it's all happening right now. Take a few minutes to really enjoy it.

Consider how you got there. What did you do with your life? What's important to you? Consider each of the different areas of your life and consider what happened to make you so happy, content and fulfilled.

Conclusion: This little exercise is great to give a quick insight into your Life Purpose.

Part B – Drawing on past experiences

Aim: To give you a bottom-up approach to discovering your purpose – uncovering instances from your past where you'll have experienced being purposeful and discovering important patterns.

Duration: 45 minutes

What you need:

- Appendix D (Past Purposeful Behaviours)

Important points:

- Be relaxed to get the most from the exercise.
- Again, write the first answer that comes into your mind; let them flow out.

Relax – Sit comfortably and be aware of your body. Feel each muscle relaxing, and your body becoming heavier with each exhalation.

1   Consider what being purposeful really means to you. What are you like when you are purposeful? Imagine being purposeful now – what would you hear, say, feel, see? You may remember times when you were really going for something, there was no stopping you, and you knew that was the thing for you. Have that feeling with you as you answer the rest of the questions.

2   Using Appendix D, consider the one thing that gave you the greatest sense of being purposeful between the ages of 0–7 – something that you did yourself, that made a big positive impact on you at the time.

Once you have such a memory answer the questions listed in the chart. Repeat for each time period of your life in exactly this way – getting the purposeful feeling and then considering the questions.

3 Take a break.

4 Look for patterns in your answers:

   a What are the key activities?

   b Which skills are frequently being demonstrated?

   c What feelings, sights, and sounds are most frequent?

   d What environment do you like to be in?

   e What types of people do you like to be around?

   f What other observations do you have?

Conclusion: Parts A and B will have provided you with insights and clarity. They are very important for the final stage (Part C) where you will consolidate all your knowledge:

Part C – Putting it all together

Aim: To consolidate your discoveries and insights by designing a personal purpose statement.

Duration: 20 minutes

What you need:

- several sheets of paper
- your Guidance Chart (Appendix A)

Important point: Be relaxed to get the most from the exercise.

Relax – Sit comfortably and be aware of your body. Feel each muscle relaxing, and your body becoming heavier with each exhalation.

Just as companies have mission statements to give a meaning to their company that employees and clients can easily recognize, you can have a *purpose statement* to aid clarity around what you really want from life, and to help you maintain a focus on what's really important to you. It's a personal mission statement that you can share or keep private.

Your statement can be just a sentence or a whole paragraph. It can be a stream of consciousness or in well thought-out English. The important thing is that it encapsulates your purpose at its current level of clarity and when you read it it gives you a great feeling of purpose and satisfaction. This positive feeling is your indicator that you're on the right track, so the stronger the feeling the better the statement is. It's best to play with the words to see what increases/decreases the feeling – it's amazing how powerful it can be to change a few words or even just rearrange the same ones.

You might find this very easy, or very difficult to do. If it's easy for you, go ahead and put yours together and move straight to point 7 below. If you find it difficult, that's fine – just follow the steps below.

1   **Relax** even more **–** be aware of your body. Feel each muscle relaxing, and your body becoming heavier with each exhalation.

2   Look at your answers in Parts A and B and jot down all the things that really resonate with you that may possibly be to do with your purpose. Pick 10–20 things that give you the most positive feelings.

3   Look for groupings within your answers so you can fit them together more neatly – maybe you'll have types of activity, environment, people, behaviour, results … or something else entirely.

4   Consider and highlight what's really important to you and why.

5   Looking at what you have already written, consider the important points, jot down phrases and sentences that resonate with you and that encapsulate them.

6   Tweak those phrases so that they give you the greatest feelings of pleasure and fulfilment. Just play around with them for a while until you stumble on the thing that really resonates with you. Then you have it.

7   Write it down in the middle of your Guidance Chart and put it somewhere that is significant for you, where you can be reminded of it and where you can easily access it for updates. (It's likely that you will need to update it as you discover more about yourself.)

Conclusion: You will now have a clearer idea of what your purpose is, or at least what it could be, and which words are really important to you.

Consider how your values and beliefs impact on your word preferences and share your discoveries with your buddy if you are working with one.

1.3.4 GOALS

'A man without a goal is like a ship without a rudder.'

Thomas Carlyle

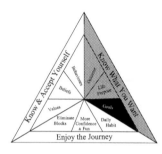

If your purpose gives meaning to your whole life then your goals are the smaller steps, the targets, towards achieving what you want. They are more challenging than a mere task, and are also achievable. They're something that you are excited about, and have full control over.

At one time or another many of us have set a goal – such as stopping smoking, losing weight, being more healthy, saving money, drinking less, etc. Some we'll have managed and some we won't. The aim of this module is to help you learn about the most effective way for you to set your goals and to help you to set them for appropriate areas of your life.

Benefits

Knowing where you are going and what you want from life is essential in the pursuit of success and happiness. If you consider all the different areas of your life and know your purpose but never set any goals, you may achieve some things but it clearly won't be as effective as if you set yourself exciting, challenging and achievable goals. On top of this, true happiness and fulfilment come from the pursuit of your purpose and goals, knowing that every step you take, every learning experience and piece of feedback you gain, is taking you one step closer to where you want to be. Realizing your goals along the way feels like a nice bonus.

What happens when we set a goal?

When we set ourselves a goal what we're actually doing is setting our mind to achieving it. We activate our Reticular Activating System, a part of the brain to 'pay attention to this' and 'fetch this'. We have all experienced this area at work – for example, after breaking up with a partner and suddenly noticing lots of couples or specific songs, or perhaps just after buying a car and noticing everyone else who has the same one. The information was always there but somehow it didn't get through, whereas by setting our RAS on what to pay attention to we start to notice it consciously.

There is no doubt that by taking action, by being committed and pursuing your goal wholeheartedly, it will one day be realized.

Sometimes when we want something and get it, it can be through sheer hard work, and at other times goals are achieved as though by magic. The real secret of goal setting is to find the method that works best for you as an individual. The most effective way of doing this is to consider experiences you've had where you've wanted something and you got it. Consider now two or three specific and different instances – they can be small and simple or large and complicated, the size and complexity doesn't matter, the fact that you wanted it and then got it does.

If you're finding it difficult to see what you were really doing compare a time that you set a goal and got what you wanted with another time where you didn't get what you wanted because the contrast will give you the blue print to the most effective goal setting method for you.

Another good consideration is from Napoleon Hill (Hill, 1960), who spent 20 years finding out the characteristics of highly successful people. He discovered that you can only achieve what your mind conceives and believes it can. I have found this to be highly powerful and absolutely true, and the biggest challenge most of us face is believing we can do it.

There are only two ways to gain a full belief that we can do something. One is to use the tools in the Blocks module to assist your unconscious mind in getting rid of the block, or the second is by using logic and your conscious mind to frame your situation in such a way that you will absolutely believe it will happen. This is what a lot of books on goal-setting refer to as being willing to 'pay the price'. It's the absolute commitment to achieving your goal, not a half-hearted 'I would like it', but a 100% commitment to persevering until you get it.

The exercise below is a method for effective goal-setting that many find useful. Use it as it is, or adapt it based on your own personal experience, so that you find the best possible goal-setting method for you.

Exercise – Discovering your goals

Aim: To learn how to set achievable and motivating goals for an area of your life.

Duration: 30 minutes

What you need:
- several sheets of paper
- One Area Chart (Appendix B)
- Your Guidance Chart (Appendix A)

Important points:
- Be relaxed to get the most from the exercise.
- Consider your successful goal-setting experiences from the past.
- Maintain an attitude of curiosity and experimentation.

Relax – Sit comfortably and be aware of your body. Feel each muscle relaxing, and your body becoming heavier with each exhalation.

Consider the area of your life you are working on and answer the following questions:

1   What is it I really want in the …
   a   short term (within 1–6 months)?
   b   medium term (within 6–12 months)?
   c   long term (5 years and beyond)?
   (The most effective way is to start small and, as you achieve what you want, set your sights higher because this builds your confidence to pursue bigger and bigger goals, and makes you more likely to achieve them.)

2   If I could have anything in the world, what would I choose for myself? (List everything you want – your goals.)

3   Go back to each goal, one by one, and make sure they are stated in the manner specified below, because that's the most effective way for your mind to be able to understand and accept your goals.
  • *Positively* (I don't want to be fat → 'I want to be thin').
  • Say it as if you have it *now* (I want to be thin → 'I am thin').
  • *Realistically* (I am thin → 'I weigh (realistic weight for you)').
  • State the *date* by which you want it.
    Therefore the goal may come out as 'I weigh 9 stone on 24/10/20XX'.

4   Ensure that you know how you would recognize having achieved your goal – set internal criteria for evaluating it rather than external. So focus on you, on the things you personally have full control over, rather than those you have little or no control over.)

5   Check that they are the best goals for you – one by one go out into the future and experience having achieved each of them. For each goal do the following:
  • Go out to that specific time in the future where you have your goal, step into your body as if it's now, (so you are looking through your own eyes) and consider: How does it feel? What can I hear? What can I see? Live it now, as if you are there. Take a few minutes to really experience it and have it wash all over you.
  • Now step out of your body so you can actually see yourself, your own body. What insights do you have? Come back to now bringing all the knowledge and empowering feelings with you. Ensure you see yourself out there in the future achieving your goal as you come back to now.
    This technique is useful in helping you to highlight to your unconscious mind that this is the thing you really want, and to help empower you to act as if you have it now. Sometimes, by going through this, people get further insights and amend their goals

accordingly and that's absolutely fine, just go back to point 3 with your new information and work through the exercises again.

6   Relax even more and go inside yourself and ask: 'Is it OK for me to have this goal? Can I achieve this? Do I believe 100% that I can achieve this?' If you get anything other that a '100% yes', it means that you have a block. Congratulate yourself for finding it and write it down on the Blocks area of your One Area Chart in the area of your life you are working on before moving on to the next goal. Then, once you have gone through each of your goals, go to the Blocks module and ensure you get rid of all the blocks and have a 100% yes. Then you'll be ready to come back and finish the rest of this exercise.

7   Take a break.

8   Go though your goals with an objective eye, looking to ensure that they are consistent with each other, and with your values, beliefs and behaviours. Inconsistencies are possible blocks. If you find any, congratulate yourself for finding them and note them down on your One Area Chart, and move on to the next one.

Conclusion: Goal-setting is a skill, and one that is unique to each of us. You will now be more aware of your method of setting goals and, as with any skill, the more you do it the better you will be at it.

Enjoy the Journey

Module	Title	Page	Exercise time (mins)
1.4.1	Enjoy the journey	74	–
1.4.2	Eliminate blocks	75	60
1.4.3	More confidence and fun each day	87	–
1.4.4	Circle of Empowerment	89	60
1.4.5	Perception Enhancer	93	60
1.4.6	Daily habit	98	30

(It will take approximately 3 hours and 30 mins to complete all the exercises.)

1.4.1 ENJOY THE JOURNEY

'Live today as though you were going to die tomorrow, plan for tomorrow like you were going to live forever.'

Thomas Edison

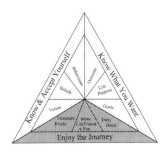

It's inevitable that there will be easy and challenging times in life, whatever course we undertake. If the journey is an unpleasant chore then when we face obstacles we'll at best have a hard time, and at worst give up. But if the journey is fun and enjoyable the challenges never seem so big or important because we tend to focus on what we want rather than the obstacles we face.

Do you remember a time in your past, maybe even when you were a child, where you needed to get something done and were truly happy and enjoying yourself in the pursuit of your goal. Imagine what it'd be like to feel like that all the time. Interestingly, most people say they enjoy, or at least make the most of, their lives. What they generally mean is that, despite all the problems they have and the hardships they face, they make the most of it. That enjoyment is all about escaping from everyday life by watching television, going to the movies, drinking, holidays, etc.

If you ask people how life is going, many will say things like 'Can't complain', 'Not so bad', 'Could be worse', or if they're trying to be positive they will respond brightly but still believe that their life, or at least some aspect of their life, is inherently tough, lonely or a struggle.

The challenge of enjoying the journey of life is easy when you know how, but nearly impossible for those who don't. The techniques in this chapter are designed especially so that you continually enjoy your journey: the module on blocks is of paramount importance in eliminating obstacles that would otherwise hinder you; the Circle of Empowerment and Perception Enhancer will help you to gain more confidence and fun, and the daily habit will help you to create effective little habits that go a long way towards enhancing your enjoyment of your journey.

1.4.2 ELIMINATE BLOCKS

'Be really whole and all things will come to you.'

Lao-Tzu

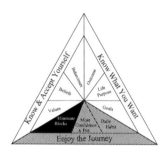

In this module we'll discover what blocks are, how they affect our lives, how we react to them and how we can get rid of them. Once we understand their structure and can eliminate them, we can move forward to happily achieve what we want from our lives.

What are blocks?

Humans are truly amazing creatures. In order to cope with the vast amount of diverse information that bombards our senses every second we develop rules based on our experiences – these are our conditioned responses. As we grow up we create a directory of these responses and continue building on it throughout our lives, for example, learning that an upwardly curved mouth is a smiling, happy person.

On the whole, conditioned responses are very useful, but unfortunately some are ineffective for us – these are our blocks, and they are disempowering and limiting. Blocks are those things that stop or hinder us from doing what we want to do and they tend to manifest themselves as negative emotions such as anger, sadness, fear, jealousy or guilt, and as limiting beliefs such as 'I can't do that', 'I'm not good enough', etc., often working together to reinforce the problem.

The formation of blocks

We all have blocks and symptoms of blocks that are unique to us, reflecting our particular experiences. If we consider how blocks are formed we can see how random and simple the process is, and yet it has a potentially devastating effect on our lives. You may have wondered how you can have a really large negative feeling about something that makes no sense to your logical mind. The problem is rooted in the way our mind stores our memories of emotional events.

Let's look at an example such as a fear of spiders. Imagine a little girl at the age of two, playing with her toys. A spider jumps out and gives her a little fright, depicted by the first star on the graph below.

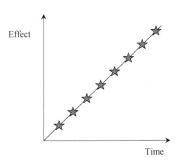

Her mind would have associated that fear with what she saw – the spider – and stored it away in her memory. Prior to this experience she might not have known what a spider was, let alone have emotions associated with it. Then later when she saw another spider, depicted by the second star on the graph, her unconscious mind would have remembered the first experience and automatically brought up the negative emotion of fear, building on the initial fear and making it stronger and more powerful.

As time goes by and she has more encounters with spiders this feeling of fear grows bigger and bigger, and may even grow into a phobia.

We can see that what may start off as a little fright can, over time, build into a very large problem that has a substantial effect on someone's life. It's the same with limiting beliefs. Over time the more experiences you have where negative, limiting beliefs are activated, the more supported those beliefs become, until they form very powerful blocks that can overwhelm us. (For more information on beliefs, see page 43.)

The effect of blocks

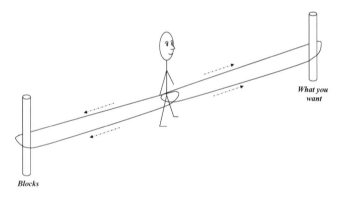

What you want

Blocks

If you stood with two large elastic bands around your waist, one pulling you towards what you want (your goal) and the other tugging you backwards, away from it, the direction you move in will depend on the power and the pull of the two elastic bands.

Sometimes the pull may be equal in strength and opposite in direction, so you're just standing still. At another time you may just be going along happily, then suddenly an elastic band is activated and you are hurled backwards, or maybe, because you have a big pull backwards, you might slowly drag yourself forwards towards your goal, fighting against the tension every step of the way. This elastic band effect is just like the effect of blocks in our lives. The effect they have depends on their structure and location. Let's look at two examples to illustrate this. First, imagine having the limiting belief 'I cannot paint'. It's just focused on one skill so the negative effect is limited and would only manifest itself when the opportunity to paint arose. Now imagine that you have another limiting belief: 'I don't deserve to be happy'. It's just one limiting belief but we can start to imagine the widespread, catastrophic effect it could have on your relationships, your work, your health … every aspect of your life, because it affects you at *identity level*. Even if you start to enjoy yourself you'll unconsciously sabotage things to ensure the belief is validated, and although it's likely that you would have no conscious awareness of this belief, you would be aware of its effect because there would be unmistakable patterns in your life.

Different ways we react to blocks

In order to spot the blocks we have it's important to be aware of the three main ways we react to them. When we've been going along happily on life's journey with the aim of reaching a goal and have suddenly been catapulted back to square one, or even further back, we'll have one of three different reactions:

1   Do it despite everything
2   Move on
3   No point in bothering

Blocks are context-dependent, which means we will behave differently in different circumstances. So we are likely to find ourselves swaying between these three reactions.

Reaction 1 – Do it despite everything

In this case, the person remains undeterred. They feel the 'pull' towards their goal so strongly that they achieve it, no matter what; alternatively, their block is such that it pulls them to their goal (i.e. fear of failure). People who react in this manner believe that even though life is hard, if you persevere you'll get there in the end, and sometimes the block even serves to motivate and drive them. They are proud of their scars because they show that they have made progress and that they have survived. Generally, these people will pay a high price and carry a big burden for getting results.

Reaction 2 – Move on

Once catapulted back, many people would deduce that that particular goal was not for them, that it didn't 'fit' with their capabilities, or some other plausible excuse, and change their goal to another, generally less challenging one that they believed they were able to achieve. They would interpret the setback as somehow showing that they weren't good enough and accept it as an unchangeable reflection of their ability.

Just as an example, a lot of people believe they cannot draw. At some point in the past they have decided, based on one or a number of experiences, that they are not good at it and from then on the belief has been reinforced every time the opportunity to draw has arisen – they either do not participate at all in the activity, or participate half-heartedly, producing just the result they know they are going to get! Instead of looking to see how they can improve their skill they put what they have to one side and move onto something else, something more achievable.

In itself this isn't that big a deal – so what if you believe you can't draw! The bigger problem comes later as this way of dealing with things gets ingrained into your way of thinking and you treat other challenges or difficult situations in the same way – leave it, take on the belief that you can't do that specific thing, and move onto something else. Over time the real problem starts to develop as more general negative beliefs, such as 'I can't do anything', are formed, 'validated' by the earlier experiences. People who react in this way inherently believe that they can't do much, and so cling desperately on to the few things they *have* learnt to do well and generally over-emphasize them at every opportunity. You can often spot this type of person from the heavy-handed way they say things like 'I'm *really good* at this'. The way it's said is the main signal, as the implication is that there are other things they aren't good at. Alternatively, they may be quietly lacking in confidence and stay very quiet, simply thinking those thoughts.

Reaction 3 – No point in bothering

There are also a small number of people who just want to stay there in the fallen position, revelling in self-pity and their failure, convinced that they will lose whatever they do, so why do anything? They delude themselves that life's just about enjoyment and pleasure (neither of which they experience to the full) and not about working yourself like a dog for nothing! These people relish others' misfortunes because it's a justification for being the way they are; it proves that if you set a goal it only ends in disappointment and so no one should bother, just as they don't bother.

Getting rid of blocks

It may be difficult to imagine getting rid of the negative emotions and limiting beliefs that we have been burdened with throughout our lives, because they can feel so much a part of us and often seem overwhelming. The truth, though, is that we can – and what's more, it's relatively straightforward to do.

Just by knowing what blocks are, we are able to look at our life from a different perspective – at least we have a reason and a purpose for having negative emotions and having limiting thoughts. We're no longer *at their effect* because we know why they're there and that they can be eliminated. Negative emotions may still consume us initially, but when we take a step back and look at them we can see that they are just the symptom level of a deeper and generally simpler problem that, over time, has gained momentum and emotional charge. As we concentrate on them further, there is soon a shift from being driven by negative emotions and limiting decisions to using them as a tool to highlight blocks and ease our journey. So instead of dreading their arrival you welcome them with open arms, as they provide another opportunity to explore, learn and grow – the positive implications of which will, in turn, make you more likely to get rid of blocks quickly and effectively.

Conscious and unconscious integration

If we want to do something simple like stand up, our conscious and unconscious minds have to work together to complete the task – our conscious mind gives the instruction 'get up' and our unconscious mind moves all the necessary muscles to bring us to a standing position. All day long our two minds continually work together as a team. Our ability to get rid of blocks involves utilizing our two minds – learning how they operate and ensuring that there is great communication between the two.

Our conscious mind

Our conscious mind is what we are most familiar and comfortable with as a society. It consists of our logical thought processes and all the things we are consciously thinking of. So, for example, if I asked you to give me the recipe of your favourite meal, one that you often cook, you'd be able to go through it with me, step by step, using your conscious mind to think it through.

Our unconscious mind

All the things we do without thinking are run by our unconscious mind. For most of us, it's something we take for granted and generally ignore. Most of what we do is actually run by our unconscious mind because the way our body functions, things such as digestion, movement, our immune system, etc., are all governed unconsciously.

Consider having to consciously figure out how to walk – you have so many muscles in your body that would need to be moved together just to lift a leg, let alone balance and co-ordinate, that it becomes clear how amazing and complicated it is. Many people are in awe of science and yet it's no match to the complexity and power of the mind and body we have. Science, with all its advancements and complexities, hasn't been able to grasp our whole capacity, let alone recreate it!

There is also another really powerful aspect of our unconscious mind – what is sometimes called our 'sixth sense'. Some people like to think of it as spirituality, being able to tune into yourself and the cosmos. However you wish to view it, it's the part of you that's connected to a higher, universal, 'all knowing' energy source, and is how you seem to intuitively know things that you couldn't have known otherwise, or how you can hope for something one day and then it miraculously happens – it brings about unaccountable coincidences and serendipity.

One of our known and accepted strengths as women is our emotional ability. Most of us instinctively know this and it is also accepted in social psychology that women are more capable than men at not only recognizing emotions in others, and within ourselves, but also in being able to communicate them. (Brody and Hall, 1993.)

We will utilize this skill, as well as tapping into the power of the mind, in the exercises for getting rid of blocks.

Preparation

There are three stages in getting rid of blocks:

1 uncovering what they are;
2 prioritizing them in the most effective order; and
3 getting rid of them.

To begin this process, you need to return to the things you have already highlighted in your One Area Charts (Appendix B) from the previous exercises – those things that have caused an unsavoury pattern in your life, behaviours you don't like, negative emotions or limiting beliefs. They are the things that you do, think or feel that are incongruent with your purpose and values, with who you are. Take five minutes to review them now.

Exercises

Aim: To prioritize the blocks so they can be effectively eliminated to give your life the greatest positive impact.

Duration: Approximately 1 hour (NB this time can vary greatly from person to person)

What you need:

- several sheets of paper
- One Area Chart (Appendix B) for each area of your life – filled in from previous exercises
- Guidance Chart (Appendix A)
- a tape recorder for Part B

Important points:

- Be relaxed, because then the integration between your conscious and unconscious minds is strengthened.
- Ask clear and precise questions and you will get clear answers.
- Go with what comes up for you straight away.
- Allow your conscious and unconscious minds to work as a team (be curious, respectful and listen openly to what comes up, without judging it).
- Some questions may appear to be a bit odd for your conscious mind. However, your conscious mind doesn't need to understand the questions – simply ask yourself the questions just as they are worded in the exercise and wait for the answer.
- Read through the exercise first because then you will know what to expect. If you wish to tape Part B, this would be a good time to do it.

Relax – Sit comfortably and be aware of your body. Feel each muscle relaxing, and your body becoming heavier with each exhalation.

Part A – Prioritizing blocks

Blocks generally have a domino effect, so by getting rid of a deep-rooted one it means the others that are connected to it will go as well. The only way of uncovering the deep-rooted ones is by getting your conscious mind to ask the specific questions and then by following the guidance of you unconscious mind. The first answer that pops into your mind – be it an image, a thought, a sound or a feeling – is the one to go with.

1   Put all your One Area Charts in locations where you can see them – if your table is not large enough you may have to use the floor. The important thing is that you are able to see all the blocks you have noted down on your charts.

2   **Relax** even more.

3   Ask yourself: 'What are the one, two or three key blocks, that, when removed, will make the most beneficial impact in my life now and help me to achieve (your objective)?'

    List them on a sheet of paper. Repeat this until you have them all (usually there are 2–4).

4   Look at your list of blocks and ask yourself: 'Which one is the most effective one to work on first?'

    Then ask: 'Which of these is the most effective one to work on next?' Put them in the order that comes up – just let it intuitively flow.

5   To ensure you have the correct ones, look at the prioritized list and ask:

    a   'Are these the right blocks for me to work now?'

    b   'Are they in the most effective order?'

    c   'Will I get the best possible results in my life by getting rid of these blocks?'

    Anything other than an absolute, congruent 'Yes' to any of these questions means that you don't have the right list, or that it's not in the right order. It's important that you get the right list in the right order because it will mean that you'll get rid of your block(s) easily and permanently.

If you don't get a definite 'Yes' then thank your unconscious mind for letting you know, and go back to the beginning of these questions, **relax** even more, and repeat them, focusing on the area that intuitively seems the right one to focus on.

If on the other hand you have an absolute 'Yes', then move to part B so you can start to get rid of the blocks.

Part B – Getting rid of blocks

Often, people find that they can get rid of blocks in under 5 minutes, but some people drag out the process to 10 or even 30 minutes! You have a choice as to which group you are in – it's purely a choice – so, if you want, decide now to be one of the people who completes it in 2 minutes.

For each of the blocks, working through them in order of priority, do the following:

1   **Relax –** Sit comfortably and be aware of your body. Feel each muscle relaxing, and your body becoming heavier with each exhalation.

2   Write down the block in the middle of a fresh sheet of paper.

3   Ask yourself: 'What is it that I need to know, the knowing of which will allow me to let go of "this block"?' Whatever comes up write it down, on the same sheet of paper, wherever feels like the right location. Keep on repeating the question until there are no more answers.

4   Ask yourself: 'What is the first event that, when disconnected, will allow this block to disappear?' Take the first event that pops into your mind – it will be right. (So if this was the fear of spiders explored early in this chapter (page 76) the first event would be at age two.)

5   **Relax** even more – feel each muscle melting and your body becoming heavier with each exhalation, then ask the 'you' from the first event to join the 'you' of now. (Going back to our example again, the mature you from now would be with the two-year-old you from your past.) They can be images (a picture of the two of you together), feelings (you can sense the two of you), sounds (you can hear the

two of you), or the two of you thinking so you can hear each other's thoughts – whatever works best for you in your own mind.

6   Have a conversation with the 'you' from then, knowing what you know now, and with all the skills and experiences you now have. How can you support and help the 'you' from your past? Sometimes all that's needed is some tender loving attention; or perhaps the perspective of an older you will help to change the viewpoint of the younger you, in effect reframing the block away instantaneously.

7   Evaluate when the 'you' from the past is absolutely happy with the event, then ask your unconscious mind: 'Is it OK to let go of this block now easily and effortlessly?'

    If you get anything other than a 'Yes' you need to have a little bit more of a chat to discover why. Then you will know what to do. After you have got a 'Yes', say: 'Great, thanks. Now go ahead and get rid of the block, and subsequent and connected blocks'.

    What will happen is that the first event and all the connected and subsequent events will all go at once, and you may feel a little different, as though there has been a physical/emotional shift – some even feel tingly all over. (This shift can last anything from a few minutes to about 2 weeks!)

8   Check to ensure that it's gone by asking your unconscious mind. Looking at the block on your sheet of paper ask: 'Dear unconscious mind, has this block completely gone now?'

    If you get anything other than an unequivocal 'Yes' it just means that you need to go back to the conversation (see point 6) and gain a few more insights before you can fully let it go. If you get a 'Yes', great! Thank your unconscious mind and move on to the final step.

9   Test your results:

    Consider experiences in your past where this block had been an issue. Go to two or three specific experiences and notice what's different now. Take a few minutes to fully experience the change

– How do you feel differently? What do you see? What do you say to yourself? Come back to now in light of your new knowledge.

Consider possible events in the future that, if they'd have happened in the past, would have caused the old block to be triggered. As you consider each one, go there now, and notice how it differs. Take a few minutes to fully experience the change – In what way do you feel different? What do you see? What do you say to yourself? Come back to now in light of your new knowledge.

Your perception of past and possible future experiences should have changed, so that you now feel empowered, have more choices and have no negative emotions associated with it.

Note: If your perception has not changed it means the block (or connecting blocks) has not gone yet. In that case just go back to point 6 and continue your conversation until the block has completely gone.

There is another situation where getting rid of blocks can be practised – in a just-in-time, opportunistic way. If something happens and you suddenly feel fear, guilt or any other negative emotion or limiting belief, you know it's just a flag indicating there is something to be dealt with, just like the 'off' smell in the fridge, and you can deal with it there and then. (If it's not appropriate you can deal with it by asking your unconscious mind to put you in a resourceful position straight away and to park the negativity – put it on the shelf by saying to yourself 'Thank you for making me aware of this I shall deal with it on [a specific day and time]. Now put me in a positive state so I can move forward with my day.') Ensure you keep to your agreement with yourself or you may find your block returns with a vengeance.

When you first try this it can feel like a lot of work, but as you do it more you'll quickly find a way that works best for you. I generally use The Glide Method (Appendix F) myself and with my clients, and it's the type of thing you want to be aiming for in the future – your own shorthand way of dealing with blocks.

1.4.3 MORE CONFIDENCE AND FUN EACH DAY

'For they conquer who believe they can.'

John Dryden

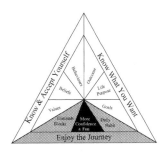

If we want the best for our lives then we need to be able to control and increase the positives. In this chapter we'll look at what we can do to ensure that we go through each day having more confidence and fun because both are critical for a happy and successful life.

The appeal

Having confidence, being happy and having fun feels great, and it's also incredibly appealing to others. If you met two people that were similar in every way except that one was fun and the other wasn't, which one would you want to have a conversation with? Which one would you rather work with? Which one would you find more attractive?

It works just the same if you substitute the 'fun' characteristic with 'confident' or with 'happy' – a deep and assured confidence that just oozes out of them. Consider again how different they would appear.

For most of us it's simple: the person who is more fun and confident is substantially more attractive and appealing than the one who isn't. And this remains true even if they are less superficially (physically) attractive than the person you are comparing them with.

The best part is that being more confident and fun feels substantially better for the person experiencing it as well. If you think back to a time when you were having great fun and/or felt confident and compare it to a less great day, it's rather like comparing sunny and cloudy days. The feeling of confidence is so empowering and nourishing that, let's face it, if we knew where we could order some, we would.

The techniques in the next two sections are designed especially so that you can do just that – have more confidence and fun. Circle of Empowerment enables you to maximize on your positive emotions and Perception Enhancer helps you to gain insight about yourself and others, thereby helping you to gain more confidence.

1.4.4 CIRCLE OF EMPOWERMENT

'Life is really simple, but we insist on making it complicated.'

Confucius

In the 1920s a psychologist named Ivan Pavlov discovered that dogs could be conditioned to physically respond in a certain way under certain conditions. In his experiments he would ring a bell just before giving them food and, before long, just ringing the bell would make the dogs salivate. (Pavlov, 1927.) This is an example of a conditioned response, which all animals, including humans, are capable of having. Interestingly, one of the most common conditioned responses in humans is avoiding going for something we want for fear of getting hurt, because of past painful experiences.

The Circle of Empowerment is an imaginary circle that uses this animal conditioning to create a stack of powerful, positive, empowering emotions so we can condition ourselves to respond in an effective way – creating a very compelling resource we can utilize whenever we want.

You may have had times in your past where you have been asked to do something and it instilled you with fear and dread, where your confidence and sense of fun went straight out of the window. Once created, the Circle of Empowerment is perfect for such a situation. All you need to do is fire it off – which you can do in your mind by imagining your Circle and physically stepping into it – and the positive emotions stacked up there will melt the fear and dread away.

Exercise

Aim: To build a very positive powerful emotional state which you can use any time you feel you need a 'boost'.

Duration: 1 hour

What you need:

- an open mind
- an attitude of curiosity and fun
- a safe, quiet environment, free of distractions and disruptions
- a sheet of paper

Important point: Be relaxed, because then you can really get in touch with your positive emotions

Relax – Sit comfortably and be aware of your body. Feel each muscle relaxing, and your body becoming heavier with each exhalation.

1   Make a list of positive emotions you want to have in your Circle of Empowerment. Ones to consider are: confidence, fun, curiosity, success, centeredness/calmness. The idea is to stack up as many positive, powerful emotions as possible because it will make your Circle more powerful. Quickly jot them down now on a piece of paper and then put them in order of priority.

2   Imagine a circle that's large enough for you to step into easily, on a specific location on the ground – you can even physically draw one if you like. This is the circle that will contain your stack of positive emotions.

3   Take the first positive emotion, e.g. confidence, and do the following:

   a   Consider a specific time in your past that you were absolutely
       confident (confident while feeling a little anxious would not be
       appropriate). It can be a special event or as simple as making
       a cup of tea. What's important is that it's a specific event in your
       personal history where you felt completely confident.

   b   Think of that event, go back to it in your mind and experience the
       emotion of confidence again as if it's now. As you feel the emotion
       building up in your body step into the Circle.

c Have the confident feeling wash all over you and then amplify the feeling. (You can amplify the feeling by making the image in your mind brighter and richer, or by imagining a dial – like a volume control – that you can use to turn up the feeling, making it stronger and stronger.) Experience it in every part of your body. When you have had enough, or if your mind wanders, step out of the Circle. It's important that the Circle is kept pure with powerful positive emotions.

d Repeat steps b and c a couple of times, so you are considering the same event, stepping into the Circle, and amplifying the feeling each time.

e Consider another time in your past when you were confident, purely confident, and repeat steps a–d until you have a very powerful Circle (for some people it means 2–3 entries and for others it's about 10).

f Test your Circle out. This will be good reinforcement for you as well as making sure you are on the right track before you start adding the other positive emotions.

Standing outside your Circle think of something that's going to happen in your future that you are apprehensive about – it should be a specific event. (If you don't have something in the future remember a specific event in your past when you felt apprehensive in advance.) Ensure your Circle has far more power and energy than the event does by asking what the strength is from 0–10 for both. If the apprehension connected to the event is stronger you need to build up the power in your Circle.

As you consider the event, step into the Circle and stay there for about a minute. Let the confidence you have stacked up melt your apprehension. Your perception of the event will be altered and you'll be left with a nicely confident feeling and a positive perspective of that event – the facts stay the same but your perception of them shifts to one that is empowering.

If this is not your experience then it means that you've missed or misinterpreted something. Thank your unconscious mind for making you aware of it now and go back to the beginning and read through all the steps until you have figured out what happened. Then repeat them.

4   Repeat the exercise for each of the emotions you want to add to your Circle. Each time, your Circle will be getting more and more powerful. Enjoy the experience and your discoveries.

Once you have completed the steps you will have a powerful Circle of Empowerment that you can pull up at will and apply to any situation. You just have to imagine stepping into your Circle – or sitting on it, having it go over your head – any image that enables your body to be in contact with the Circle in your mind.

A great way of increasing the positive power of your Circle is to stack positive experiences into it as you have them – just imagine stepping into your Circle as the experience happens.

1.4.5 PERCEPTION ENHANCER

'When one door closes another door opens; but we so often look so long and so regretfully upon the closed door, that we do not see the ones which open for us.'

Alexander Graham Bell

Most women are naturally good at forming and keeping relationships, but even so, there are moments of crisis in relationships, when our emotions run riot and we are at a loss – emotionally hijacked.

For example, imagine two scenarios: in one your partner does something that really upsets you and in the other someone else does the same thing, but it doesn't emotionally affect you. If you had to communicate your thoughts it's likely that you would be far more objective and effective with the person who isn't your partner because, when we get involved with someone, we often lose our objective perspective and our natural ability to connect may suffer.

The technique below, Perception Enhancer, is a great way of ensuring that you have a full and informed perspective of any relationship – it has consistently proved itself to be one of those little gems that helps people across the board because it helps them to understand their relationship, their role within it, and what they can do to improve it.

Consider a relationship you have that's not going well, with someone at work who really annoys you perhaps, or a relative who always seems to get under your skin, even someone from your past. Select someone that you want to get more insights about, either so you can let them go from your past or so you can have an easier relationship with them in the future.

Once you have someone in mind go through the following exercise.

Exercise

Aim: To enhance your perception of your relationship with a specific person – how you behave, how they perceive your behaviour, and vice versa – and discover what you can do to improve your relationship.

Duration: 1 hour

What you need:

- an open mind
- an attitude of curiosity and fun
- a safe, quiet environment, free of distractions and disruptions

Important point: Be relaxed, because then you can get the most insights.

Relax – Sit comfortably and be aware of your body. Feel each muscle relaxing, and your body becoming heavier with each exhalation.

In your mind have a clear idea of where, on the floor, you would like Positions 1, 2 and 3 to be, as shown in the picture below: Position 1 is you in your own body; Position 2 is 'being in their shoes'; and Position 3 is an objective position where you are observing how the person in Positions 1 and 2 relate to each other.

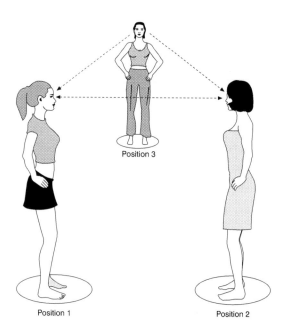

Position 3

Position 1

Position 2

1   Step into the location for Position 1, into your own body looking at the person you have in mind (imagine they are looking back at you from Position 2). Just enjoy being in your body and consider:

a   How do you feel?

b   What do you see?

c What do you hear?

d What do you say outwardly and to yourself?

When you feel you have fully experienced all that there is to experience, leave the 'you' there (because that belongs in Position 1). You can do this easily by shaking your shoulders slightly and moving out of the location for Position 1.

2 Move along and step into Position 2, into the other person's body so that you are looking (in your mind's eye) at your own body in front of you, in Position 1, behaving the way you do, saying what you say, interacting with the other person as you would interact. This is truly being able to step into another person's shoes, so by being here consider:

a How does if feel to be him/her?

b What does this person see?

c What does this person hear?

d What does this person say outwardly and to himself/herself?

Really experience it from the other person's perspective. Then, when you feel you have fully experienced all that there is to experience, leave that position – fully clear yourself of the other person, again by shaking your shoulders slightly.

3 Now step into Position 3, the observer position, so you can see the 'you' in Position 1 behaving, thinking and feeling the way 'you' do, and the other person in Position 2 behaving, thinking and feeling the way they do, and you are in the position of objective observer, viewing the interaction between these two people. Consider:

a What do you see?

b How do these two people interact? How do they relate to each other?

c What works well?

d What could improve?

e What's needed by you in Position 1 to assist you in the interaction? (Go back to a time when you had what you needed and imagine it in your body now.) Once you have learnt as much as you can in this new position, leave it by shaking your shoulders slightly and moving out of the location.

4   Take all your new insights and resource(s) and go back to Position 1, into your own body, observing the other person in Position 2. Now apply your new knowledge and behaviours, and observe how you have changed:

a   How do you feel?

b   What do you see?

c   What do you hear?

d   What do you say outwardly and to yourself?

Once you have fully experienced this, shake it off and move out of the position.

5   Step into the other person's shoes, Position 2, be the other person again, with this new behaviour and interaction from 'you' in Position 1, observe the changes that are happening in the other person:

a   How does this person feel?

b   What does this person see?

c   What does this person hear?

d   What is this person saying outwardly and to himself/herself?

Once you have fully experienced this, shake it off and move out of the position.

6   Move on to Position 3, into the observer position, and look at the new way these two people are interacting together.

If you don't consider it to be good enough, or feel that it can be even better, repeat all the steps again.

Otherwise go back to Position 1, into your own body, and stay there for a minute to enjoy your accomplishment. (Its always best to end up in your own body!)

(*Please note* that sometimes you can even have a Position 4, which is a perspective even further away, a galactic view of Positions 1, 2 and 3. For some people this can be a very useful addition; for others it is very similar to Position 3. The best thing to do is to try it out and if it adds value for you then to use it.)

Whilst going through the exercise you will have found some of the positions to be far easier to get into than others. Generally we are very good at one, OK at the other and very weak at the third (our 'blind spot'). It's good to know which ones come naturally for you and which is your 'blind spot' – your area for growth. For example, if someone has experienced a lot of emotional upset at an early age, they may not be able to easily connect with their own feelings, so Position 1 will be a struggle for them. Equally for 'emotional' people Position 3, the observer position, can be very difficult to get into, especially when upset.

This simple exercise is wonderful for effectively managing relationships and developing our relationship skills. The most effective people have the skill of gaining information from all three of these positions and making decisions in Position 3.

1.4.6 DAILY HABIT

'We are what we repeatedly do.
Excellence, then, is not an act, but a habit.'

Aristotle

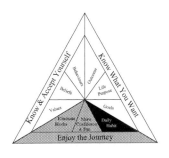

Imagine you are at the beach and want to build a sand castle, one that you will be really proud of. You get rid of any blocks you might have that would stop you, visualize your castle and set your goal to build it. You then need to take action, either to start building it yourself or to recruit other builders; otherwise it's unlikely you'll get your sand castle.

Getting rid of our blocks frees us from what holds us back and setting goals gives us clarity for what we want. Then, by taking action – doing something on a daily basis that supports our purpose and our goals – we immediately feel good and know that we are on our path. One day, after a little while of being 'true to our path', and when we least expect it, we become aware of how blissfully happy and fulfilled we are from just living our everyday life. What were mundane activities in the past are transformed into purposeful ones – stepping stones on our path, our personal adventure.

Doing something for yourself every day (a daily habit) that's fun, empowering, and in line with who you are and what you want from life is very powerful because it increases your 'pull' towards achieving what you want: a habit that gives you a great sense of accomplishment and of purpose. It's a confirmation that you are on your path, and that in itself is highly pleasurable.

For each area of your life the question to ask yourself is 'What enjoyable thing can I do on a daily basis to help support my life's purpose and my goals?' The two critical success factors for effective habit creation are for it to support the future you want, and for you to be 100% sure you can, and will, keep to it. Only take on as many as you can definitely keep to.

There are two general daily habits which you may wish to look at: Habit 1 – Positive Thought Habit (Appendix G) and Habit 2 – Visualizing Your Goals (Appendix H). They have been tried and tested and are very effective.

Ideally, you want to select daily habits that are initially small and pleasurable that will have a definite positive effect over the weeks, months and years. Doing something for yourself every day is very important – you can enjoy creating the life you want to have, letting it grow with you.

It should only take about half an hour to decide what your daily habits will be and the habits themselves need to be very quick – a few minutes at most – so they can easily be absorbed into your day.

I love this passage by Buddha. it describes the real power and impact of a simple thought and habit:

'The thought manifests as the word;
The word manifests as the deed;
The deed develops into habit;
And the habit hardens into character;
So watch the thought and its ways with care;
And let it spring from love …
As the shadow follows the body,
as we think, so we become.'

From the Dhammapada (Sayings of the Buddha)

Conclusion to Part 1

Just being aware of the techniques in Part 1 is empowering in itself, because they offer you choices in situations where previously there were none: you can choose to gain clarity, or not; you can choose to deal with your negative emotions and limiting beliefs (your blocks), or not; you can choose to live your life in balance, or indeed not. Ultimately, there is no greater gift than the gift of knowing you have choices and that there are other ways of seeing and doing things.

PART 2

Dealing with Specific Life Challenges

Introduction to Part 2

Each module in Part 2 describes a fairly common problem or challenge from the various phases of a woman's life and is followed by a solution, using the techniques from Part 1, that's practical and has worked for others in the past.

Each solution section is preceded by a 'Top Tip', which points out the one thing that's most important to focus on within the context of that challenge. The 'Getting results' section gives an overview, a road map, of the appropriate modules in Part 1 that you'll need to apply to get the result you want, so you can apply them to your own situation. It takes you step-by-step through an exercise to help you gain clarity and deal with your challenge in the best possible way for you. It also demonstrates the usefulness of the technique being described with a case study, so you can see how it has worked in practice.

Please note that these are wide-ranging solutions that have been designed in a way which is holistic and general so as to work for as many people as possible. It's therefore important that you consider these exercises as guides and adapt them as you feel appropriate for your own unique situation.

Relationships

Module	Title	Page	Exercise time (mins)
2.1.1	The secret of finding the *right* man	113	215
2.1.2	Keeping your man, or not!	122	185
2.1.3	Is your man cheating on you?	128	460
2.1.4	Starting to date again	135	215

2.1.1 THE SECRET OF FINDING THE *RIGHT* MAN

Fed up with going out with overgrown boys, bastards and commitment-phobes? Wondering if there ever is a 'Right Man'? Does he really exist or is he just a character in a fairytale? Are all the good men married? Should you settle for a mediocre relationship or hold out for Mr Right – soul mate or no mate?

There's a world of loving, wonderful women out there, all with different backgrounds and ages, but with the same problem – they're single and would like to have a partner, someone to love. They've met many Mr Wrongs but somehow Mr Right has evaded them. If you're one of these women you are in good company.

Sarah Clarke is an ambitious, fun-loving and caring 30-year-old. She's attractive, intelligent, has a great job, her own home, a wonderful circle of friends and is completely at a loss.

'What am I doing wrong? Why can't I find a decent guy who'll love and respect me?'

Sarah has been in love four times. Each time, when she least expected it – Bam! – she fell head over heels. Then a few years down the line, when it was screamingly clear to her friends, she noticed that perhaps all was not well.

Her last relationship was the worst. They met at a colleague's leaving drinks and were instantly attracted to each other. He was five years older than her – fit, great fun, and good looking. They had a wonderful romance for three years but over the last twelve months she started to realize there was something wrong. He was always away on business and, though she didn't think much of it initially, slowly she became more and more suspicious. In the end she discovered that he'd never left his last girlfriend! She felt that she should have realized the truth earlier. What kind of a fool was she? How did she get sucked in by his bare-faced lies?

Was she attracting Mr Wrongs because she is Miss Wrong, or Miss Not Good Enough?

Hilary Jennings is very happy with her life. She has a beautiful daughter and grandchildren – Kate, 6; and Peter, 14. Her mortgage is paid and although she isn't wealthy she is financially independent, and over the years she's built a core circle of friends that she cherishes very dearly.

Generally her life is relaxed and peaceful but with occasional pangs of longing. Her husband died 20 years ago and up until now she has not considered having another man in her life. She was always far too busy raising her daughter and her daughter's needs always came first. But now she craves someone she can share her life with.

'I'd be quite happy never to have sex again, but I really would like to have a man take care of me, and have someone I could take care of. It's the little things I miss,' she says, looking lost. 'But how do I find someone so late on in my life? I'm so out of practice – I don't do the things youngsters do!'

Many of us have, at one time or another, gone out looking for a man. Generally it doesn't work: the thing you pursue resists. It's when we stop looking and get on with life that relationships come along. The adage

'A rose does not chase a bee' is the fundamental essence of finding Mr Right. Grow, blossom, take care of yourself, exude your uniqueness and wait for Mr Right to come to you.

If you are thinking about beauty treatments and perfume, think again. That's not it. It's about exuding the essence of you – really discovering who you are; what you want in a relationship; being the confident, fun 'you' you know you can be, and observing the results. Physically taking care of yourself is great, but that's just the icing on the cake.

TOP TIP

The secret of finding the right man is by simply finding yourself and what you truly want.

Getting results

So how do you find yourself? What do you have to do so the right man is attracted to you? Below is a process that will help you to do just that.

1 Outcome
2 Behaviours
3 Beliefs
4 Blocks
5 Values
6 Goals
7 Feedback

1 – Outcome

To be able to find your Mr Right you have to know what you're looking for and ensure you're ready to have it. The Outcome Model will help you do that.

For Sarah this module was the most helpful one because it highlighted the root cause of her problem. You can see how the limiting beliefs below would have made it difficult for her to find Mr Right! (You will find outcome model answers for Sarah in Appendix E.)

> *Sarah's limiting beliefs are:*
> * *'When you have the right man "something inside you dies"';*
> * *'There's no "excitement" when you are in a relationship';*
> * *'The excitement of the struggle and chase goes when you are in a relationship'; and*
> * *'Opportunities are endless when you are single; when you're attached you know what you've got'.*

It is clear that unless she deals with these limiting beliefs she'll never be in the type of relationship she wants, because she has an unconscious vested interest in staying single (secondary gain). Unless dealt with, these beliefs will always be sabotaging her efforts.

Go to page 57 to go through the Outcome Model for yourself. Pay particular attention to the final section, questions 11–16, because this will highlight any secondary gains you may have from staying single. If you do have any secondary gains note them down and put them to one side ready for when you go through the Blocks module.

2 – Behaviours

Just as a doctor looks at symptoms to find the root cause of a problem, behavioural analysis enables you to look at your behavioural patterns in or around relationships and uncover possible root-level problems that are stopping you from finding, or keeping, Mr Right.

When Sarah looked at her relationships this way the pattern became crystal clear.

- *She doesn't fancy the guy initially.*
- *Then, in conversation, when she least expects it, she would become captivated and in awe.*
- *She is always under the influence of alcohol when she 'falls' for him.*
- *The relationship is initially euphoric, then problems begin to appear – she starts to find out who he really is and the more she finds out the less she likes.*
- *The relationship lasts between two and three years, and the last six months are extremely difficult.*
- *She lets her feelings rule her head and doesn't take proper stock of the situation.*
- *She never listens to her friends' advice, just to her heart.*

So what does this pattern mean? What's the root cause? We can't always tell for sure from this information alone. These are like jigsaw pieces indicating that there is a problem but not giving a clear picture. All we know at this stage is that Sarah is attracted to men who are not right for her. There has to be something driving her to do this – and that will be the root cause.

Go to page 47 for more information on behaviours or, if you prefer, go straight to the behaviours exercise on page 48 and discover your own behavioural patterns in relationships.

3 – Beliefs

Beliefs are the foundation of behaviour. Positive beliefs will help you find and keep Mr Right and limiting beliefs will hinder and sabotage you. The Beliefs module will help you to uncover all your beliefs around relationships, both positive and limiting.

It's important to highlight limiting beliefs because then we can eliminate them using the Blocks module. Highlighting positive beliefs will help you understand yourself far better and enable you to exude your unique essence that much more effectively.

For Sarah her top three positive relationship beliefs are:

- *'I will find my soul mate';*
- *'I am a good catch'; and*
- *'I deserve to be happy'.*

Her top three limiting relationship beliefs are:

- *'I don't deserve to be loved';*
- *'Men use me'; and*
- *'Men are all bastards'.*

The plot thickens – we know there is a root-level problem causing Sarah to pick the wrong men, so the question is: 'Is one of these limiting beliefs the root cause of the problem or is there something else?' Again, we keep the information we have so far and investigate further.

Go to page 43 for more information about beliefs or, if you prefer, go straight to the beliefs exercise on page 45 and discover your positive and limiting relationship beliefs.

4 – Blocks

Getting rid of limiting blocks is essential for getting your man. You can create as much positive essence as you like but if it's contaminated with negativity your essence will be muddied and not effective. The Blocks module will help you to highlight and get rid of those areas that stop or hinder you from getting your Mr Right.

The limiting beliefs and negative emotions you have already uncovered from the earlier exercises will be highlighted and worked on in this section so they can be eliminated.

The blocks that Sarah worked on are:

- *'When you have the right man "something inside you dies";*
- *'If I was in a relationship then I'd lose the excitement of being single';*
- *'There's no "excitement" when in a relationship';*
- *'The excitement of the struggle and chase goes when you are in a relationship';*
- *'Opportunities are endless when you are single; when you're attached you know what you have got';*
- *'I don't deserve to be loved';*
- *'Men use me';*
- *'Men are all bastards';*
- *negative emotion of being alone – loneliness; and*
- *negative emotion of fear.*

This is a compilation of her answers from previous modules and her results from going through the Blocks module. Having worked on her blocks Sarah was able to get rid of them and as a consequence looked as though she'd grown a foot taller, just because of the new way she held herself!

Go to page 75 for more information about blocks or, if you prefer, go straight to the blocks exercise on page 85 and start to get rid of the unconscious blocks stopping you from finding, or keeping, your Mr Right.

5 – Values

Values provide the torch to guide you whilst you consider if you want to go out with someone or not; they are at the core of our very being and by being consciously aware of your relationship values you'll be able to project your true self.

> *Sarah's relationship values are:*
> - *growth*
> - *integrity*
> - *empowerment*
> - *fun*
> - *sex.*
>
> *If Sarah were to go out with someone and simply have a great time with them – having fun and lots of sex – and felt completely empowered to do anything she wanted, it would not work out. However hard she tried to convince herself that he was great for her, she would be missing someone with whom she could have a good conversation and someone with integrity that she could trust. Anything less than that is Mr Wrong.*
>
> *You may be wondering how someone can leave love out of relationship values. Sarah simply felt that if she had all of these that there would be love anyway.*

Page 39 will give you more information about values or, if you prefer, go straight to the exercise on page 41 and discover your own relationship values. The most important thing here is that there's no right or wrong, whatever comes up for you is right for you, for now.

6 – Goals

The Goals module will help you to maximize your sense of self and greatly increase your levels of attraction for Mr Right.

Sarah set the following goals:

> - 'Meet and be going out with her Mr Right by the end of the year'; and
> - 'Be married with a family within ten years'.

Go to page 65 for more about goals or go straight to the goals exercise on page 68 to define your relationship goals.

7 – Feedback

In this module you will learn how to use the fundamental concept of feedback to ensure you achieve your goal of finding Mr Right.

Sarah, after a couple of enhancements to her goals, is now going out with a man she believes to be Mr Right. She's not absolutely sure yet – time will tell – but she's happy to get to know him more and see how it goes (though in her heart, after two months, she is 99% sure he is the one for her).

Go to page 26 to discover the feedback-not-failure concept and how it can work for you.

Once you have gone through these modules you'll have gained a far greater understanding of yourself and your past relationships – you'll know what you really want and will have got rid of any blocks. As a result you'll naturally be giving out that wonderfully unique essence of you and attracting your Mr Right.

2.1.2 KEEPING YOUR MAN, OR NOT!

Our relationships are very important to us and our relationship with our intimate partner is usually one of the most important. So it's perhaps unsurprising that many women feel they want to go the extra mile to keep their man – using anything they have at their disposal to keep him from straying – everything from threatening, controlling and overpowering behaviour to coaxing and being indispensable (a doormat) or, indeed, trying to be perfect.

It's ironic that when we first start to date, it's often the man who does the chasing, with the woman remaining more aloof, and yet once there's some sort of commitment, the roles completely reverse, with the woman changing her behaviour and becoming the opposite of what the man was attracted to in the first place! On top of this, keeping her man can be a standard by which the woman evaluates her self-worth.

Amy Peterson has recently started to date Michael. They met at a friend's party and she didn't like him at first – she thought he was full of himself – but as they were the only smokers they frequently ended up outside together. By the end of the evening she had really started to like him and when he called the following week she knew the feeling was mutual.

It's been two months since the party and they are getting on incredibly well, even talking about going on holiday together. It's all going along swimmingly except that Amy is now worried about him straying and cheating on her, even leaving her. How can she make sure she keeps him?

Harriett Kempton has been going out with Paul for three years. The first two years were great, but over the last year the relationship has had its difficulties – they don't talk so much and generally when they do it tends to end up in an argument. Now he spends more time at work to avoid her. Even so, Harriett feels that she should try to make the relationship work – she's invested a lot of time and effort and doesn't want to let it all go, but doesn't know how to improve the situation.

When we find something good we tend to want to keep it forever, but by holding on too strongly to someone we can kill the relationship and end up holding on to something that has died. There are tricks and techniques you can use to keep someone with you but they are superficial and ultimately disempowering. We don't cover them here. What this module aims to do is show how you can get the most from your relationship so you both **choose** to stay together, rather than one person manipulating the other. This will mean you can be confident and happy within yourself and your relationship.

TOP TIP

Accept that your man is not your possession to keep, just as you're not 'his'. If you let go of the need to keep him and be totally, naturally and positively yourself, then if you choose to stay together you'll have a truly wonderful relationship.

Getting results

The process below will guide you towards getting the most from your relationship. As with all things, the more you put in to it the more you'll get out.

1   Outcome
2   Blocks
3   Strategy
    • Values
    • Perception Enhancer
4   Feedback

1 – Outcome

This is a simple model to highlight whether you truly want, and are ready to keep, a partner. It will flush out any secondary gains you may have from being single – i.e. hidden unconscious benefits that breaking up may have for you. These have to be uncovered and addressed before any other work is done, or the work will have to be repeated.

> Amy initially wanted to have a relationship with a partner who doesn't cheat. Then after turning it into a positive she realized that what she really wants is to have a fun relationship where the trust is inherent. Amy also discovered that she had a block – the fear of being badly hurt.

Go to page 57 to go through the outcome model for yourself. Pay particular attention to the final section, questions 11–16, because this will highlight if you have any secondary gains from losing your man.

2 – Blocks

Getting rid of limiting blocks is fundamental to having a healthy relationship. This module goes to the root causes of your negative emotions and limiting beliefs, highlighting them and helping you tackle them so you can move forward free of blocks.

The blocks Amy worked on are:
- *fear of being vulnerable to being truly hurt;*
- *fear of loss;*
- *fear of betrayal;*
- *jealousy; and*
- *a feeling of not being good enough.*

Interestingly it was the last one she worked on first – getting rid of the negative feeling that she was not good enough. After dealing with this the others lost their charge, although she went through them one by one anyway, just to be absolutely sure.

Go to page 75 for a more detailed explanation of blocks and how they affect us or, if you prefer, go straight to the blocks exercise on page 85 and start to get rid of the unconscious blocks that are stopping you from having a great relationship.

3 – Strategy

Getting rid of limitations and blocks leaves you with a clean canvas to start creating an effective strategy for having a wonderful relationship. We all have our own unique way of relating to others and it's important that you keep that. However, you should find that the process and tools below can help enhance it.

1 Discovering your own and your partner's values is incredibly important because it's like having the blueprint of what's really important

to you both. Either go through the Values module on page 39 for further information on values or go straight to the exercise on page 41 and discover what your and your partner's relationship values are. (You can either go through this exercise individually and then share your findings with your partner or go through it together – whichever works best for both of you is fine.)

2   Perception Enhancer is a wonderful model to help you see your relationship from a different perspective; the more you are able to enhance your perspectives the better your relationship will be. Go to page 93 for more on Perception Enhancer or, if you prefer, go straight to the exercise on page 94 and see what discoveries you make about yourself, your partner, and how you interact in your relationship.

3   Communication in a relationship is as vital as water is to our bodies – without it we wither and die. We all have different ideas about the best way to communicate – some have to strike immediately when an idea comes into their head, whilst others like to take time and reflect before speaking. Get to know your partner's and your own preferences and be flexible in your approach – the best way to do this is to be absolutely honest, be truly present in what's happening in the moment, to listen to your partner and hear what is truly being said.

4   We each have our own unique way of demonstrating how we love, respect, and value our partner. Equally we have a unique way of recognizing how our partner loves, respects and values us. Generally this is all unconscious and we just expect the other person to telepathically know – a bit like going to a foreign country and expecting the culture and language there to be the same as ours!

The most effective way forward is to find out how you and your partner demonstrate and recognize that you love, respect and value each other. The quickest way to do this is for both of you to independently sit down and answer the questions below, because then your answers are free of any possible influence:

- How do I know I am loved?
- How do I demonstrate that I love my partner?

Then repeat these questions for the other two areas – respect and value. Once you are happy with your list of answers, share them with each other. *It's very important there are no negative judgements made when you are sharing your discoveries, so phrase everything positively.*

Initially, Amy found the strategy rather simple; it was only later that she understood its full power. Knowing her values meant she had very clear boundaries for what she would and would not accept; the Perception Enhancer helped her to understand Michael and herself more, especially why he retreats into his work and how she has responded to that in the past. The thing that made the biggest impact for Amy, though, was discovering her love strategy and also his – one of Michael's ways of demonstrating his love for her was by solving her problems. Interestingly, one of her ways of knowing she was loved was by being listened to – there had been a mismatch in the past where he had tried to solve her problems far too soon for her to feel loved! It all started to fall into place for her.

3 – Feedback

In this module you will learn how to use the fundamental concept of feedback to ensure you get the outcome you desire, because knowing there is a fallback position often makes you less clingy and gives your current relationship a better chance of succeeding.

Go to page 26 to discover the feedback-not-failure concept and how it can work for you.

Amy didn't think she'd need to use feedback but discovered that she liked the fact that she had a fallback position – somehow making the concept of a break-up less painful and more of a positive learning experience.

Once you have gone through the modules outlined above you'll have gained a far greater understanding of yourself, your partner and how you relate to each other (how you know you're loved, respected and valued) and will have uncovered and eliminated any blocks stopping you from having a great relationship – leaving you free to truly discover each other and your relationship or, if need be, that you need to move on.

2.1.3 IS YOUR MAN CHEATING ON YOU?

Ever wondered if your partner is cheating on you? Even if it's just a fleeting thought, it cuts to the very core. Could he do this to me? Would he? Would I know? Do I know? Surely he wouldn't blatantly lie or risk our relationship? Others have – would he?

Besides hiring a private investigator or just accidentally catching him out, is there another way you can find out if your man is true or not? If you're a women in this situation the biggest obstacle you face is yourself, or more specifically, your perception of reality. We all go about our day deleting, distorting and generalizing reality – we can't help ourselves, we've had to learn to cope with the two million bits per second of information thrown at us and it's the only way to manage.

As women, we tend to ignore the signs of infidelity if it's not what we want to see – we distort truths and make plausible excuses to ourselves and to others to keep what we have.

Susan Pryor, a school teacher, had been married for seven years when her husband turned around and said he wanted a divorce because he'd met another woman, was in love with her and no longer wanted to be married to Susan.

Susan had met Peter whilst doing her degree and, five years into their relationship, he proposed. She was 25 and completely besotted with him – he was charismatic, sensitive, great fun, and intelligent; he took risks but she was grounded enough for the both of them. Together they made a great team. What else could a girl want? She was happy with her life and they'd been talking about having a baby. When he broke the news she was devastated, the floor went from under her and her world fell apart.

Mary Potter had been going out with Steve for two years and they were deeply in love, or at least so she thought. He spoke about them buying a home together and even getting married, but something inside Mary had said 'Wait – this isn't right yet'. It was a slip-up on his part that initially got her suspicious – his stories didn't match up. Did she hear right? Unlike other times she decided not to challenge him straight away, she wanted time to think. She was starting to get a really uneasy feeling in the pit of her stomach.

At first she felt very uncomfortable checking up on him – if she didn't trust him the relationship should stop now and she shouldn't be spying on him, or anyone for that matter. They had to break up, she was not the type of person to stay with someone she suspected of cheating. Even so she wanted to know – she **had** *to know.*

Besides ignoring the signs the other common problem for many women as that we place a lot of the blame on ourselves: What kind of a woman am I to even suspect him of cheating? What kind of a relationship is this? It somehow becomes a reflection of the woman and her relationship. Generally the truth is very simple – either your partner is cheating on you or your insecurities and jealousy are such that you suspect it to be so. The challenge, of course, is to figure out what the truth really is, because then we can protect ourselves from sabotaging our relationships, or indeed from wasting our time with emotionally backward, deceptive, game-playing partners.

TOP TIP

Be honest with yourself. You already know the truth – the process below will help you to confirm it.

Getting results

Women can be very intuitive. It's a well accepted feminine skill and yet when it comes to our own personal lives we can completely miss the signals, become doubtful, and get ourselves confused. Below is a process that has helped clients, friends and myself in the past; hopefully you'll find it equally useful in finding out if your partner is cheating on you.

1 Outcome
2 Behaviour
3 Perception Enhancer
4 Strategy
  • Blocks
  • The secret of finding the *right* man
5 Feedback

1 – Outcome

This is a simple model to highlight whether you are truly ready to uncover the truth. It will flush out any secondary gains you may have – i.e. hidden unconscious benefits to you of not knowing the truth or mistrusting your partner. These will have to be uncovered and addressed before any other work is done, otherwise the work will have to be repeated.

> Mary realized that her real outcome is to understand her relationship and herself more. She was doubtful about him and even more so about herself – he always had a clever answer for everything and she had to know if he was being honest. At the time she didn't trust herself to go with her gut feeling – she had to know for sure. She needed to investigate.

Go to page 57 to go through the outcome model. Pay particular attention to the final section, questions 11–16, because this will highlight if you have any secondary gains from not knowing the truth, whatever it is.

2 – Behaviour

Just as a doctor looks at symptoms to find the root cause of a physical problem, behavioural analysis allows you to look at your behavioural patterns in or around relationships to highlight possible relationship problems.

Divide up the time you have spent with your partner into 8–10 time periods; for each period consider:

1 Generally what is happening within your relationship?
2 How frequently do you see each other?
3 What do you spend most of your time doing?
4 What do you like about your relationship and about him?
5 What don't you like about your relationship and about him?

6   Are you happy?

7   Are you getting what you want from a relationship?

8   If you were an outside observer looking into your relationship with your partner what would you notice?

> *This module gave Mary immense confidence to keep quiet when she noticed the inconsistency – for two years she had eight time periods of information. She knew that her feelings had been covering over her perception of the relationship – what she actually had with him was less than a glimmer of what she had previously thought. She definitely preferred the perception to the reality, but she was still emotionally connected to him and didn't want to walk away.*

Go to page 47 for more information about behaviours or, if you prefer, go straight to the behaviours exercise on page 48 (using the questions on page 131) and discover your behavioural patterns with your partner.

3 – Perception Enhancer

When we are in a relationship it can sometimes be difficult to be objective about the situation – to know if we are being reasonable or not. This model helps you to gain insight into your relationship by helping you to see it from different perspectives. Look for patterns and inconsistencies. When you are open to seeing what's there, rather than just what you want to see, it's amazing what you start to notice.

> *Mary realized that she'd been far too trusting and giving in her relationship and that she should have been more challenging.*

Sadly she realized she hadn't been getting what she wanted from that relationship for two years! She had let an intelligent, manipulative man with low integrity into her heart and had found it amazingly difficult to be objective, until now. Even at the end when she knew he was not right for her she had to find the evidence, to have the external validation, proof, which she eventually got.

Go to page 93 for more information about Perception Enhancement or, if you prefer, go straight to the Perception Enhancer exercise on page 94 and see what discoveries you make about yourself, your partner, and how you interact within your relationship.

4 – Strategy

The emotional turmoil of suspecting your partner of cheating can be immense but, interestingly, the strategy for dealing with is remarkably simple.

1   If you suspect at any level that your partner may be cheating, know that this is just like a flag signalling that you need to pay attention to it – it's a message saying 'look at this, pay attention to this'.

2   It's time for you to look deep within yourself and also at your relationship. You may be feeling the way you are because he is in cheating on you, or because of a completely different reason, e.g. your own fear/insecurity – blocks from your past. The important thing is to deal with it because, if you leave it, it will only fester and gain strength.

3   Acknowledge the flag and work through the Blocks module on page 75. Then, if appropriate, go through The secret of finding the *right* man module above (page 113) because it will help you to ensure that he is the 'right' man for you.

4   Trust your gut feeling/intuition. You *know* if he is or isn't cheating – have confidence, trust yourself. Relax your body completely. Ask

yourself the question, listen to your first response and be open to believing it, whatever it may be.

5   Look at the evidence. The behavioural analysis will help as will the Perception Enhancer. Objective friends can also be very useful because if you are particularly open, loving, trusting and believe other people are like you, you will have a large blind spot.

This section gave Mary the greatest insight of all – she realized the signs were there in her gut, that uneasy feeling as soon as she met him, but had suppressed it thinking she was being silly. He was obviously a great catch and there was no evidence of anything to the contrary. By the time the evidence came along she was already in love and completely oblivious to it – it took the behavioural analysis to show her how blinded she had been. At first she was embarrassed at having made such a blunder, but then she realized that it was a great lesson – a very painful one but one she she'll always remember, teaching her to listen to her gut and trust herself above all else.

5 – Feedback

In this module you will learn how to use the fundamental concept of feedback to ensure you discover whether your man is cheating on you.

Mary is using this feedback process to get more confident about her gut feelings – she found the absolute evidence she needed to prove to herself that she was right, and she's decided to use it in the future to become more in tune with herself.

Go to page 26 now to discover the feedback-not-failure concept and how it can work for you.

Once you have gone through these modules you'll have a far greater understanding of yourself, your relationship, whether your partner is cheating on you or not, and indeed what you intend to do. Most of all you'll have developed your skill of intuition and found a way to use your emotions as a flag for further investigation into any situation – to use your emotions to your advantage rather being at the effect of them.

2.1.4 STARTING TO DATE AGAIN

If the thought of going back to dating instills you with fear, dread, apathy or frustration, then it is important to recognize that you are not alone – it's common to feel uncomfortable when starting a new phase in our lives, especially when it's something we've done before. We feel we ought to be able to get back on the dating bike and ride off into the future with ease. Unfortunately it's not that simple, because both you and the dating scene will have changed.

As with all the phases of our lives there are things that are great about it and things that are not so great. Dating can be a wonderful way of meeting new people and experiencing new things; It can be a truly adventurous time and it helps to have an open mind and a positive perspective on the possibilities.

Jo is 56. She has been married for 30 years, her children are at university, and she and her husband were planning to move house so they could start afresh in the autumn of their life to-gether. Then her husband dropped a bombshell – he wanted a divorce! It's taken her a long time to get over the shock and now that the divorce is nearly finalized she wants to start to date again but doesn't know what to do – all her friends are in couples and her life has revolved around her family and friends for so long.

Jo has redecorated her home, got herself a new car and gone on a diet, but is running out of ideas fast.

'It's so difficult because although the boys are away I am still focused on them and my friends. The nights can be really tough, even though my ex was hardly at our family home during the week. I am not sure if I am ready yet but my friends keep on insisting that I get out more and go on dates. I feel so uncomfortable about it, though – it just doesn't feel right. But I don't want to get too old before I find myself a new man.'

Susan is single again after a long term relationship ended six months ago. It was a long time coming and the last year had been the most difficult but it was clear they wanted different things and that the relationship had to come to an end. Almost immediately she started to date – she's attractive and there's a world of good men out there – she just has to find one.

There's no doubt that it can be difficult to get back into dating. You can easily find yourself being ineffective with your efforts – basically stumbling over yourself – or lack of them. This is generally compounded by the fairytale syndrome – expecting your knight in shining armour to come to you and for you to just fall in love, and that's it, with no consideration or planning – it *should* all be effortless and perfect.

Imagine what it would be like if you decided to cook a meal after not cooking for a long time, though. Would you just expect it all to work, without putting in the effort to consider and plan your meal? It's possible that, depending on your character and previous experience, you may stumble on a reasonable meal, but if you want to be effective it's worth taking a little time to ensure you are prepared and to give yourself the best chance for success. The solution below is all about that – giving yourself the best opportunity to enjoy dating and be successful at it in your own unique way.

TOP TIP

Treat dating as you would going out with a new possible friend – go out with those that you value and enjoy spending time with.

Getting results

We all have our own way of dating and ultimately if your way works for you – that's great. But if it doesn't then the process below has been designed to help you get the most from your dates so that you can really enjoy yourself and be effective. It works best when you take the general structure and adapt it to create your own style.

1 Outcome
2 Blocks
3 Strategy
   • Circle of Empowerment
   • Perception Enhancer
4 Feedback

If you are looking to a serious relationship then it's important that you also go through 'The secret of finding the *right* man' module above (page 113).

1 – Outcome

This is a simple model to highlight what you truly want from your date and whether you are ready to get it. It will help you to focus on your objective and flush out any secondary gains you may have from not dating or having bad dating experiences.

> *Jo's very clear that she wants to have some time and space for herself and, although she'd like to go out on a date now and again, she's not interested in anything more. Her outcome for dating is to enjoy going out and add some variety to her life. She has no secondary gain.*

Go to page 56 for more information about the outcome model or, if you prefer, go straight to the outcome model exercise on page 57 and discover if you are truly ready to date, and if so, what you want to achieve by dating.

2 – Blocks

Getting rid of limiting blocks is of paramount importance to having good dating experiences. This goes to the root cause of all the negative emotions and limiting beliefs that come up for you when you consider dating.

> *The blocks Jo worked on are:*
> * *fear of betrayal;*
> * *fear of hurt;*
> * *feelings of abandonment and sadness associated with it; and*
> * *the limiting belief 'I am too old to start dating'.*

Go to page 75 for more information about blocks or, if you prefer, go straight to the blocks exercise on page 85 and start to uncover and get rid of the unconscious blocks stopping you from dating or being able to enjoy dating.

3 – Strategy

Getting rid of your limitations and blocks leaves you with a clean canvas to start creating an effective strategy for having good dating experiences. The process below is designed to be used before, and during, every date:

1   Have your outcome in mind before, during, and after your date because it will help you get what you want very quickly.

2   Use the Circle of Empowerment to build your confidence so that you can truly let yourself shine in your unique and special way. If you're not familiar with this go to page 89 to read more about it or to page 90 to go through the exercise.

3   Match and mirror non-verbal communication in a natural way – so that your voice, posture, gestures and your energy levels are similar – because doing this initially will help you relax and enable you to be yourselves.

4   Once on the date, find a subject that he feels very passionately about and find something within it that you are truly interested in – the aim is to find common positive interests. You can do this by asking questions like 'What's really important to you?'

5   Every so often throughout the date go through the Perception Enhancer positions and see if you have any insights – perhaps have a bathroom 'time out' break to reflect. If you are not familiar with this, go through the process on page 94 – it's a great technique for improving your awareness and increasing your communication skills.

6   Treat the date for what it is – a first date. At most your objective is to see if you want to go on a second date.

Depending on where you are with your confidence and your awareness of who you want to be with, it may be wise to do some preparation beforehand by reading other possibly beneficial modules 'Boosting your confidence' (page 229) or 'The secret of finding the *right* man' (page 113).

> Jo's confidence is very low because it was her husband's choice to leave her – she wanted to make it work and would have done just about anything to have him stay. It's important for her to work on her confidence and to build up her self-esteem. Finding the right man is not an issue for her as she is not looking for a serious relationship, so she chose to miss that out. She loves the overall strategy for dating because it gives a manageable structure for something that is daunting and emotionally challenging for her – it's the simplicity and common-sense side of it that she really finds surprising and practical.

4 – Feedback

In this module you will learn how to use the fundamental concept of feedback to ensure you get the outcome you desire.

> Jo has been on two dates with members of her tennis club – both were friends of friends and one she liked more than the other. He was far more fun, yet she decided to carry on dating both to ensure it didn't get serious.

Once you have gone through these modules you'll have given yourself the best opportunity to enjoy and get the most from your dates.

Work

Module	Title	Page	Exercise time (mins)
2.2.1	Gaining respect at work	143	275
2.2.2	Discovering if you're in the right job/career	153	265
2.2.3	Making the most of redundancy	162	90
2.2.4	Starting work with a boost	166	435

2.2.1 GAINING RESPECT AT WORK

We live at a time when women are respected more than ever before; we have a seemingly equal standing in society to men and the freedom to do what we wish, and yet there is still a disparity between men and women's pay as well as minimal representation of women in senior roles. Yes, we have more respect – but evidently not enough!

Ever had that feeling that you've been passed over, not acknowledged, or not respected for your contribution? It can be incredibly frustrating and disheartening to put your heart into your work, produce great results and have your less worthy male colleague get the promotion! Is this sexism, though, or is it something else?

There's no doubt that sexism still exists in some organizations and it's important to be aware of it, but to blindly blame sexism would be both false and incredibly disempowering, because there is very little we can do about others' belief structures. For the purpose of practicality we shall leave sexism and focus on the factors over which we have more direct control.

Some people are of the opinion that you should be respected for who you are, no matter what. It's a lovely idealistic way of looking at the world but unfortunately one that doesn't generally reflect reality. Most of us judge other people's behaviour very harshly and yet can give lots of reasonable excuses for our own. Whenever you've seen someone behaving badly, maybe a mother shouting at a child or even smacking them, a married man flirting with a young woman, or having an affair, or even a crazy driver verging on road rage, the chances are you made a decision about the type of person they are, pretty quickly and rather harshly: bad mother, adulterer, lunatic! If, however, you find yourself in a situation where you've behaved the same way, you'll probably excuse yourself with reasons such as lack of sleep, being tired, lonely, confused, pressured, deceived. The way we behave is judged by everyone, and more harshly by those we know the least.

At work it's not just how good we are at our job that helps us to gain respect but also how we behave. Imagine if someone who is great at their job also goes about moping the whole time, talking negatively about others, behaving inconsistently and wearing inappropriate clothing. There may be 101 good reasons why the person acts that way but generally what will be judged by others is the behaviour. In most jobs the image you portray and how you behave is as important, if not more so, than what you are able to do, assuming you have reasonable skill and competency for the work.

Jill Cook is working well above her current grade and yet she is being overlooked at promotion time. Three of her colleagues have been promoted after delivering on similar projects and being recognized for their efforts, but she's not! She is naturally asking herself 'What do I need to do to get noticed and promoted?'

How can an organization which prides itself on equality and fairness let this happen?

Alice Brown has been a researcher for a large retailer for over seven years, and this year she turns 45. Although she loves what she does she can't help but feel frustrated because she's being constantly overlooked for pay increases promotions. Her work is crucial for the future of the business because she's responsible for designing and interpreting the market research on customer buying patterns. She loves taking the complex raw data and putting it in a way that her company can easily understand to make wise decisions about. Although she wouldn't want to leave, she does want the acknowledgement and respect she deserves for what she's doing.

TOP TIP

Respect yourself to the degree to which you want others to respect you.

Getting results

Working through the process below, in the order given, is a great way to help you get respect in the work place, as well as making you feel good about yourself and what you do.

1   Outcome
2   Values
3   Behaviours
4   Beliefs
5   Blocks
6   Strategy
7   Circle of Empowerment
8   Feedback

1 – Outcome

This is a simple model to highlight what you want to achieve from your job and to ensure you are able to get it. It will flush out any secondary gains you may have from not being respected – i.e. hidden unconscious benefits of being undervalued. These will have to be uncovered and addressed before any other work is done, or the work will have to be repeated.

Jill realized whilst going through this module that she'd not been specific enough by thinking that she just wanted more money and the next grade up. Now she wants that as well as having a clear idea of the skills and experience she wants to gain from her job.

Go to page 57 to work through the outcome model for yourself. Pay particular attention to the final section, questions 11–16, because this will highlight any secondary gains you have from not being respected. If you have any secondary gains just note them down and put them to one side ready for when you go through the Blocks module. You can now concentrate on progressing through the Values section.

2 – Values

Values are at the very core of who we are and because of this, being consciously aware of them will provide the torch to guide you throughout your career by helping you make decisions and enforcing your boundaries.

> *Jill found working together on her values incredibly useful as in the past she'd felt that she had to stretch the truth to clients. She became much more content in herself and far more effective in her job. She discovered that she'd been seen as a bit of a doormat, but now she's holding her ground and setting her boundaries according to her values. She's more consistent and, because of this, more respected.*
>
> *Also, because of her strongly held fairness value, she had felt that she shouldn't have to ask for promotion – that they should see how good she is at her job and give it to her. Afterwards she realized that she'd have to change her behaviour to move up.*

Go to page 39 for further information about values or, if you prefer, go straight to the values exercise on page 41 and discover your own work values before moving on to the Behaviours module.

3 — Behaviours

Just as a doctor looks at symptoms to find the cause of a problem, this exercise in behavioural analysis will allow you to look at your behavioural patterns at work so you can find out what's going on beneath them, and how they are affecting the level of respect others have for you.

> Jill found she had a pattern of letting things be, of not asking for promotion, of saying yes and working late to get her work done. She was so busy getting things done that she didn't have time to reflect back on what happened each day. The thing that made the most difference for Jill was to look at her behaviour objectively and realize how she was being judged by others on the back of it.

Go to page 47 for a more detailed explanation of behaviours or, if you prefer, go straight to the behaviours exercise on page 48 and discover your behavioural patterns for gaining respect at work, before looking at your belief structures in the next exercise.

4 — Beliefs

Beliefs are the foundation of behaviour. Positive self-beliefs will help you behave in a way that gains the respect of others (and of yourself), and limiting beliefs will hinder and sabotage you. This section will help you uncover all your beliefs around the subject of work – both the positive and limiting ones.

It's important to highlight limiting beliefs because then we can eliminate them in the Blocks module. Equally, highlighting positive beliefs is important because they will help you understand yourself far better.

> *Jill's top three positive beliefs about the workplace were:*
> - *'Everyone deserves respect';*
> - *'I am very committed to my work'; and*
> - *'I will work as hard as need be'.*
>
> *Her top three limiting beliefs about the workplace were:*
> - *'I feel unworthy';*
> - *'I don't deserve respect'; and*
> - *'I am not good enough (and will get found out if I stand out too much)'.*
>
> *It's a very powerful thing for Jill to recognize how her beliefs had been affecting her behaviour.*

To do this for your own beliefs go to page 43 for a more detailed explanation or, if you prefer, go straight to the beliefs exercise on page 45 and discover your own positive and limiting work beliefs before going on to the Blocks module.

5 – Blocks

Getting rid of limiting blocks is vital to gaining respect. You can do as much work as you want, but if you are clouded by negativity, your efforts will be muddied and ineffective. This module will help you to highlight and get rid of those areas that hinder you from getting respect.

The limiting beliefs and negative emotions you have already uncovered from the earlier exercises will be highlighted and removed in this section.

> *After working through the previous modules, Jill uncovered and worked on the following blocks:*
> - *'I feel unworthy';*
> - *'I don't deserve respect';*

> - *'I am not good enough (and will get found out if I stand out too much)';*
> - *fear of rejection;*
> - *fear of success; and*
> - *fear of failure.*
>
> *Jill was able to get rid of these blocks relatively quickly and found getting rid of her fear very liberating – it was as if she was somehow lighter.*

Go to page 75 for more information on blocks or, if you prefer, go straight to the blocks exercise on page 85 and start to get rid of the unconscious blocks stopping you from gaining respect at work. Then you can move on to the Strategy module.

6 – Strategy

The strategy below is a powerful one for ensuring you achieve and maintain respect in the workplace:

1   Have a clear idea of what you bring to the organization: what are your core skills? How do they compare with those of others in the company and in the industry? What is your market value? (Remember your worth to your company is greater than your basic market value because if you were to leave it would cost them money to recruit a replacement, time for learning the new business, plus the risk factor of the new person not being good enough.)

2   Look at who is getting promoted and what they have done to be recognized. Specifically, what they are doing differently to you.

3   Market and sell yourself at appropriate times. You may do the best job ever but if you keep it a secret no one will know. This is all about taking credit for the things you do and even asking for a promotion or pay rise if you believe you should have it – make it easy for your boss to promote you.

4   Have a clear set of work boundaries that are empowering and that you can, and will, enforce because they demonstrate the respect you have for yourself. (It helps, if at all possible, to have a buffer of money on which you could survive for 2–6 months without a job, because this will give you the confidence to walk away if you ever have to. Most people don't leave but they find that the knowledge that they they can means they can be more assertive for the business and with their own boundaries.)

5   Choose to be there, doing your job, and if you ever wish you weren't find a way of moving on.

Jill noticed that she'd never done a single one of these things – she had always believed that if she did a good job she would be recognized for it. Jill was constantly observing others' performance and therefore assumed that's what her bosses would also do! She'd not considered it her role to make it 'easy' for her boss to promote her – surely that was a part of the job description of being a boss – and when she considered it, she realized that if her objective was to get respected and acknowledged for what she does she'd have to go above the 'noise' level to get noticed. She was able to cover almost all of the points straight away apart from saving for her buffer, which took her three months.

Go through this strategy for yourself and see how it works for you before you move onto the Circle of Empowerment module.

7 – Circle of Empowerment
Most of us are unaware of our internal emotions let alone the effect they have on how we are perceived – our bodies reflect what we think and

feel. When we meet someone for the first time, within the first five seconds we have already made a decision about who they are (intelligence, schooling, character) just by the way they look. What we wear, our posture, how we move ourselves, and the sound of our voice combine to make up over 93% of how we are perceived – with the content of what we say contributing only about 7%. In a study at UCLA in 1967, Dr Albert Mehrabian found that when there is conflict between what is said (verbal content), the way it is said (vocal) and the way the speaker is seen (visual) then the visual is overwhelmingly dominant. So, in face to face communication it's 7% verbal content, 38% vocal and 55% visual; over the telephone it's 16% verbal content and 84% vocal. These percentages change as we get to know someone but, even so, the unconscious messages we give out are critical to the way in which we're perceived. For example, if we feel confident we stand up straighter, our voice is more measured and clear – what is going on inside is unconsciously displayed outside and we look and sound more confident. That is why people who give the right 'impression' but do not have the content/experience can do so well in life.

For women, managing our emotions is even more important than for men because we tend to let our insecurities affect us. Luckily, however, we find it easier to tap into our emotions. For this reason women generally find this module easier than men.

Whilst going through this module consider all the positive emotions you need to feel to be respected in the workplace. If you believe you already have some of them, that's a bonus – this module will help you make those feelings even stronger.

The emotions Jill felt she needed in order to get respect were:
- *confidence*
- *fun*
- *curiosity.*

For Jill, using the Circle of Empowerment was like using magic – she was at last determining and controlling her emotions rather than having her emotions control her. She was delighted to have this combination to call upon and meetings became far more interesting and fun, and she got a lot more out of them. Her change in behaviour and attitude was noticed and the next time reviews came round she asked for a promotion and a pay increase and gave the reasons why she believed she should have them. This time she got what she wanted.

Go to page 89 for more information about the Circle of Empowerment or, if you prefer, go straight to the exercise on page 90 and build your own personal circle of empowering emotions. When you have finished, and are happy with how to use it, move on to the Feedback module.

8 – Feedback

In this module you will learn how to use the fundamental concept of feedback to ensure you gain respect in the workplace.
Go to page 26 to discover the feedback-not-failure concept and how it can work for you.

Jill initially decided to use the feedback model to gain more and more respect – the change in behaviour was recognized within a month of the initial work and by the time she had fine-tuned her use of the model, six months had gone by and she already had her first promotion.

Having gone through all of these modules you will have gained a far greater understanding of yourself, you'll have got rid of any blocks, and because of this you will naturally ooze confidence, have clearer boundaries, and will gain the respect you deserve.

2.2.2 DISCOVERING IF YOU'RE IN THE RIGHT JOB/CAREER

Are you better suited for a different career path? Are you wasting your time in your current job? Should you be doing something different with your working life? It's only natural to take the time to wonder whether life has more to offer – that maybe you're not fulfilling your potential and you could improve your working life.

Depending on how much you like your current job you may even daydream about another career – how your life would be different, and how much better it would be – if you were an artist, chef, restaurateur, teacher, financier, entrepreneur … The chances are, if you've been fantasizing about other careers you've been imagining all the perceived benefits and comparing them with the harsh reality of your current job, which you know inside out.

How great it would be to have your own restaurant, to be in charge of your own destiny, designing the layout, the menu, the uniforms. But, is it so great when you consider the reality of 16-hour days, 6–7 day weeks, and the risk of investing every penny you own in a new venture that might fail? It's the 'the grass is always greener' mentality and having it as a way of life merely means we are permanently dissatisfied. People that think in this way have often stumbled into a job, or even a career, and then tried to keep it or sometimes progress within it.

Susan Clarke still questions what she should be doing for a career. She's a single mum who has her own small business, and she's also a good artist and earns some money through that too. And yet she's dissatisfied with her lot. Deep down inside she believes that there is something else for her – she yearns for something more worthwhile but hasn't found it yet.

Susan loves her painting and wants to keep it as a hobby, whereas her company is just a way of earning money to support her family; if she could find another way of paying all the bills she would. She likes helping her kids learn, so she's thought of being a teacher, and most of her friends ring her for help and advice so she's also kind of an agony aunt – so maybe she could also go into counselling? She jumps from one idea to the next, hoping that she'll stumble on the right career. Surely if she comes up with enough dreams then one of them will come true?

Kate Brown has been working as a recruitment consultant since gaining her degree, but now it's all getting too much for her – getting up early, being pressured at work, as well as late nights out partying. In her industry you're only as good as your last month's results.

At first it was fun, always exciting, and she was earning more money than she ever dreamed of whilst still being able to go out socializing. But at some point a few years back she realized she was unhappy with her career at a general level. She didn't really fit in and, to be honest, never had, which was part of the reason why she drank so much – to escape from her trapped existence.

She knows the market well, has her personal contacts, and knows she's very good at her job, and yet it feels like something's missing, that she's wasting her life, that something more rewarding is out there for her – if only she knew where to look.

Some people know the job they want from a young age and are consistent in their desire throughout their lives. They are the lucky few, though. Others find the right career but later wish to change because it's no longer right for them, so they seek out a new direction. For most of us a career is just pot-luck, based on a decision we evaluated for about as long as buying an outfit to wear, perhaps even less!

Finding the right career and being in the right job for you, one in which you are happy and fulfilled, is actually simpler than you might imagine, although at first it may sound daunting. Imagine you were given the challenge of finding your favourite meal – what would you do? If you don't already know the answer you'd probably consider all your favourite ingredients, list possible favourite meals, and either imagine what they would taste like or go the whole hog and taste them to properly evaluate what you really like the most. Figuring out what's the best career for you is very similar.

TOP TIP

Consider and evaluate your dream. If you really want it, then make it a reality – live your dream.

Getting results

Working through the process below, in the order given, has helped other women find their true career path; for some it's a quick revelation, for others it takes longer, but everyone has great insights even if they're not 100% sure of which career they want straight away. The process highlights your favourite 'ingredients' as well as furnishing you with a list of possible 'favourite meals', if not your absolute favourite.

1   Outcome
2   Values
3   Life Purpose

4   Beliefs
5   Blocks
6   Goals
7   Feedback

1 – Outcome

Go to the outcome module on page 57 to assess whether you are truly ready to discover the right career for you. Completing this section will flush out any secondary gains you may have – i.e. hidden unconscious benefits of not finding the right career for you. These will have to be uncovered and addressed before any other work is done, otherwise the work will have to be repeated.

> *For Kate, the outcome model clarified that she was fine to go ahead with the rest of the modules; there were no additional insights into her possible career. However, she did get a much clearer idea of what it will feel like when she is in her new job and was absolutely confident about her new resolve. Then she had to find a way to make a change from her current job.*

When you go through the model yourself pay particular attention to the final section, questions 11–16, because this will highlight any secondary gains you may have. If you do have secondary gains, just note them down and put them to one side, ready for when you go through the Blocks module. But for now, concentrate on progressing through the Values section.

2 – Values

With the outcome module complete you are now absolutely clear of what it is you want from your career, which is a great starting point for moving on to your career values. These are at the very core of who you are and because of this, being consciously aware of them will provide you with a torch to guide you whilst you consider your different career options.

Kate's top five career values are:
- *results*
- *money*
- *creativity*
- *empowerment*
- *synergy.*

Interestingly, in her current job Kate is able to satisfy each of these values: placing candidates in jobs is all about getting results; the commission structure is very lucrative and has the double benefit of tracking the 'results' as well as satisfying her money value; she's able to manage her clients and candidates as she sees fit, so she's able to satisfy her last three values as well. All in all, being a recruitment consultant fits very well with her top five career values. Her dissatisfaction with her life is definitely not due to a conflict with her values, which is a very common occurrence. For Kate, the conflict must lie elsewhere.

Go to page 39 for more information about values or, if you prefer, go straight to the exercise on page 41 and discover your own career values before moving on to the Life Purpose module.

3 – Life Purpose

Knowing your values gives you clarity and focus. This module will build on that to give you more information about what you really want. By the end of it you'll have a much clearer idea of possible career options, or at the very least, a list of criteria you need in your career, and some that you definitely want to avoid.

If there's an ultimate driving force that fires up your career path then it's your Life Purpose – your reason for being is the single most powerful driver you have.

Kate found that working through the exercises gave her lot of new insights into her life. Until this point she'd been confused: her career was perfectly in line with her values so why did she feel dissatisfied? When Kate answered the question, 'When you are old and grey, lying on your death bed, absolutely happy with your life and what you've done with it – what would that be? How have you lived? What have you done in your life?' In an instant the cloud lifted and it was clear – she wants to help people improve their lives; she wants to make a difference to individuals' lives in a fundamental way.

Recruitment is good in that she helps candidates get jobs, but she wants to do more. When she went through the bottom-up approach it started to become clearer. She has a consistent pattern of helping/teaching her friends, her colleagues, and even sometimes strangers – even the transition into management went smoothly because she 'taught' her team to be successful in their own individual way. She's a natural born teacher and it seemed amazing that she hadn't realized it before. But surely this couldn't be right – she wasn't even sure she liked teachers, let alone wanted to be one, and teaching is such a poorly paid profession, so it couldn't be the career for her. Or could it? After going through all of the exercises she was clear about a number of points.

- *Environment is important.*
- *The job has to involve interaction with people.*

> * *She needs to help people on an individual basis.*
> * *A teaching/workshop type of situation fits well.*
> * *Flexibility, freedom and control of her own destiny, as she has in her current job, are important.*
>
> *Ultimately, Kate wants to make a difference to individuals' lives in a fundamental way but she was still unclear as to which particular area to pursue. So for her, the possibilities are:*
>
> * *teaching;*
> * *dating/match-making specialist;*
> * *events organizing;*
> * *her own head hunting business; or*
> * *personal coaching.*

Go to page 59 for more information about Life Purpose or, if you prefer, go straight to the Life Purpose exercises starting on page 62 and discover what you really want before moving on to the Beliefs module.

4 – Beliefs

Having insight about, or indeed discovering, your Life Purpose is essential for knowing what you really want from your career. Now that you have that insight it's important to understand what beliefs you have around work – uncovering your enhancing and limiting beliefs will help you gain further clarity about your career and assist you in achieving a happy, successful career. It's also important to be aware of negative, limiting beliefs because then you can get rid of them and give yourself a clear path in your pursuit of your ideal career.

For each of your possible career options, list your positive and limiting beliefs. After you've done this, go through to the blocks area to get rid of the limiting beliefs that are hindering you.

> *Kate realized that she had a lot of stereotypical limiting beliefs and that she needed to do some research to see what her true career options were. She wasn't convinced that her limiting beliefs were blocks, e.g. teachers do not earn much money. After we worked on this she realized that, yes, although many teachers don't earn a high salary, private schools charge a lot and therefore there has to be a market for high-earning teachers. She even considered starting a school herself.*
>
> *Kate's top three positive career beliefs are:*
> - *'I can do anything if I want it enough';*
> - *'I will find my life's true path'; and*
> - *'I get results'.*
>
> *Her top three limiting beliefs are:*
> - *'I won't be able to earn big bucks doing something I love';*
> - *'Caring and business do not go together'; and*
> - *'I am too old to start something new'.*

To do this for your own beliefs go to page 43 for a more detailed explanation or, if you prefer, go straight to the beliefs exercise on page 45 and discover your own positive and limiting career beliefs before moving on to the Blocks module.

5 – Blocks

Getting rid of limiting blocks is vital for finding the right path. This module will help you to highlight and get rid of the limiting beliefs that you have already uncovered in the earlier exercises.

> *The blocks that Kate worked on were:*
> - *'I won't be able to earn big bucks doing something I love';*
> - *'Caring and business do not go together';*

- *'I'm too old to start something new'; and*
- *fear of failure.*
This is a compilation of her answers from previous modules and the results of going through the Blocks module. It's useful to compile your own list in the same way.

Go to page 75 for more information on blocks or, if you prefer, go straight to the blocks exercise on page 85 and start to get rid of the unconscious blocks stopping you from having the career you desire. Then you can move on to the Goals module.

6 – Goals

Now that you have eliminated the blocks that were in your way and have clarity around what you want from your career, you are ready to create specific goals, appropriate to your situation and desires. This process will enable you to get what you want, quickly and effectively.

Kate's goals are:
- *to know which career is the right one for her in five months' time;*
- *to have started the transition into her new career in one year's time; and*
- *to be in her new career two years from now.*
She found it very exciting to be thinking about her future in such tangible ways.

Go to page 65 for more information on goals or, if you prefer, go straight to the goals exercise on page 68 and set your own career goals before moving onto the Feedback module.

7 – Feedback

Having set your career goals you need to ensure you achieve them. You can do this by using the fundamental concept of feedback.

> For Kate the seed is sewn; she has taken the first step, evaluated where she is, and taken a path that will give her more clarity. The feedback concept is fundamental to her achieving her ultimate objective – feeding back her learning so she's able to home in on what works best for her, because then she will be able to find a career that truly satisfies her.

Go to page 26 now to discover the feedback-not-failure concept and how it can work for you to ensure you get all the things you want.

Having gone through all of these modules you will have gained a far greater understanding of what you want, you'll have got rid of any blocks, and set career goals that will help you to get the career that you want.

2.2.3 MAKING THE MOST OF REDUNDANCY

Please note: If you have serious financial difficulties and are not sure how you are going to survive, then this section is *not* for you – you need to focus on getting the best job possible for the skills you have, as soon as possible. Working through the Circle of Empowerment and Perception Enhancer modules will empower you for your job hunting; also going through the Feedback module will help you to ensure you take precious insights from this experience too.

This module is for those who are financially stable, at least for a period of time, to help you to get the best possible results for your time and money. Redundancy is one of those bitter-sweet occurences in life. On the one hand it's an experience of rejection, which may cut to your very core, bringing up dark feelings of low self-worth and fears of lack of ability, and on the other it's a great opportunity to do something different and expand your experience of life as well as having a sum of money to use in whatever way you see fit.

Depending on your perspective the loss of job security and the uncertainty of the future can either be incredibly debilitating or euphorically exciting. For some it can even be a mixture of both, though generally people tend to be at one end of the spectrum or the other.

Harriett Adams found her work challenging – the late nights and weekend hours just seemed like a necessary element. Her hard work had been paying off too – she'd been promoted twice in a row and had had four large pay rises within four years. Life was tough but rewarding.

When she was offered voluntary redundancy she was devastated. She kept on rereading the letter as she couldn't quite register the facts. She saw rejection and her failure. What would she do? How would she cope? She was at a loss and needed help.

Belinda Brown headed a sales team for a small software house. She had a great team and loved her job, even though it was a male-dominated area – she was able to differentiate herself and use her femininity, intellect, and people skills to her advantage.

Unfortunately for her the small software house was acquired by a larger company and she was made redundant within days. She was even told that she didn't have to work her notice, just to the end of the day would be fine and would give her time to pack up her stuff!

She was angry and jobless, and yet she had a strange, excited feeling in her gut – maybe this was the break she had been waiting for, to take some time out and re-evaluate her life.

Redundancy can be a very difficult and emotionally draining time where you can find yourself swinging wildly through the emotions of denial, anger, loss, excitement and hope for the future. This cycle is natural to go through and how positively or negatively you look at it will depend on your personality and situation.

Neither outlook is necessarily more accurate, they are just perspectives – like viewing the glass of water half full or half empty. How you choose to see it, is up to you. (See page 24 for more on this.)

If you imagine your life from the 'half empty' perspective, what do you say to yourself? What are the things you notice? What has happened to your energy levels? How do you think you come across to others? Are you in a good place to decide what you should do next? Does your future look sunny or bleak?

Putting that to one side, imagine your life from the 'half full' perspective. What do you say to yourself now? What are the things you notice? What has happened to your energy levels? How do you think you come across to others? Do you think you are in a good place to decide what you should do next? Does your future look sunny or bleak?

Mostly the latter perspective is far more energizing and motivating. Being made redundant is a fantastic opportunity to re-evaluate your life and your career. In effect, your old company is paying for you to find the best possible life for you. Some find it a confirmation of what they initially wanted to do and carry on in their previous career, and others find this a great opportunity to reinvent themselves and do something different.

> **TOP TIP**
> *Keep a 'glass half full' perspective and treat the redundancy as an opportunity to discover what you really want.*

Getting results

If you're thinking this is all well and good but you're in the pits of despair, and although you can see the 'glass half full' perspective, you don't own it – it's somehow just a mirror image of reality with no impact on your life – then please acknowledge this deep feeling. Give it as much space in your life as you need, because then you will be able to get rid of it by going through the Blocks module (see page 85). Ideally you will then be ready to have at least a neutral, if not positive, perspective on your life.

The process below is designed to help you to get the best possible results for your time and money. The first thing on the list is great fun and it's very important for ensuring that you spend your money as you truly want to and not fritter it away, and to give you a clean slate from which to start a new chapter in your life. The list is one that others have found useful and you may also wish to use and/or adapt it.

1 Put aside time to evaluate your career – one week minimum.
2 Put aside time before starting a new job (2–12 months depending on your situation).
3 Put aside a percentage of the money for:
    a savings;
    b a holiday – to go somewhere or do something where you can completely relax for a week or two;
    c a present for yourself – something you wouldn't otherwise have bought;
    d presents for family and friends;

    e a party/wake/celebration – whatever you want as a significant event that says goodbye to the last job, thanks for the money, and hello to the rest of your life!

Ensure you have enough time and money to finance whichever of these you wish to do and once you have decided, just relax and let it all fall into place, enjoying every bit of it.

Even if you believe you are in the right career, this is a perfect time to objectively re-evaluate, and it's important that you work through the 'Discovering if you are in the right job/career' section above (2.2.2), because even if you end up choosing the same career again, you are very likely to get insights about yourself that will be beneficial when choosing your next job.

Once you've done this, go through the Feedback module on page 26 and ensure you include everything you've learnt from your last job, as this will help you achieve what you want in your future career.

2.2.4 STARTING WORK WITH A BOOST

We spend a large part of our life at work, so it's important that you find it fulfilling – you want to be energized by the thought of your work, and excited about your career rather than finding it a drain and a chore. Making sure you have the best possible start is like setting the right foundation – it's essential.

Embarking on a new phase in life can be stressful and starting to work can be doubly so, because the people around you seem to be doing it all so effortlessly. It's a bit like being in a foreign country with everyone speaking a language you are not quite fluent in. There are rules – you just haven't figured them out yet. Depending on your character and situation it can be one of the most daunting or exciting things you can do.

It's important that you don't let your negative emotions get the better of you during this early phase, or you could end up putting yourself and your abilities down. If you can learn to utilize your positive emotions it can give you the boost you need.

There is now more career advice than ever for students starting work but even that is limited and there is still no substitute for taking full responsibility, truly discovering your Life Purpose, and taking action. Whatever your ambition or desire for your career, being aware of what you want and what you can give is of paramount importance in finding happiness and success at work.

Julia Keep has two children and now that the eldest is going to university she feels it's time she started to work outside the home. The extra money would come in useful, especially with the kids' education, but more importantly she wants to keep herself busy and do something useful.

She went to university and studied English Literature but it was a long time ago.

'I feel like I am going to be competing with graduates because I have no work experience and am older than others going for the same role – why would anyone give me a job?'

Her feelings of inadequacy are overwhelming in the face of the perceived competition and she just doesn't know where to start.

Katie Henderson is lucky in that her father is a successful businessman who is already exploring his contacts to see how he can help her in her career, even before she finishes her education. Despite being in a far better position than many of her friends she's still pretty much at a loss because she just doesn't know what job she would like to do.

'There are so many opportunities and options and I know it's really important I make the right choice, but I just don't know which way to go. I want to be successful and happy but I'm not sure which career to go for.'

Whatever your personal situation, starting to work can be as easy or as difficult as you make it. Ultimately, your decisions will open some doors for you and close others – all you can do is to gather as much information as possible so you can make the best decisions possible – for you, for now.

Imagine what it would be like to know that you've done the best that you can do to prepare yourself for your working career: to have a good idea of and perhaps even fully know your Life Purpose, your strengths, and your areas for improvement; to choose a career that fits in with your purpose and what's really important to you about work – your work values; to have awareness and confidence about what you bring, your market worth and how you intend to progress.

TOP TIP
Be aware and honest with yourself about what you want to do, what you can contribute and your market worth.

Getting results

Working through the process below, in the order given, is a great way to help you start work with a boost.

1   Outcome

2   Blocks
3   Know what you want
4   Purpose
5   Values
6   Goals
7   Blocks
8   Strategy
9   Feedback

1 – Outcome

This is a simple model to highlight what you want from your working life and whether you are truly ready to have it. It will flush out any secondary gains you may have from having an unsatisfactory career.

> Julia's outcome for her career is to get more clarity about what she wants, why she wants it, and what she can do to help herself. She wants to make a difference, be successful and know that she's doing the right thing. She's hoping the rest of the work we do will help her gain clarity. She has no secondary gain.

Go to page 57 to work through the outcome model for yourself. Pay particular attention to the final section, questions 11–16, because this will highlight any secondary gains you have. If you do have secondary gains, just note them down and work through them in the next module.

2 – Blocks

Getting rid of limiting blocks is vital to having a successful career. This means going to the root cause of all the negative emotions and the limiting beliefs which come up for you at this time – highlighting and getting rid of them so that you can move forward without these blocks:

The blocks Julia worked on are:

- fear of failure;
- fear of change and of the unknown;
- limiting belief 'I'm not good enough'; and
- limiting belief 'I'm too old'.

This is a compilation of her answers from the Outcome module as well as the results of going through the Blocks module. It's useful to compile your own list in the same way.

Go to page 75 for more information about blocks or, if you prefer, go straight to the Blocks exercise on page 85 and start to get rid of the unconscious blocks hindering you. Then move on to the next module – 'Know what you want'.

3 – Know what you want

Now that you have eliminated any blocks that have been working against you, you're ready to move forward. This module highlights the importance of knowing what you want in life and is the foundation for the following modules.

Julia's very excited about sharing this module with her boys at university. She knows it's going to have a very positive effect on them, hopefully giving them a better start because it will help them gain clarity about their lives and about what they want. They are likely to be more successful and, hopefully, happier too.

Go to page 54 for more information on the concept of 'knowing what you want' and how it can work for you.

4 – Life Purpose

Now you are aware of how important it is to know what you want, you will be able you to make the most of discovering your Life Purpose, which is vital to truly enjoying and being successful in your career. This module takes you through the exercises for discovering your Life Purpose and helps you to understand the full impact of this discovery.

> *Julia is absolutely delighted because she's realized that she's got a lot of skills, that her 20 years of raising her boys and running a household as well as all her charity work has given her a wonderful skills base that she can use in just about any environment. Finding her Life Purpose was really straightforward – to raise her family in the best way that she can.*

Go to page 59 for more information about Life Purpose or, if you prefer, go straight to the exercise on page 62 and start to uncover your own before moving onto the Values module.

5 – Values

This module helps you to discover what your career values are. Ascertaining these values is important because they are truly important to you. If they remain unfulfilled you will be affected in a negative way.

> *For Julia this was a straightforward and interesting exercise to go through because it highlighted why she feels the need to go out to work. Now that her children are grown up her active role has diminished. Her top five career values are:*

- *integrity*
- *making a difference*
- *fun*
- *money*
- *recognition.*

Go to page 39 for more information about values or, if you prefer, go straight to the exercise on page 41 and discover your own work values before moving on to the Goals module.

6 – Goals

Setting achievable career goals is an incredibly powerful method of achieving what you want. This module goes through how you can best get results when setting goals. Only set goals for things you know you will persevere with until you get. It's wisest to start small and build up rather than set too difficult a goal from the outset and risk overwhelming yourself.

Julia wanted to set one goal for herself – to be in a job that she enjoys within six months – and one for her kids – to discover what they really want from their lives.

Go to page 65 for more on goals or, if you prefer, go straight to the exercise on page 68 and define your own work goals before moving on to the Blocks module.

7 – Blocks

Getting rid of limiting blocks as they come up is hugely important. The reason this module is here again is because, when you set new goals, sometimes there are blocks stopping you from achieving them and it's important that you go to their root cause and get rid of them straight away. If you find that you set yourself a goal but 'something' always happens to stop you from getting it – look within yourself, find the root cause, and then take action.

> *The blocks that Julia worked on were:*
> * *limiting belief 'I can't do that';*
> * *fear (of change); and*
> * *limiting belief 'Happiness and work don't go together'.*

Go to the blocks exercise on page 85 to get rid of any blocks that you've discovered from setting your goals. Then move on to the Strategy module.

8 – Strategy

Now that you have set your goals and cleared your blocks, how do you ensure you are on track and doing the right thing? There are many ways of achieving results, and starting a career is no different. The process below is one that others have found useful and that you may also like to adapt and use. It's a simple and powerful way of ensuring you are absolutely confident that you have done the best you can do and that the decisions you make are the most informed possible.

a   Get a mentor (at least one; more if you can find them) – someone who's an expert in the area you wish to be in and whom you admire, respect and trust; someone you can go to for advice and guidance once a quarter or twice a year. It's important that they have your best interest at heart and make no personal gain from what you decide to do except by contributing to your life.

b Research areas of possible interest yourself as well as soliciting advice from your mentor and others who may be able to help you. Find out what different jobs are really like and what type of character traits are needed. Industry magazines are also a great source of insight into different areas of work.

c As you do your research make a list of possible careers. Write a list of the pros and cons of each career and then finally, when you have a shortlist, go back to your contacts list again – who do you know that can help, or who do they know?

d Annual/quarterly review – get yourself into a routine of reviewing your career for yourself:
   • What have you liked and disliked?
   • What have you learned?
   • What do you want to do differently next time?
   • What do you need to learn/do to achieve the next level?
   Review your goals and create new ones based on what you've learned. This strategy can benefit you for the whole of your career – continually reviewing, learning and growing as you go.

Julia realized that there was good reason for feeling the way she did – there's a lot to do that she hadn't even recognized before because there is a long list of careers she could possibly do. Now that things are clearer and she's in less of a hurry to work straight away she's very excited about taking on the task of finding herself a career that's right for her.

Go through this strategy for yourself and see how it works for you before moving on to the final module in this section, Feedback, to tie everything together and ensure it works.

9 – Feedback

In this module, you will learn how to use the fundamental concept of feedback to ensure you get the outcome you desire.

> *Julia has found the whole process useful in that she now has focused on herself and her kids and is aware of what's really important to her. Now she is using the feedback process to help her to fine-tune what she specifically wants to do.*

Go to page 26 to discover the feedback-not-failure concept and how it can work for you.

Having gone through all of these modules you will have gained a far greater understanding of what's really important to you about your work, what your Life Purpose is or at least which direction to move in; you will also have got rid of any blocks and learnt a strategy that can be adapted and used throughout your working life – you are ready to start your career with a boost.

Family

Module	Title	Page	Exercise time (mins)
2.3.1	Making the most of your time with a new baby	179	310
2.3.2	Getting the most out of being a stay-at-home mum	184	140
2.3.3	Maximizing your relationship with your kids	190	215
2.3.4	Dealing with infertility	196	185
2.3.5	Juggling kids, partner, home and work effectively	202	175

2.3.1 MAKING THE MOST OF YOUR TIME WITH A NEW BABY

When we go through a permanent change we undergo the most severe stress. Many women don't connect having a baby with stress until after they have had their first, and even then some don't recognize it as stress.

When you become a mother, you have just been through the equivalent of a major operation and straight afterwards, instead of resting and recovering (which is what your body physically needs to do), you start a new full-time job where you are on call 24 hours a day! Your hormones are all over the place, you're physically exhausted, you may be suffering a great deal of discomfort as a result of the birth, and you are on an intense emotional rollercoaster – from euphoria and wonderment at having such a lovely little baby, to feelings of enormous responsibility, even anger, fear, misery, guilt and possibly depression.

Your overall experience will depend on many factors including your character, past experiences, the difficulty of your pregnancy and childbirth, and how supportive your partner is. It's likely to be the most wonderful and yet most challenging time of your life.

Andrew and Sara were going out when she became pregnant and because of the rush to get married they hadn't really had time to think fully about being parents.

'The drive back from the hospital was when it really dawned on me – this really lovely, tiny, perfect person is 100% reliant on me. It was overwhelming!'

The first two weeks were like being in a wonderful euphoric bubble for Sara – Andrew took time off work, she had time to rest, and together as a family they even went out to the park a few times. It was everything she had hoped for and more.

The night before Andrew went back to work the boiler broke down, which meant that Sara had to stay in and wait for an engineer the whole of the next day. All day she worried about horrible scenarios of what could happen if Katie needed something and she couldn't go out and get it.

A few days later when she thought of going out she was absolutely in shock – what would she do with the buggy? Where would she go? How would she breast-feed? What if Katie didn't stop crying? She now tends to stay in and waits for Andrew to come home.

'I never thought I would be a clock watcher but I have to admit that throughout the day I do tend to watch it a bit too much and it's taking away from my enjoyment of my time with Katie.'

Charlotte Thompson has been married to Greg for two years and has just become a mum. Greg is a 'man's man' which, to him, means he doesn't do any household chores or help with the baby. Charlotte never used to mind before – she stayed at home so it seemed reasonable that she managed the house. But since giving birth to Sally she feel she needs some help. She's beyond tired and still sore with the stitches – she's a 24-hour-a-day mum and housewife and the pressure is just too much. Greg expects everything to be the same as it was, just with the addition of a baby; but it's not, and he's having a tough time adjusting.

Charlotte says 'I don't know what to do – there's just not enough hours in the day and I am so shattered it's beyond anything I've ever experienced before. He won't go shopping or even stay with the baby while I go in case she needs changing! I get so angry sometimes that I even scare myself. I know something has to change but I don't know where to start!'

There's no doubt that coping with a new baby is tough, perhaps the single toughest experience we will ever experience, but its rewards are such that pretty soon we laugh at the difficulties and only really remember the pleasurable times – perhaps that's nature's way of ensuring we carry on having children!

TOP TIP

The quicker you accept that the 'normal' life you took for granted is no more and that your life has changed forever, the easier your transition will be.

Getting results

There are many books on the practicalities of parenting, but what this section focuses on is the most important aspect – you, because when you take care of yourself you are in the best position to care for others.

Working through the process below, in the order given, is a great way to help you empower yourself, because then you'll be in the best position to get the most from your life and be as great a mum as can be.

1   Outcome
2   Strategy
   • Eliminating anxiety, worry and stress

- Blocks
- Cause or Effect
3   Feedback

1 – Outcome

This is a simple model to highlight whether you are truly ready to be a happy mum and enjoy this phase of your life. It will flush out any secondary gains you may have from being anything less than a happy mum at this stage of your life.

> *Sara is very clear on her outcome – she wants to do the best for Katie and the only thing stopping her is her limiting belief that she's not good enough.*

Go to page 57 to work through the Outcome model for yourself. Pay particular attention to the final section, questions 11–16, because this will highlight any secondary gains you might have. If you do have secondary gains just note them down and put them to one side, ready for when you go through the Blocks module. Then you will be ready to progress to the next section, Strategy.

2 – Strategy

There are many ways of empowering yourself through the transition to motherhood but the strategy below has been effectively used by others. Alter it as you need to to make it work best for you. It's been divided into two sections: points 1–3 are for initial preparation; points 4–6 can be used as and when needed.

1   Go through whatever process you would like to, to grieve for the life you no longer have, and celebrate your new life – being a mother. Some like to have a celebratory party; others like to treat themselves

to a present. Do whatever is right for you as long as it marks this time as a momentous transition.

2   Acknowledge that you are going through a major change – physically, hormonally and emotionally

3   Be gentle with yourself – being a mother is a new job with lots of new things to learn. Don't expect yourself to know everything straight away and allow yourself room to learn and grow, happily and naturally – the more relaxed you are the more relaxed your baby will be.

4   Go through the Eliminating anxiety, worry and stress module on page 292. Depending what the situation is you may wish to look at other modules in this chapter, and those in 2.4 Finding a path in life and, possibly, 2.6 Health.

5   If you have a specific negative emotion or limiting belief go through the Blocks module on page 75.

6   If you feel that things are happening to you and around you but you don't have any control then go through the Cause or Effect module on page 15.

Sara knew that the physical effect of the hormonal changes in her body were affecting her perspective of life – her reaction to the boiler problem was distorted and emotionally charged yet she couldn't control herself. She liked the new tools because they gave her a structured process to work through any problems she may have, and because she could do it in her mind whilst stealing a few minutes here and there. Ultimately, for her, the thing that made the difference was to learn to be gentle with herself – doing so resulted in a more loving and relaxed atmosphere all around.

Go through this strategy for yourself and see how it works for you before moving on to the final module in this section, Feedback, to tie everything together and ensure it works.

3 — Feedback

Wanting to be the best mum you can be is an internal driver that most mothers have. In this module you will learn how to use the fundamental concept of feedback to ensure you achieve the outcome you want.

> *Sara found it reassuring to know that what she's going through is 'normal' and to have a way of ensuring she's as relaxed as possible – when she finds herself getting overtired, or under strain, she stops what she's doing, takes a few deep breaths, and reminds herself to be gentle with herself. On a weekly basis she's using the feedback model to ensure she's doing the best she can for Katie.*

Go to page 26 now to discover the feedback-not-failure concept and how it can work for you.

Having gone through all of these modules you will have gained a far greater understanding of your situation, learnt new techniques to eliminate any specific problems, and ensured that you are as gentle with yourself as you are with your baby.

2.3.2 GETTING THE MOST OUT OF BEING A STAY-AT-HOME MUM

To choose and be absolutely happy to stay at home and take care of your family is fantastic, and if that's how you feel then this module isn't designed for you. Equally it's not for you if you are looking at this decision from a purely logical perspective; that if you pause in your career it will compromise what you have done; if there is no negative charge to it and you are happy to make that sacrifice.

On the other hand, this module is for you if you chose to stay at home because you felt that there was no other real option, and somewhere inside you feel bad about what you have given up to stay at home. Depending on your character, your past experiences and how your partner behaves, you may feel that you are the only one making big sacrifices and may suffer from either suppressed anger, which comes out in different (passive/aggressive) ways, or overt anger, where you take out your frustrations and anger on those around you, with the ensuing feelings of guilt and remorse that are likely to follow.

Jane Richards is the mother of two boys, Harry and John. When she first became pregnant it was all very exciting, and it seemed to make sense for her to stop working as she earned half what Peter, her partner, did. Paying for a child minder would pretty much wipe out what she could earn anyway, so it was a logical step.

Initially she found the adjustment difficult, but she accepted that it was a transitional period and the first couple of months flew by, with so many things to do and just not enough time in the day to do them. It wasn't so bad because Peter was home by bath time, and at weekends he looked after the boys for half a day so she had some time for herself.

Then Peter got a promotion and started to travel more. Jane was stuck at home, sometimes going for days without seeing him, her whole life revolving around being a mum. She's now starting to resent being the one making all the sacrifices.

'I know I am far more irritable now and I'm taking it out on my family.'

> *She knows she needs to stay at home but something inside is rebelling and she's not sure what to do.*

Until you work through and resolve your situation your internal conflict will continue. It appears that men who stay at home rarely experience such problems because they tend to think it through thoroughly beforehand, whereas women can become swept away by the flow of events and what's expected of them, without thinking through what they really want. The exercise below is designed to help you to uncover what you really think, feel and want.

TOP TIP

The sooner you make a conscious choice the sooner the conflict will go away.

Getting results

This section is not about whether you go back to work or be a full-time mum; it's aimed at getting you to a position where you are absolutely happy with the choice you make – it's the conflict that causes the unhappiness. Working through the process below, in the order given, is a great way to get you to that place.

1   Outcome
2   Strategy
    • Blocks
    • Cause or Effect
3   Feedback

1 – Outcome

This is a simple model to highlight what you really want and whether you are truly ready to make a decision you will be happy with.

> *Jane's outcome is to decide what she really wants and be happy with her life. She has a secondary gain of being a 'martyr' – if she is the one who sacrifices, then she is nice and good. It's what her mother did and she feels she should do it too.*
>
> *Please note that sometimes you will get answers that are other people's expectations of you rather than your own wishes. The way to spot these is to note where you use words such as 'should/ought/obliged/have to' – it's where you think or feel you have no option, as in Jane's case, where she feels she should stay at home. Jane may choose to stay, but at this stage her perception is that there is no other choice, which is far less empowering.*

Go to page 57 to work through the Outcome model for yourself. Pay particular attention to the final section, questions 11–16, because this will highlight any secondary gains you have. If you do have secondary gains just note them down and work through them in the first part of the Strategy module below.

2 – Strategy

The strategy below is great for helping you get to a position in your life where you are fully in control and are absolutely confident and comfortable with the decision you are making for yourself for now.

1   Turn your focus inward and consider the option of giving up your work and staying at home. If you have any negative emotions or limiting beliefs, list them all and go to the Blocks module on page

75, working through until you eliminate them. Do that now before moving on to the next point.

2   Go through the Cause or Effect module on page 15 and note the level of control and influence you feel you have about your decision to work. (If it's anything less then full control and influence then note the limiting belief around that, and either read more on Blocks on page 75 or go straight to the exercise on page 85.) Do that now before moving on to the next point.

3   Get a sheet of paper and draw a line down the middle. On the left-hand side write at the top 'Reasons why I want to stay at home and be a full-time mum' and on the right-hand side write 'Reasons why I want to go to work'. Then write down all the ideas that come to mind about each of these options, leaving some space between your comments. When there are no more ideas take a few minutes' break.

4   Look at your two lists objectively and highlight the points that are really important to you as a mum. Then do the same considering yourself as a partner, and then repeat it again considering yourself as an individual.

5   Consider why those highlighted things are important to you – make a quick note in a different coloured pen around the highlighted points in the space you left before.

6   Consider what else you can do in your life now that will help you get the things you value on either side.

7   Consider the two sides and decide what's the best option for you, at this point in your life.

8   Consider what's really important to you and then take action accordingly.

9   Test your decision by imagining yourself in ten, even twenty years from now looking back at this point in time. What advice does the future you give to the current you? Dwell on this for a few minutes

and ensure both the current and future you are happy with your decision.

> *Jane used this strategy and was surprised at how quickly she realized that she was actually doing what she really wanted – she just needed to consider it for herself and 'own' the decision. Of course, getting rid of the martyrdom block was instrumental in achieving that. Although there are some things she doesn't have in her current life that she wants, her stay-at-home reasons were so much longer and more important to her than the go-to-work ones. She is delighted and has a new zest for her life. Although her situation hasn't changed, she feels incredibly differently about it. 'It's like I've found the energy of "me" again', she says.*

Go through this strategy for yourself and see how it works for you before moving on to the final module in this section, Feedback, to tie everything together and ensure it works.

3 – Feedback

In this module you will learn how to use the fundamental concept of feedback to ensure you get the outcome you desire.

> *Jane found it useful to really look at the cause of her frustration and deal with it. For her, the strategy of objectively looking at the pros and cons of being at home really helped her to see how important it is for her to be there for her boys. She doesn't expect to need the feedback model but if she does she's got it to hand.*

Go to page 26 now to discover the feedback-not-failure concept and how it can work for you.

Having gone through these modules you will have gained an insight about what's really important to you, why it's so important, and whether you are content and happy with your decision to be at home or want to plan your route back into work. Whatever it may be for you, ultimately you have the choice and you are empowered to make it.

2.3.3 MAXIMIZING YOUR RELATIONSHIP WITH YOUR KIDS

Raising a family takes a large portion of your life and is the foundation of your children's future. Ensuring that you make the most of this time and give them the best of yourself is what this module is about.

Being able to get on with your kids is vital in helping them to learn effective relationship-building and communication skills – they will instinctively learn these from you. The quality of all your lives will be enhanced by a greater understanding of each other, giving you more ease and pleasure.

One of the main challenges within families is effective communication. We tend to believe that because we say something that *we* understand, others should too, and when we hear something or observe a behaviour from others our interpretation of it is based on our understanding of the world, which may or may not be in line with theirs. In any relationship there is either a positive spiral, where the relationship is growing and getting stronger, or a negative spiral, where it is becoming weaker. Generally, the better the communication within a relationship the more positive the spiral is and vice versa. In families, communication difficulties are often compounded by the parents' expectation that their offspring will be the same as them, when of course they have their own personalities and characters.

Angela Thompson has two daughters, Stephanie and Katie. Angela decided to go back to work when the girls started school. The family had moved into a bigger house and had financially over-extended themselves so it was the only real option.

The work is great – Angela's confidence has gone up and she feels as if she is doing something useful. But her relationship with her kids and her partner is under strain. She's the last to leave the house and always ensures it's clean and tidy; yet, by the time she comes back home, the kids have messed it up again.

'They just don't appreciate me. If they did they would tidy up after themselves.'

Angela gets very upset and shouts at the kids quite often. They generally retaliate at first then just sulk for the rest of the evening. Then everyone walks around on eggshells for a few days until they all relax – and then the cycle is repeated all over again.

Paula Peterson is mum to Sam and Susie. She's a housewife and loves to do domestic things like baking cakes and sewing. Kevin, her husband, is very much a 'man's man', and though in private he is very affectionate and considerate, in public and even in front of the kids he is quite bossy and rude.

This was not a problem before they had children – Paula ascribed his behaviour to his being a 'man' and she didn't mind it too much because he was wonderful at home. Now, however, her children are behaving towards her in a similarly aggressive way, and it's becoming increasingly difficult for her to keep control of her family and get things done.

> 'The girls just don't listen to me. They do whatever they want and answer me back! I feel like I am already losing them. What can I do?'

Getting on well with your children is extremely challenging because there are a lot of expectations around what things 'should' be like, based on your upbringing and that of your partner, as well as what you see in the wider community. It involves a minefield of feelings – being unloved, misunderstood, unappreciated, attacked – which can easily develop into a negative spiral. The challenge is to convert the experience into a positive spiral, so relationships within your family relationship and family grow positively.

TOP TIP
Remember that your children are individuals with their own character, beliefs, values, goals and motivators.

Getting results
Work through the process below, in the order given. It has helped others to improve their relationships with their children and most of the steps can be used to improve relationships with others as well.

1 Outcome
2 Blocks
3 Strategy
   • Values
   • Perception Enhancer
4 Feedback

1 – Outcome

This is a simple model to highlight whether you truly want, and are ready to have, a great relationship with your children. It will flush out any secondary gains you may have from maintaining an average or bad relationship.

> Angela's objective is to be able to have a loving and respectful family life. Going through this model she realized that her behaviour towards her daughters was a reflection of how they behaved towards her. For Angela her environment is significant, and having it clean and tidy is very important, whereas for the girls that's not important but the way Angela behaves is.

Go to page 57 to work through the outcome model for yourself. Pay particular attention to the final section, questions 11–16, because this will highlight any secondary gains you have. If you do have secondary gains just note them down so that you can work through them in the next module.

2 – Blocks

Getting rid of limiting blocks is vital to having a healthy relationship. You have to go to the root cause of all the negative emotions and limiting beliefs that come up for you at this time – highlighting and getting rid of them so that you can more forward with your life:

> The blocks Angela worked on are:
> - 'If they don't tidy up they don't love me';
> - fear of being unloved; and
> - fear of being alone.

Go to page 75 for more information about blocks or, if you prefer, go straight to the exercise on page 85 and start getting rid of the unconscious blocks hindering you from having a successful relationship with your children. Then you'll be ready to move on to the Strategy module.

3 – Strategy

Getting rid of limitations and blocks leaves you with a clean canvas to start creating an effective strategy for having wonderful relationships. We all have our own, unique way of relating to others and it's important that you keep your uniqueness. Many have found that the process and tools below can help to enhance their unique way as well as facilitate better communication with others.

1 For successful child development it's essential that there are clear boundaries and rules that are consistently enforced and within which freedom and choice remain.

2 Spend quality time together doing something of mutual interest – it will be fun, increase your understanding of each other, and provide a wonderful bonding experience.

3 Go through the Values module and find out what your and your children's and partner's 'family' values are, because then you will have the blue print of what's really important to all of you. For an explanation of values go to page 39, or to go directly to the exercise on page 41.

4 Perception Enhancer is a wonderful model for helping you to see your relationships from different perspectives – the more you are able to enhance your perspectives the better your relationship will be. The Perception Enhancer exercise can be found on page 94. (Please note that another's view of a given situation will probably be different from your own and as you go through position 2 you are likely to see this difference – it's not right or wrong it's just different, and being aware of it empowers us because it gives us more choice.)

5   Communication within a relationship is as vital as the air we breathe. Recognizing its importance is essential, as is understanding that we all have different preferences as to when, and how, we communicate – some have to strike while the iron is hot whilst others prefer to reflect and consider before talking. Knowing your and your children's preferences, and being flexible in your approach, will greatly enhance your communications. This is a large subject and if there is one thing to focus on it's to be truly present, to listen to your children and to discover who they really are:

   • What's really important to them?
   • What do they need and how will they know they have it?
   • How do they know they are being loved?

6   Treat yourself and all your family members with courtesy and respect, and expect the same in return. Sometimes this can be really difficult and we find ourselves behaving in a way that's inappropriate. If you find yourself in such a situation the most effective thing to do is to rectify it straight away by using open and clear communication. However difficult it may initially appear it's generally a very empowering and bonding experience.

Angela was delighted with her insights from this process. She, like most mums, had previously assumed that she knew herself and her children, and the discovery that she didn't was a shock. Angela now understands that her daughters have a different view of what is important, and that they were scared of when she might 'blow up'. She hadn't realized that although a clean environment was important to her, for the kids it was how she behaved that was important. It was quite overwhelming for her, so she prioritized and dealt with the most important thing first – how to show her daughters that she loves them.

Go through this strategy for yourself and see how it works for you before moving on to the Feedback module, to tie everything together and ensure it works.

3 – Feedback

In this module you will learn how to use the fundamental concept of feedback to ensure you get the outcome you desire.

> *Angela will be using this feedback model to really understand her kids. Each time she goes through it her understanding of them grows, along with her ability to communicate more effectively.*

Go to page 26 to discover the feedback-not-failure concept and how it can work for you.

Having gone through these modules you will have dealt with any blocks you may have had from your past, used strategy to improve your understanding of and communication with your children, and used the feedback model to enhance your evolving relationship with your children.

2.3.4 DEALING WITH INFERTILITY

Infertility can be one of the most destructive issues in a person's life – the misery of not being able to conceive is intense and can have a profound effect on your relationship, with both partners going through different and yet equally powerful emotions of despair and unhappiness. When a couple face infertility they experience a great deal of stress, dealing with it in the best way they can, according to their personalities and past experiences.

Girls know from a young age that they have the potential to be a mother when they are older, and motherhood is still the accepted norm for adult women in most societies. Our identity, womanhood and reason for being can easily become tied up with the ability to be a mother.

Our bodies are designed to conceive and because we spend such a long time worrying about falling pregnant when we don't want to, as soon as we decide we want a child it seems reasonable that we should be able to become pregnant almost immediately. Interestingly, according to *The Relate Guide to Better Relationships*, only about 60% of couples conceive within the first six months of trying, and 15% try for over a year before conceiving. When we stop to consider the wonderful complexity of a human being it's baffling that we expect it all to happen at the drop of a hat. The word 'infertile' sounds so absolute, and so negative, that it becomes scary in itself. In fact, the definition of infertility is being unsuccessful at getting pregnant after having unprotected sex for a year. Many women go on to get pregnant after this period, so 'infertility' is really not as conclusive as the word suggests.

Whatever the statistics or 'logic' of the situation, the reality is that once you've decided that you want a baby you'll have mentally started to prepare yourself for motherhood and, unless you are very careful, not conceiving will soon begin to have a negative effect on you, your partner, and your relationship. In fact the stress often becomes a vicious circle, as stress has been found to impede conception. There are many couples who, after 'giving up' on conception (and thereby reducing the stress they feel), then conceive.

This module is about what you can do for yourself to help you through this difficult time and give you the best chance of success.

Sarah Herford has been with Peter for three years, of which the last year has been the most difficult of all. Sarah wants to have a child, and Peter, who already has one from a previous marriage, is not that bothered about it. Sarah's not been able to get pregnant and has been getting increasingly upset.

'I feel so isolated. Peter's so relaxed about the whole situation whereas I feel like there's been a death. I just want a baby of my own.'

Sarah's whole focus is now directed towards getting pregnant and she wants to do what she can to ensure she has the best chance of having a baby.

Karen Sumerford got married to David last year. They wanted to have a family straight away, thinking it would be good to have two children and ideally before Karen turned 40, but they have been trying for over a year now and each month their disappointment grows deeper – Karen is getting more and more depressed.

'It seems quite ironic when I've worried about contraception so much in the past. I can't seem to think about anything else now – the thought of never having a child is unbearable.'

When we've always just expected something and then discover we can't get it (at least for now) we have a deep sense of loss. The process below is designed to help empower you to cope with this situation.

TOP TIP
Acknowledge and deal with what you are thinking and feeling because then you'll be in the best position to make decisions and get results.

Getting results

The process outlined below will help you and your partner to get rid of past baggage and limitations whilst equipping you with effective techniques for moving forward through this difficult time.

1 Outcome
2 Blocks
3 Strategy
   • Values
   • Cause or Effect
   • Circle of Life
   • Goals
4 Feedback

1 – Outcome

The outcome model is a simple tool for highlighting what you truly want and whether you are ready to get it.

> Sarah found it very difficult to even consider that she maybe sabotaging her chances – the thought was unthinkable. Even so, she worked through it and was happy to find that her outcome is to have a healthy happy baby and family. She doesn't have any secondary gain.

Go to page 57 to work through the outcome model for yourself. Pay particular attention to the final section, questions 11–16, because this will highlight any secondary gains you have. If you do have secondary gains just note them down so that you can work through them in the Blocks module.

2 – Blocks

Getting rid of limiting blocks is of paramount importance in being able to deal with this situation. You need to go to the root cause of all the negative emotions and limiting beliefs that come up for you at this time – highlighting and getting rid of them so that you can move forward with your life.

The blocks Sarah worked on are:
- *hurt*
- *fear*
- *pain*
- *sadness/loss*
- *anger.*

Go to page 75 for more information on blocks or, if you prefer, go straight to the blocks exercise on page 85 before moving on to the Strategy module.

3 – Strategy

Getting rid of limitations and blocks leaves you with a clean canvas to start creating an effective strategy for dealing with your situation.

1   Grieving for the loss, or even the potential loss, of your ability to have a child is essential for moving forward. Grieve for as long as you need before moving on.

2   Make a list of what you have now that you are taking for granted – everything in your life that you value and that, if you were to lose it, would upset you, i.e. your partner, family, friends, job, home.

3   Go through the Values module (page 39) and find out what your values are for each area of your life, because then you will have a blue print of what's really important to you.

4   Make a list of the options available to you now and in the future. Focus on the main logical points and consider each in turn, going through the Cause or Effect module (page 15) and noting the level of control and influence you have in each option. Discuss the options with your partner and decide together what you really want. Even make an option for your worst-case scenario – if you can never have a child of your own – do you want to adopt/foster?

5   Go through the Circle of Life and Goals modules (pages 11 and 65) and set yourself short-, medium- and long-term goals that you wish to achieve for all the different areas of your life.

Go through other modules as you need them – for example, 'Eliminating anxiety, worry and stress' (page 292) may be useful for you at this stage.

Sarah found this strategy incredibly hard but rewarding to go through. Facing the prospect of life without a baby was horrific but she also realized that she has an amazing relationship with Peter and the thought of possibly losing him was greater still. She is still deeply saddened by her situation but now has clarity about what she will do, and when, along with a sense of hope about the future, whatever it may bring.

Go through this strategy for yourself and see how it works for you before moving on to the final module in this section, Feedback, to tie everything together.

3 – Feedback

In this module you will learn how to use the fundamental concept of feedback to ensure you get the outcome you desire.

Sarah has decided to try for a baby for another year and then use this feedback model to evaluate what they should do at the end of that time. It gives her a feeling of safety to know that she has a plan for the possibility that she is still unable to conceive by that point and then they can decide what they are going to do next. For now she can relax.

Go to page 26 to discover the feedback-not-failure concept and how it can work for you.

Dealing with infertility is very difficult and hopefully these techniques have helped you to feel more empowered and objective, so you can deal with your situation in the most effective way for you.

2.3.5 JUGGLING KIDS, PARTNER, HOME AND WORK EFFECTIVELY

If you go back to work after having a child, your partner's willingness and ability to share the workload at home as well as your support network (family and close friends) will all have a big impact on how you experience the combination of going to work and being a mum.

There is no doubt that it's an incredibly challenging time but it can be as rewarding as it is challenging, and those that have managed it often comment on how wonderful it is to have their independence, saying that it builds their self-confidence immensely, gives them something else to focus on, and means there is always going to be a sense of achievement in one area of life, even if the other is not going so well.

Sandy Parker is mum to two-year-old Harriett, and Toby, who's 8 months old. She also works full-time, with her mother-in-law taking care of the little ones three times a week. Sandy has everything planned out and organized, and except for illnesses and accidents, things are going along according to plan. But the strain is building – working a full day, bringing work home, and having to come back and be a mum, cook, cleaner, gardener and wife is just getting to be too much. She's not able to be as focused on her paid employment as she used to be and feels that she's letting everyone down. More often than not she is up at two in the morning, finishing stuff off because yet another disruption during the day got in the way.

'Its all getting too much. My life is full of guilt – when I go to work I feel guilty about leaving the kids at home and when I finish work I feel guilty about leaving on time, so I take work with me. I've got to change something – soon!'

Journalist Jenny Henderson has a daughter, Amy, who's 14 months old. Jenny is lucky in that she can do a lot of her work from home so she doesn't have to pay for child care, but as good as that is, it's impossible for her to do her work whilst Amy is awake. Her challenge is to effectively juggle these two very different roles and cope with the constant trade-offs that they involve – and to enjoy her life as she does so.

'I am working all day, every day, with no time off. God knows what I'd do if I was ill. There must be a better way of doing this!'

At whatever stage you return to work you'll have two jobs. Depending on your partner's contribution one may be a part time job, but nevertheless it'll be a challenging time. For those women who choose to go back to work after their children have left home the challenge of juggling is largely removed, but they have other challenges, such as adapting in a market which has changed dramatically and issues of confidence, to deal with.

TOP TIP

Expect to work differently to the way you did before you became a mum.

Getting results

Working through the process below, in the order given, is a great way to help you find an effective way to juggle all the things you need to do in your life.

1   Outcome
2   Strategy
   •   Blocks
   •   Cause or Effect
   •   Perception Enhancer
3   Feedback

1 – Outcome

This is a simple model to highlight whether you are truly ready to enjoy your life whilst juggling work and home. It will flush out any secondary gains you may have from being unhappy.

Sandy's outcome is to enjoy what she is doing when she is doing it. Her belief that if only she could be more effective then she would be able to enjoy things more is a limiting one because although it appears to be reasonable at first, its actually limiting her from being happy because being more effective never ends – one can always do better. What's interesting is that most people who worry about this, or have this as a limiting belief, actually end up being less effective because they are focusing on improving something that's not there, an abstract concept of 'better', rather than what is. Out of all the work we did together this was the single most powerful shift for Sandy and it transformed the way she saw herself. She also had other blocks around guilt, and fear of doing the wrong thing, which had a compounding effect on the earlier block.

Go to page 57 to work through the Outcome model for yourself. Pay particular attention to the final section, questions 11–16, because this will highlight any secondary gains you have. If you do have secondary gains just note them down and work through them in first part of the Strategy module below.

2 – Strategy

The process below is great for helping you get to a position in your life where you are fully in control and are absolutely confident and comfortable with the decision you are making for yourself for now.

1   Focus inward and consider your situation – juggling home, work, family and your partner. If you have any negative emotions or limiting beliefs go to the Blocks module on page 85 and work through it until you eliminate them. Do that now before moving onto the next point.

2   Go through the Cause or Effect module (details on page 15; exercise on page 16) and note the level of control and influence you feel you have when you are at your paid employment and then for your home

life. If it's anything less then full control and influence then go back to the Blocks module with whatever belief you have that's getting in your way. Work on this until you have full control and influence in each area of your life. Then when you are ready move onto the next point below.

3   Consider your life 20 years from now. Imagine the you from the future and ask yourself, 'Knowing what you know, with all that additional wisdom, what advice would you give to you now, so you get what you really want?' Take the insights and consider them – if you are to take on board your suggestions how different will your life be? Take action to do what you think is best for you.

4   Consider how others in your family view you going back to work by working through the Perception Enhancer module (details on page 93; exercise on page 94).

5   To help make the most of this very challenging and rewarding time other women have used the 'essential' list and you may also wish to incorporate it into your life.

- Make a pre-going to work 'Agreement' with your partner and kids (if your kids are old enough).
- Actively cultivate a good partnership with your partner.
- Plan thoroughly for every day and for other times, such as what to do in case of sickness, holidays, etc.
- Ask for help or pay for services that will make your life easier when you need it, not just when you're desperate.
- Create quality time for all the family, as well as for your relationship with your partner and kids individually. Just as importantly, though, make time for yourself. If you would like to improve your relationship with your kids then also go through the Maximizing your relationship with your kids module on page 190.

Go through this strategy for yourself and see how it works for you before moving on to the final module in this section, Feedback, which ties everything together and ensures it works.

Sandy found it amazing to have a process that she could use quickly to find solutions to her everyday problems, especially for dealing with negative emotions and limiting beliefs. Interestingly, though, it was the exercise dealing with blocks that took her the longest time. When she managed it, it transformed her perception of her life, as she found that she was happy with it. The things that had overwhelmed her before just became tasks to be dealt with.

3 – Feedback

Juggling work and home life is highly challenging and it's to be expected that there will be a lot to learn along the way. This module can help you to ensure you get the most from your life as you juggle.

Sandy has decided to review her situation on a monthly basis – feeding back each month on the things she likes, what she'd like to improve, and all the things that really stand out for her. She has also decided to hire a gardener and a cleaner to see if they make the difference she needs.

Go to page 26 now to discover the feedback-not-failure concept and how it can work for you.

Having gone through all of these modules you will have gained a far greater understanding of yourself and what's important to you, got rid of any blocks, and have a process in place that you can build on as you become truly effective at juggling all the responsibilities of kids, partner, home and work.

Finding a
Path in Life

Module	Title	Page	Exercise time (mins)
2.4.1	Discovering the something that's missing in your life	211	155
2.4.2	Re-evaluating your life	217	375

2.4.1 DISCOVERING THE SOMETHING THAT'S MISSING IN YOUR LIFE

Ever thought there must be more to life? It's one of those small, nagging concerns that's like a buzzing in the background – you get so used to it that most of the time you don't even notice it's there. Sometimes, though, when you dwell on it, you can feel uneasy – that all is not as it should be. And as you pay attention to it you can hear the buzzing – the discontentment in your heart – that there has to be more to life than what you currently have, that something is missing.

Many people keep busy to avoid hearing the buzzing, preferring to focus on the nearest external distraction, such as shopping, holidays, family, partner, work.

Those who attempt to fill the gap at a superficial level, outside of their own core, soon discover that the cycle only repeats itself, leaving you with more achievements but with the same old feeling that something isn't right. Papering over the cracks initially feels good because it makes you feel like you are doing something, being proactive, taking control, but unfortunately it's a false sense of happiness because trying to find what's missing this way is like trying to catch bubbles – as soon as you think you have one, it pops, leaving you with yet more bubbles to chase.

Local science teacher Karen Pryor is single and lives with her dog, Toby, who keeps her active. Together with playing the violin and her 'green' activities she's always been busy. And yet, she has felt for a long time that something is missing – but she didn't know what. She didn't know how to look for it, let alone find it!!

Her gut feeling was that when she found her soul mate she wouldn't long for whatever the missing thing was. Everyone else appeared to be just getting on with everything, so that's what she did too.

Mandy Keet has two daughters: Claire, seven, and Sarah, five. She loves being a stay-at-home mum and although she wouldn't change anything she constantly feels that something is missing. From the outside it's not obvious at all. They live in a lovely cottage. The girls are well behaved and healthy. Peter, her husband, is very supportive and makes sure that at least once a week Mandy gets time away from the kids. They have holidays together and are surrounded by loving friends and family. She has it all – and yet she feels something is lacking.

Mandy's always thought her family should be enough and felt bad for wanting more, so she's suppressed her feelings for over seven years. But now that Sarah's five and ready to go to school Mandy is comfortable with focusing on herself a little. She wants to find out what's missing in her rather idyllic and comfortable life.

Knowing that something is not right with your life can be difficult to deal with when you think you are the only one in that position. Equally, it's very easy to pass the buck and blame a part of your life that's obviously not working and sidetrack yourself from the real culprit. To be able to find the root cause of your problem and deal with it at that level is the most effective way of filling the gap and setting your course to becoming truly happy and content within yourself.

> **TOP TIP**
>
> *The answer lies within you – look within to find what is missing.*

Getting results

Working through the process below, in the order given, is a great way to help you uncover what's missing in your life. People who are able to relax and let go find it an easy and surprisingly pleasant process. There is something magical about starting off knowing something's definitely missing and at the end discovering that you are complete within yourself and everything else in your life is a bonus – even if there may be things you still want in your life that you don't yet have.

1 Outcome
2 Strategy
   • Blocks
3 Feedback.

1 – Outcome

This is a simple model to highlight whether you are truly ready to find out what it is that's missing and to be complete within yourself. It will flush out any secondary gains you may have from feeling that something is missing in your life.

> *Karen found the outcome model useful in helping her think more positively about what she wants. When she started, all she could focus on was the empty, something-is-missing feeling – she wanted it to go away which meant she had been focusing on a negative representation of the feeling. She quickly realized that what she really wanted was to feel whole within herself, for the*

> *something-is-missing feeling to dissolve and to be happy and*
> *content within herself, that's her 'outcome' and she is ready to*
> *get it.*

Go to page 57 to work through the outcome model for yourself. Pay particular attention to the final section, questions 11–16, because this will highlight any secondary gains you have. If you do have secondary gains just note them down and you can work through them in the Blocks part of the Strategy module below.

2 – Strategy

Once you are ready to discover what's truly missing in your life dwell on the thought for a few minutes then go through the steps below.

1   Go through the Blocks module to highlight and deal with any of your negative emotions and limiting beliefs about having something missing in your life and ensure they have all completely gone. Go to page 75 for more information on blocks or, if you prefer, go straight to the blocks exercise on page 85.

    NB Blocks are the single most important thing to focus on if you feel there is something missing and don't know what it is.

2   After the blocks work, the deep general sense of something being missing should have gone. However, if you still feel that there are some things that you really want, go through the following point (point 3). If not, move on to point 4.

3   List all the areas of your life where you think something is missing and for each consider the following questions:

    • What do you already have that you're taking for granted?

    • Why is it that you don't already have what you want – what's the cause?

    • For each cause what would take you one step closer than you are right now to getting what you want?

- Consider the worst-case scenario and ensure you are truly happy with dealing with it if it were to happen.

4 Take an overview of where you are now: what you have in your life; what you have taken for granted; what actions you are going to take. Truly know in your heart that you're on the right path and being 100% true to yourself right now.

Karen loved this part because she was able to change her perspective on her life within a few hours. It was as though it had been a grey and cloudy day and suddenly the clouds dissolved and the sun shone through, lighting up and warming her whole life. The areas of her life she had blamed were:

- *not having a partner;*
- *not having career progression;*
- *being physically bigger than she wanted to be; and*
- *not achieving more in her life.*

The negative emotions connected to the something missing in her life were:

- *emptiness*
- *loneliness*
- *loss*
- *fear – specifically fear of the unknown.*

She also had a limiting belief that she must suffer – life was hard and she was alive therefore she should suffer.

As soon as she started to air her problems the clouds started to dissolve and her perspective shifted. It's very common for this to happen but important to continue to the end of the exercise, because sometimes the feelings are so great you think it's OK to stop; but to absolutely ensure it's worked it's best to go through to the end.

Karen realized how much she had going for her that she had taken for granted – she loves her job, has peace and comfort at home, is absolutely free to do as she pleases, is an OK-looking woman, with generally good health. Then there are the really simple things that, when she considered what life would be like if she didn't have them, made her realize that she's a very fortunate peron – things like the warmth of the sun on her skin, the smell of freshly cut grass, the birds singing first thing in the morning and her big family gatherings.

Her action points for moving forward are to:
- *stop watching TV*
- *start going out and doing things that she's not done before – just for fun*
- *exercise throughout the week by driving less and walking more, and take Toby out for a very long walk once a week; and*
- *get her home into a state that she is happy with and start to have the types of dinner parties she's dreamed of.*

Go through this strategy for yourself and see how it works for you before moving on to the final module in this section, Feedback, to tie everything together and ensure it works.

3 – Feedback

In this module you will learn how to use the fundamental concept of feedback to ensure you get the outcome you desire.

For Karen, this module was useful in giving her absolute confidence that she's going to be able to get what she wants, because she's able to use it to monitor and keep to her action points.

Go to page 26 now to discover the feedback-not-failure concept and how it can work for you.

Having gone through these modules you'll have uncovered and eliminated any blocks you may have had and worked through appropriate areas of your life to uncover what's missing, dealing with this directly at the root-cause level.

2.4.2 RE-EVALUATING YOUR LIFE

Sometimes we find ourselves living a life and not knowing how we got there, as if the tide of life just swept us away and when we opened our eyes we discovered a new and different place. If we're happy with the discovery that's absolutely fine, but sometimes we find ourselves somewhere feeling trapped, lost, frustrated, possibly confused about what we want, or just knowing it's not where we want to be. It's all too easy to get caught up and lose focus of the big picture – our life and what we want to do with it. Generally when this happens in one or more areas of our life we feel the urge to take stock and re-evaluate, or sometimes it's prompted by a major birthday or big external event in our lives which forces us to truly reflect.

Not knowing what you want from your life can be incredibly frustrating – like being a ship without a sail in a fog. For some people it's absolutely fine to go with the flow and see where life takes them, but for others it's wearisome, annoying and a trap they'd like to get out of. They know that the most successful people tend to know what they want and go for it, staying focused and making sure each step takes them closer to their objective.

Ultimately, the most fulfilling path is usually a combination of the two – knowing where you are going, and setting a course, and then letting life throw what it may at you whilst you enjoy flowing through it towards your destination. To be able to do this you have to be sure you know what you want in life, whether that's having a baby or not, being in a relationship or not, following a career, etc … It's important to know what you want in each area of your life because then you can work towards them effectively.

Taking the time to gain clarity is essential to being happy and successful because if you know what you want, why and how you intend to get there, you can confidently invest time and effort into achieving it. If you continue with your life without re-evaluating you run the risk of regretting things you 'should' or should not have done because you were focused on other less important but possibly more urgent things – each day taking you further away from your true course in life.

Sandra Henderson is happy with her career in that she's earning more money than she ever thought she would, and the work is challenging, but it feels like such a soulless thing to do. She is dating Peter, who she really likes, but she's not absolutely sure if she should carry on seeing him – something doesn't feel quite right but she can't put her finger on it. Generally she's getting on with life and feels she's done well but she would like more direction and focus.

'I have some big decisions to make over the coming year and really don't want to make a mistake. Should I stay in my job or change completely? Is Peter right for me or not? Do I want to have kids? There are so many things to decide and I really don't know what's the best thing to do.

Helen Clarkson has been widowed after 20 years of marriage. She's financially comfortable and appears to have a nice life – there are no demands on her and she is free to spend her day

> *as she wants – but after spending so long focusing on taking care of one man she is now at a loss as to what to do.*
> *'I want to change my life. I will never get over Rupert, he was such a lovely man, but I know I need to move on and want to do what Rupert would call a "stock check" – you know, to see what I have and what I really want.'*

For some, taking time out to re-evaluate life is a luxury they believe they can't afford. Although this is a false economy there is no right or wrong time to re-evaluate your life – whenever you think or feel you are ready is the right time for you.

It's all about getting clarity about who you are, where you've come from, what you want in your future. The solution below is full of useful tools and techniques to help you do all this but you may find others you prefer to use in this book – that is absolutely fine as long as you are able to get the clarity you need.

TOP TIP
Be open to observing your past and to the possibilities of the future.

Getting results

Working through the process below, in the order given, is a route specifically designed to give you a very thorough evaluation of your life, because then you'll get to the best possible solution, but it also gives you the choice to cover as much or as little as you want at any one time.

1   Outcome
2   Blocks

3   Who am I?
4   Accept yourself
5   Know what you want
6   Life Purpose
7   Circle of Life
8   Values
9   Goals
10 Blocks
11 Feedback

1 — Outcome

This is a simple model to highlight what you want and whether you are truly ready to re-evaluate your life and get what you want. It will flush out any secondary gains you may have from keeping your life as it is.

> Sandra is clear about her objective and has no secondary gain stopping her – she wants to feel passionate about her life, to feel confident that she's doing the right thing and isn't wasting her life.

Go to page 57 to work through the outcome model for yourself. Pay particular attention to the final section, questions 11–16, because this will highlight any secondary gains you have. If you do have secondary gains just note them down, as you will work through them in the next module.

2 — Blocks

Getting rid of limiting blocks is essential for having a great life. This module goes to the root cause of all the negative emotions and limiting beliefs that come up for you at this time – highlighting and getting rid of them so that you can move forward with your life:

> *The blocks Sandra worked on are:*
> - *fear of making a mistake;*
> - *fear of change and of the unknown;*
> - *limiting belief 'I don't deserve to be happy'; and*
> - *limiting belief 'I can't do this'.*

Go to page 75 for more information on blocks or, if you prefer, go straight to the exercise on page 85 and start getting rid of the unconscious blocks hindering you, before moving on to the next module, Who am I?

3 – Who am I?

Understanding who you *think* you are as well as who you really are is of paramount importance to re-evaluating your life. As you go through this module be aware of how your perception of your identity starts to change and make particular note of what's important to you.

> *Sandra found this module quite mind blowing. She hadn't thought about herself in such an objective way before and had been giving herself a hard time because of some behaviours in the past – such as being short with and rude to the people she loved the most. She's particularly intrigued by how much she associates her identity with her job – she is her job, or at least that's what the exercise in this module highlighted, but she doesn't think that's right.*

Read through the Who am I? module on page 32 to make your own discoveries before moving on to the next module – Accept yourself.

4 – Accept yourself

Understanding who you are is the first step to being able to accept yourself – by knowing and accepting yourself you build the foundation for being able to objectively re-evaluate your life. If you have any problems accepting yourself treat it as a block and go back to the Blocks module (page 85).

> *Sandra was quite flippant about being able to accept herself. Her attitude was one of dismissive acceptance – of course she accepted herself. After working through the exercise, though, she realized that it wasn't quite as straightforward as she'd imagined. She found it difficult to accept behaviour that didn't fit in with her perception of herself.*

Go to page 36 for more information on accepting yourself before moving on to the next module – Know what you want. (It's important to be absolutely honest with yourself because only then will you have the best possible situation from which to improve your life.)

5 – Know what you want

This module highlights the importance of knowing what you want in life. It doesn't have any exercises – they appear later, in other relevant modules.

> *Sandra found the concept interesting and it increased her curiosity about what we did next which helped her maintain momentum.*

Go to page 54 for more information on knowing what you want before moving on to the next module – Life Purpose.

6 – Life Purpose

This module helps you to understand the full impact of discovering your purpose and goes through exercises to assist you in discovering yours.

> *Sandra was completely amazed by her discoveries about herself. She wants in her lifetime to have a family – she's not quite sure if she wants it with Peter yet, but it's clear to her that that's her Life Purpose.*

Go to page 59 for more information on Life Purpose or, if you prefer, go straight to the Life Purpose exercise on page 62 and start to discover yours. Then move on to the next module – Circle of Life.

7 – Circle of Life

This module highlights where you think you are in the different areas of your life and gives you a holistic picture of it.

> *Sandra was very surprised by how unbalanced her life was – she was far more focused on her career than on any other part of her life. Although it made sense to her, considering her identity was wrapped up in her job, now that she is consciously aware of it she wants to take action to redress the balance, especially in light of her Life Purpose.*

Go to page 11 for more information on the Circle of Life or, if you prefer, go straight to the Circle of Life exercise on page 11 and start to discover what the balance in your life is like. Then move on to the next module – Values.

8 – Values

This module helps you to discover your values for each of the different areas in your life that you wish to work on, so you know what's truly important to you and what your main drivers are in each area.

> For Sandra this was a straightforward and interesting exercise to go through. It was also quite time consuming because she wanted to know her values for all of the different areas of her life.

Go to page 39 for more information on values or, if you prefer, go straight to the exercise on page 41 and start to discover your own values before moving on to the next module – Goals.

9 – Goals

Setting achievable goals in each of the areas of your life is an incredibly powerful tool for achieving what you want. This module goes through how to get the best results. Only set goals for things you really want, and know you will persevere at until you get them. It's wise not to aim too high at first and then build up, than to tackle too much at once and risk overwhelming yourself.

> Sandra had great fun setting her goals and benefited from setting them for the different areas of her life. For the time being, though, we agreed for her to set only one small goal per area.

Go to page 65 for more information on goals or, if you prefer, go straight to the exercise on page 68 and work on setting your own goals before moving onto the next module – Blocks.

10 – Blocks

The reason the blocks module is here again is because if you have a block when you set new goals it will only manifest itself then and not before – with something like 'I can't do that' or 'That's not for people like me'. It's important you go to the root cause and get rid of these feelings straight away, otherwise you'll be hindering yourself from achieving your goal. Equally, if you find that you set yourself a goal but 'something' always happens to stop you from reaching it – look within, find the root cause, and take action.

> Sandra had a big block about moving house to a really nice location in town. Immediately after deciding on the goal she had the thought 'People like me don't live there' and the negative emotion of fear. She worked through both, quickly, so that they were no longer an issue for her.

Go to page 75 to refresh your memory on blocks or go straight to the exercise on page 85 and start getting rid of the unconscious blocks hindering you, before moving on to the final module in this section, Feedback, which will tie everything together and ensure it works.

11 – Feedback

In this module you will learn how to use the fundamental concept of feedback to ensure you get the outcome you desire.

> Sandra found the whole process useful and has decided to use this feedback process to help her to stay on her true path – a periodic sanity check.

Go to page 26 now to discover the feedback-not-failure concept and how it can work for you.

Having gone through all of these modules you will have gained a far greater understanding of what's really important to you about your whole life, your Life Purpose, values and goals for each of the areas of your life you wish to work on, and have got rid of any blocks hindering you from pursuing the right path for you.

Self-esteem

Module	Title	Page	Exercise time (mins)
2.5.1	Boosting your confidence	229	185
2.5.2	Discovering the attractive and wonderful you	235	540
2.5.3	Reversing feelings of self-hatred	241	505
2.5.4	Making life less difficult	248	230

2.5.1 BOOSTING YOUR CONFIDENCE

True confidence is an enviable quality; anyone who has ever felt insecure, fearful, uncomfortable or at a loss in a situation – and let's face it, that's probably all of us – will have either wished for a hole to swallow them up or for more confidence to deal with all that life throws at them. Generally, once our confidence is rocked it can be very debilitating and even feel like we're in a quicksand of negative emotions and negative thoughts – I am not good enough, I can't do that, I can't do anything! This book can't provide you with the hole to dive in to but it can help you take control and become more confident.

> *Kate Armstrong, on the face of it, is an absolute marvel – she'll bend over backwards to keep everyone in her life happy: she goes on holidays she doesn't really want to go on just to please her husband; she works late, and sometimes even at weekends, to please her boss; and she helps out with her friends' chores even though it infringes on her life. Kate has very low self-esteem and because of this she's letting herself be a prize doormat to everyone in her life – putting everyone first but herself. She doesn't feel that she is good enough to be around, to be loved, if she is truly herself, so she is too eager to please.*
>
> *It's become a bigger problem since she got married because her husband doesn't want her to be so self-sacrificing towards her friends, and also she doesn't have enough time for her work. Her marvellous life is quickly turning into a logistical nightmare.*

Many women lack confidence in at least one of the following three areas: their physical appearance, their identity, their career/work. At its most extreme it can drive us to despair or make us go into denial and escape from the thing that we lack confidence in, pretending all is well.

Strangely, many of us believe that confidence is one of those things you either have or you don't; that a fortunate few are truly confident within themselves whilst, for the rest of us, every day's a struggle.

I'm sure you'll have had times in the past when you specifically lacked confidence – maybe over a big event like a first date, going to college or university, leaving home, giving a presentation, or it could have been a simple event like cooking, going on a trip, or going to a meeting and for some reason you lacked confidence.

On the other hand, though, you'll have had plenty of other personal experiences where you were absolutely confident, doing something very simple like making a cup of tea, cooking, or tending the garden, or perhaps something more challenging – you'll certainly have tackled some things with 100% confidence. Being able to tap into that supreme confidence and apply it to any area of your life that needs a boost is what this module is about.

Imagine what it would be like to be confident all the time, to feel empowered and able to do whatever you wanted. To replace fear, anxiety, and feelings of low self-esteem with strength, clarity, confidence and a sense of curiosity and excitement about life in general. Imagine how your life would be different: What you would do differently? How you would behave differently? What you would see and hear around you? How you would feel?

TOP TIP

View confidence as a skill that you can learn, because it is, and if you consider it as such you'll be able to build it to whatever level is appropriate for you.

Getting results

The process below is a very simple and powerful way of helping you to gain confidence. The more you work with it the more powerful it gets and the more confidence you'll have to tap in to.

1   Outcome

2   Blocks

3   Circle of Empowerment

4   Strategy

5   Feedback

1 – Outcome

This is a simple model to highlight what you want and whether you are truly ready to have it, and it will flush out any secondary gains you may have from lacking confidence.

> *Kate wanted to not be a failure, to not let her family and friends down. Interestingly, though, she had a secondary gain stopping her from being truly confident – her husband always takes care of her and shows her love and support when she lacks confidence. We had to go through the Blocks module and then come back to setting her outcome that was, in the end, to have inner peace and confidence in every situation she finds herself in.*

Go to page 57 to work through the outcome model for yourself. Pay particular attention to the final section, questions 11–16, because this will highlight any secondary gains you have. If you do have secondary gains just note them down and work through them in the next module.

2 – Blocks

Getting rid of limiting blocks is vital to gaining confidence. You have to go to the root cause of all the negative emotions and limiting beliefs that come up for you at this time – highlighting and getting rid of them so you can move forward with your life.

> *The blocks Kate worked on are:*
> - *fear of failure;*
> - *limiting belief 'I'm not good enough'; and*
> - *limiting belief 'I'm not confident'.*
> *This is a compilation of her answers from the Outcome module as well as the results of going through the Blocks module. It is useful for you to compile your own list in the same way.*

Go to page 75 for more information on blocks or, if you prefer, go straight to the exercise on page 85 and start getting rid of the unconscious blocks stopping you from building your confidence. Then move on to the next module – Circle of Empowerment.

3 – Circle of Empowerment

This is a simple yet powerful module that will help you to begin learning the skill of confidence. As you go through it focuses on those emotions that are essential for you to be confident so that you can become the type of confident person you want to be.

> *Kate put these emotions into her Circle of Empowerment:*
> - *confidence*
> - *fun*
> - *curiosity*

> • *calm.*
>
> *When we started to work on this module Kate's level of confidence was so low that she found it very difficult to find a time in her past where she'd felt confident at all, but bit by bit she was able to relax and make progress. The exercise took four times longer for Kate than it usually does but the reward at the end was unbelievable – she was ecstatic. Her whole attitude to life shifted and now she's actively looking for another job whilst also considering starting her own company – something she wouldn't have dreamed of before.*

Go to page 89 for more information on the Circle of Empowerment or, if you prefer, go straight to the Circle of Empowerment exercise on page 90 and start to develop your confidence-building skills before moving on to the Strategy module.

4 – Strategy

Creating and being able to use the Circle of Empowerment is great for building your confidence and the strategy below ensures that you make the most of it.

1   If you are about to do something where you feel that you are not 100% confident, fire up your Circle and step into it as you think of the thing you are about to do. The Circle will change your perspective.

2   As you are about to start, fire up your Circle for an extra boost. Some people even like to go to a room in private (toilets are the easiest option in most places!) and let your Circle flow all over you and go for it.

3   When there is a big rush of positive feeling reflect on what happened after the event, or even during it. This is a great time to stack up your Circle. Equally, if there are areas that perhaps didn't go so well use your Circle to make sure you are well prepared for the next time.

Kate's main 'Eureka!' moment was at the first stage. She found this module useful but was more matter of fact about it. Later, though, she admitted that she forgot to use the preparation for an important interview but as soon as she remembered, waiting in reception, she imagined her confidence circle going over her and covering her fully – it gave her just the confidence boost she needed.

Go through this strategy for yourself and see how it works for you before moving on to the final module in this section, Feedback, to tie everything together and ensure it works.

5 – Feedback

In this module you will learn how to use the fundamental concept of feedback to ensure you get the outcome you desire. The use of feedback will make sure that, no matter what happens, you will persevere until you have the level of confidence you want for every aspect of your life.

Kate decided to use this module to help her ensure that she's building on her confidence over time, periodically observing where she is.

Go to page 26 now to discover the feedback-not-failure concept and how it can work for you.

Having gone through all of these modules you'll have gained a far greater understanding of what's really important to you about being confident, highlighted and eliminated any blocks you may have had around your confidence and learnt a powerful yet simple technique that you can apply in any situation to boost your confidence.

2.5.2 DISCOVERING THE ATTRACTIVE AND WONDERFUL YOU

Ever had a 'fat and ugly' day? Many of us at one time or other have felt we are not attractive enough, not good enough or even downright ugly and bad. We live in a society that puts a lot of emphasis on the way we look, and our identity is often, at least on some level, tied up with how we look.

The media's preferred images of women are airbrushed, pubescent stick insects that do not reflect the rich and beautiful diversity of women that exist in the world. The result of this wide gulf between glossy magazine portrayals and everyday reality is that many women are left feeling dissatisfied and longing to look different. We are inherently social creatures – we want to fit in, to be accepted, to have others appreciate and value us – and we unconsciously or consciously compare ourselves and others to these unrealistic images of what's 'attractive'.

Some women deal with this by completely cutting out the things they feel 'beautiful women' typically do – so they don't wear make-up or they choose hair styles that are convenient rather than flattering, and generally keep themselves away from the 'frills' of physical beauty, believing it's not the thing for them because they're not that type of woman.

Some others believe they're not attractive enough or good enough but try to emulate the 'look', and so put on lots of makeup to hide behind, constantly checking to make sure their mask is fully intact.

Then there are those women who were 'beauties in their day' and now believe they've lost their looks just because they're getting older, so with each passing year they try more desperately to hold on to what they had, believing that their current, mature beauty is just not enough.

Stephanie Peters is the mother of three boys. She is a full-time stay-at-home mum and for the last ten years has put on make-up about three times, and that included her wedding day!

She doesn't have time to bother about such things. She's intelligent, practical, fun mum and doesn't want to worry about something she doesn't think she even has an outside chance of being good at.

Or at least that was her attitude until the father of one of the kids at school left his family and ran off with another woman. It was a shock to the whole community and for Stephanie it was like a lightening bolt, it brought up all her insecurities, including all the ones about not being attractive enough, and now the fear of losing her family is overwhelming her.

She's convinced she needs to work on herself, that she's not good enough as she is, that the thirteen years they have been together could now be a reason why her husband would want someone else, someone better looking. She's absolutely at a loss and her insecurity and worry is affecting her relationship and causing tension.

Angela Thompson, 29, is exceptionally good at her job. She's incredibly hard working, conscientious and greatly respected by those who have worked with her. She's also a practical realist – she knows she's not stereotypically beautiful, she wouldn't even classify herself as pretty or average. She just sees a short, slightly overweight woman with pale blotchy skin and angular features.

She takes care of her appearance, wearing nice clothes, having her hair styled every six weeks, and using make-up to make the most of herself, but deep down, she believes she isn't good-looking enough: 'No man would want to go out with some-one who looks like me.'

She takes compliments badly, turning them round to support her views – so, her friends say nice things because they love her and not because they mean it, or a man who compliments her is only after one thing!

The reality is that Angela is an attractive, voluptuous, kindly looking woman who most men would want to date but for the large chip on her shoulder. She unwittingly gives out a negative message that puts men off, and then when they're not interested, it confirms her belief that she's not attractive enough.

As we are growing up we deal with the hurt life throws at us in different ways. In our society the concept of physical beauty surrounds us and yet most of us can't do an awful lot about what was given to us at birth. What's considered beautiful varies across time and culture but what's not transient is the true beauty that radiates from within: the lighthearted joy and energy of youthful beauty, the depth and breadth of mature beauty, and the many different types in between.

Is an oak more beautiful than an apple tree? Perhaps for some, but for most they are both beautiful in their own way, and an oak pretending to be an apple tree just doesn't make sense – much better to discover which type of tree you are and allow yourself to grow and blossom.

TOP TIP
Find the beauty within and let it shine out.

Getting results

Being able to radiate your own inner beauty is all about self-knowledge, self-acceptance and confidence. Working through the process below, in the order given, will enable you to achieve that.

1 Outcome
2 Blocks
3 Strategy
   • Who am I?
   • Life Purpose
   • Values
   • Beliefs
   • Perception Enhancer
   • Boosting your confidence
4 Feedback

1 – Outcome

This is a simple model to highlight specifically what you want and whether you are truly ready to discover how attractive and wonderful you are.

> Angela was amazed at her shift in perspective. Initially she was very sceptical about the work we were doing together – she had wanted to focus on getting a man – but it became obvious that her main issue was her limited perception of herself. After going though this model she was able to see that her true aim was not to look like other people but to take further what she was already doing – making the most of what she has, but doing it in a far deeper, more fundamental way.

Go to page 57 to work through the Outcome model for yourself. Pay particular attention to the final section, questions 11–16, because this will highlight any secondary gains you may have. If you do have secondary gains just note them down and we'll work through them in the next module.

2 – Blocks

Generally the belief that 'I'm not attractive enough' is a limiting one connected with one or more negative emotions. The Blocks module enables you to go to the root-cause level and get rid of these limitations so you can allow your inner beauty to shine through.

> *Angela worked on her belief that she's not attractive enough and the negative emotions of fear and sadness. By getting rid of these the concept of beauty lost its charge and is no longer so important to her.*

Go to page 75 for more information on blocks or, if you prefer, go straight to the exercise on page 85 and start getting rid of the unconscious blocks preventing you from discovering how attractive and wonderful you are. Then move on to the Strategy module.

3 – Strategy

The strategy below is very powerful for helping you to be truly happy with who you are and the way you look. As with many of these exercises, though, it's a great start but it's important to tweak and adapt it to your own requirements.

1 Read through the Who am I? section (page 32) to ensure you are happy with the general concept of 'self' and then consider how you view yourself. It would also be useful to work through the Life Purpose (page 59), Values (page 39) and Beliefs (page 43) modules to gain more clarity, but these are not essential.

2 List all the things you:

- like about your character;
- like about your body; and
- have done/achieved that you are proud of.

3   Go through each of the positions in the Perception Enhancer (page 94) to acknowledge what you have achieved, who you are, and all the things you like about yourself. You will need to place a significant person in your life in Position 2 because it will enable you to see yourself as someone else sees you and also, of course, objectively.

4   If confidence is an issue for you go through the Boosting your confidence module on page 229.

This strategy was a revelation for Angela. In the past she had just covered up what she considered to be her inadequacies but now she's happy with who she is and what she offers the world, and has decided to concentrate on the practical dos and don'ts of what styles and colours to wear for her height, shape, and colouring, because then, as she put it, 'my outside can reflect my inside'.

Go through this strategy for yourself and see how it works for you before moving on to the final module in this section, Feedback, to tie everything together and ensure it works.

4 – Feedback

In this module you will learn how to use the fundamental concept of feedback to ensure you get the outcome you desire.

Angela has decided to use the feedback process to help her ensure she continues to build on her inner confidence.

Go to page 26 now to discover the feedback-not-failure concept and how it can work for you.

Having gone through all of these modules you will have highlighted and eliminated any blocks that may have been stopping you from really appreciating yourself and started to discover how attractive and wonderful you are – letting the beauty within shine through.

2.5.3 REVERSING FEELINGS OF SELF-HATRED

To truly hate yourself is very isolating. Most people who feel this way keep it hidden, sometimes even from themselves, considering any such thought that may present itself as trivial and unimportant, so no one can see how bad (sometimes even evil) they think they really are and will not hate them as they hate themselves. Some may even ignore the problem, hoping it will just go away – but alas, it just gets bigger and stronger as time goes by, even if the person pushes it into the background, and feels better for a while.

Although self-hate may be, and generally feels like, the cause, it's a symptom of a deeper problem, but because it resides at identity level, it can also be the cause of, or support mechanism to, other problems as well, as shown in the example below.

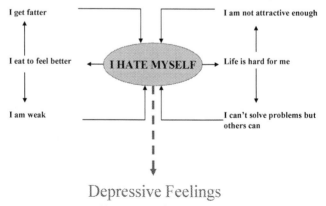

Depressive Feelings

*No way out, stuck, trapped
and emotionally low*

Louise Brown, a florist, is single and shares a flat with an old school friend. She's attractive, slim and very considerate to her family, friends and colleagues, but despite the apparent support, she's got to a stage where she can't cope any more. She's over £20K in debt, fears losing her job all the time, has trouble with her landlord, and has a sexual hunger which she never manages to quench so she sleeps with men but then feels awful and hates herself for it. 'I don't know how I got here but I know I can't carry on like this,' says Louise.

Louise is at the end of her tether. For the last five years she's been spiralling out of control, getting deeper and deeper into a cycle of self-loathing, and it's affecting every aspect of her life. She's desperate to get out before she drowns. She's even starting to fall out with friends. 'It's like I am in quicksand, the harder I try to get out the deeper I go!' she says.

Travel agent Janet Porter is married and has children, and feels her life is an ongoing drudgery – she has to do all the household chores, otherwise they don't get done, and hold down a full-time job in order to pay for the things she needs and wants – healthy food, clothes, and toys for her son. Her husband does nothing to help around the house except pay the big bills, and as soon as he comes in from work he showers and is off to the pub or sits in front of the TV.

Janet's tired of carrying so much of the burden, of feeling alone, of crying herself to sleep. Most of all she hates herself for being the way she is and staying in her situation.

Generally, when we have these feelings of self-loathing it's because we are doing something in our lives that conflicts with our beliefs of who we are. The challenge is to find the area of incongruence and take appropriate action to resolve the conflict.

TOP TIP

Look at the feeling of hating yourself as a flag, an indication that something's not right.

Getting results

The process below can be used repeatedly whenever you find conflict in your life and, because of all the things you discover about yourself, the more you use it the easier it gets and the less you'll need to use it.

1 Outcome
2 Beliefs
3 Blocks
4 Strategy
  - Who am I?
  - Life Purpose
  - Values
  - Perception Enhancer
  - Boosting your confidence
  - Cause or Effect
5 Feedback

1 – Outcome

This is a simple model to highlight whether you are truly ready to let go of your 'I hate myself' feelings and start to like and appreciate yourself. It will flush out any secondary gains you may have from hating yourself, which is necessary before any other work is done or the work will need to be repeated.

> *Louise has no secondary gain issues. Her outcome is to like herself and her life – she just doesn't believe it's going to happen because her life is so far removed from what she'd like it to be.*

Go to page 57 to work through the outcome model for yourself. Pay particular attention to the final section, questions 11–16, because this will highlight any secondary gains you have from hating yourself. If you have any secondary gains just note them down and put them to one side ready for when you go through the Blocks module, but for now, move on to Beliefs.

2 – Beliefs

Beliefs are the foundation of behaviour: positive beliefs support you and help you to achieve what you want in life, whereas limiting beliefs hinder and sabotage you. It's important to uncover all your beliefs about yourself because then you'll have much more information about where the real problem lies.

> *Louise's top three positive beliefs related to this issue are:*
> - *'I can do anything I put my mind to';*
> - *'I will persist until I succeed'; and*
> - *'Sometimes I like myself'.*
>
> *Her top three limiting beliefs are:*
> - *'I hate myself';*
> - *'I don't deserve to live'; and*
> - *'I deserve to suffer'.*

To do this for your own beliefs, first go to page 43 for a more detailed explanation or, if you prefer, go straight to the exercise on page 45 and discover your own positive and limiting beliefs. Then move on to the Blocks module.

3 – Blocks

Getting rid of blocks such as the limiting belief 'I hate myself' and its associated feelings and starting to truly love yourself involves going to the root of the problem. Once you are rid of your blocks – lightening a load you will have carried since you were very young – you can move forward with your life.

> *The blocks Louise worked on are:*
> * *'I hate myself';*
> * *'I am not worthy';*
> * *'I don't deserve to live';*
> * *'Men just want to use me';*
> * *'I am evil';*
> * *'I am trapped'; and*
> * *'I deserve to suffer'.*
>
> *For Louise 'I am evil' was the root of her problem and when we got rid of that belief the others just lost their charge and importance. It's important to mention that Louise's belief doesn't mean she was evil at all, it's just an association she made when she was three that she has unconsciously carried with her all these years.*

Go to page 75 for more information on blocks or, if you prefer, go straight to the exercise on page 85 and start getting rid of the unconscious blocks stopping you from letting go of your feelings of self-hatred and truly being able to love yourself. Then you will be ready to move on to the Strategy module.

4 – Strategy

Getting rid of limitations and blocks leaves you with a clean canvas to start creating an effective strategy for liking yourself and continuing to like yourself in the future. The strategy below is a useful starting point.

1   Read through the 'Basic structure of a person' on page 32, and make sure you are happy with the concept of 'self'. It may be of value to work through the modules on Life Purpose (page 59) and Values (page 39) too, because these will give you a greater understanding of yourself and help you to appreciate yourself more – but they aren't essential.

2   List all the things you:
   • like about your character;
   • like about your life; and
   • have done/achieved that you are proud of.

3   Go through each of the positions in the Perception Enhancer on page 94 to acknowledge what you've achieved, who you are, and all the things you like about yourself. You will need to place a significant person in your life in Position 2 because it will enable you to see yourself as someone else sees you and also to see your whole situation objectively.

4   If confidence is an issue for you go through the Boosting your confidence module on page 229.

5   For each area of your life list all the things you hate at the moment. (To get more information on the different areas of your life, see the Circle of Life on page 11.)

6   Put them in order of priority by asking yourself 'What's really important to me?'

7   Go through the Cause or Effect module on page 15, and for each item note the level of control and influence you have.

8   For each item either decide on an action to deal with the issue appropriately, or decide who to approach for advice and ideas – people you know and trust who have achieved what you want to achieve. Ensure each action has a time limit attached to it and that you are happy/congruent within for achieving it. If you're not happy, treat it as a block and go through the Blocks module on page 85 to resolve the lack of congruence.

9   Take action and keep to your agreement.

10 Make alterations as necessary.

Louise had dealt with her problems by sweeping them under the carpet – it was only a matter of time before the dirt built up. She found the strategy outlined above incredibly useful for focusing on all the things she had been avoiding, and getting herself to tackle them. The thing that really amazed her was that when she got down to it, they really were not so bad after all, but somehow, by avoiding them they'd appeared far more difficult than they actually were. For example, not facing up to her financial problems had meant she spent money to feel better, which only fuelled her problem further. By looking at her situation objectively she was able to manage to stop overspending and start to pay back what she owed.

Go through this strategy for yourself and see how it works for you before moving on to the final module in this section, Feedback, to tie everything together and ensure it works.

5 – Feedback

In this module you will learn how to use the fundamental concept of feedback to ensure you get the outcome you desire.

For Louise this module was useful in giving her absolute confidence that she will be OK moving forward, because if she ever has that old feeling of not liking herself again in the future she'll know it's a flag that something needs to be dealt with and she knows how to find the root cause and get rid of it. She's 100% sure that she will be able to love herself more and more and that her understanding and acceptance of herself will grow as time goes on.

Go to page 26 now to discover the feedback-not-failure concept and how it can work for you. (Remember the feeling of self-hatred is a flag – it just indicates there are more blocks to remove, nothing more.)

Having gone through these modules you'll have uncovered and eliminated any blocks you may have had, and worked though appropriate areas of your life to deal with the root cause of what's stopped you from truly appreciating and loving yourself. You'll also have a strategy to help you to truly start loving yourself and knowing that, as time goes by, your self-love and acceptance will get deeper and stronger.

2.5.4 MAKING LIFE LESS DIFFICULT

Feeling that life is overwhelming, that things have stacked up against us – relationship troubles, a life change, work stress, trying to manage work and home life, or a bereavement – is bound to happen once in a while. It can afflict you whatever your age, sex, intelligence, social standing and level of affluence. Often it's when you're just managing to 'cope' and then there is a change in your circumstances and your world is thrown into the abyss of losing control; it can even happen to people who have quickly come into a lot of money. Or it can creep up over time without us really knowing when it started. Somehow the weight of life overwhelms us and it's just too much. We are drained, and the light at the end of the tunnel just seems to lead to another tunnel. It can be incredibly debilitating and life can have very little meaning; the simple joy of being alive doesn't exist – even positive events are overshadowed by the belief that what goes up must come down – and we see deep, dark despair just around the corner.

The worst characteristic of such experiences is that generally we don't realize we are lost; it just feels like this is what life's supposed to be like. And those who *do* realize it's not right may feel they just have to get on with it, and carry on, whilst falling deeper and deeper into a problem-ridden, painful life; they simply learn to cope with the painful symptoms.

Our responses to such things are deeply individual, though; three people could go through the same life events and one might come out absolutely fine, one a little lost, and the third completely overwhelmed, based on their past experiences, ability to deal with the events, their support structure, and their character.

Generally, in our society we tend to treat the symptoms and not the cause. We focus on treating chemical imbalances rather than the root cause of those imbalances: a lack of effective beliefs and strategies with which to deal with life's experiences.

Angela Stubbs has been promoted twice in as many years, which is very unusual and a reflection of her hard work and tenacity. She works 100% during the week and sees friends and catches up on chores at the weekends. She has money but very little time.

Angela's surviving but deep down she's lost and finds life incredibly hard. She doesn't know what to do to be happy, so in the meantime she's just trying to make the most of it, working hard and going out and enjoying herself. But underneath it all she's frustrated and tired of constantly picking herself up and coping. 'When do I start to live?' she often wonders.

After leaving college, Rachel Peters went straight to work at a training company specializing in software applications. She'd wanted to go travelling for a while but had debts and no way of raising extra cash, so going out to work was her only option.

It had taken her a long time to figure out the education system and just when she had mastered it, and was successful, she had to move on! It was a strange experience having to apply her mind during set hours and not having the flexibility to skive and make up the time later. In the business environment, the rules were not so easy to see and people didn't always say what they meant. Although she gave it 110%, somehow she just didn't feel in control. On the one side life was easier because she only had to work the set hours and she got paid, but somehow it was much harder and so much shallower than she had expected. Two years on and she is still asking herself 'Is this it for the rest of my life?!'

In Rachel's eyes everyone else seems to cope OK, so she feels very alone, in a gulf of despair. She knows that even when she gets out of this blue feeling it's sure to return. She is starting to ask her herself 'If this is what life is about – the highs and lows and at the end we all die anyway – is it worth living?' She knows she needs help but she wants to be able to help herself.

Rachel's case, though quite extreme, is not uncommon. Feeling that life is getting too much happens to all of us at one time or another – with the right triggers it can happen to anyone.

TOP TIP

The natural state of humankind is to be happy with life. As children we do it without thinking, but somehow, as we grow up, we forget how to enjoy the simple things and just focus on problems, effectively learning how to be unhappy. But we can regain what we once knew – how to be happy, deep inside.

Getting results

The feeling that life is too much is a flag, an indication that something in you or your life isn't right and has to change. Working through the process below, in the order given, will help you to deal with these negative emotions at their cause level, as well as helping you to gain new strategies to turn the negative spiral into a positive one.

1 Outcome
2 Blocks
3 Strategy
   • Cause or Effect
   • Blocks
4 Feedback

1 – Outcome

This is a simple model to highlight whether you are truly ready to let go of your feeling that 'life is too much' and to start truly enjoying being alive and dealing with what may come up easily and effectively. It will flush out any secondary gains you may have from feeling that life is overwhelming.

Initially Rachel found it incredibly difficult to put her desired outcome positively; she wanted 'life to not be a chore, for life not to be a burden and a hassle to her'. As we worked on stating it positively she realized what we were trying to achieve and how difficult it was for her. She instinctively thought in negatives and found it very tough to change her way of thinking. She was delighted when eventually she came up with a positive outcome: 'to truly enjoy life and for living to be easy'. It was a major shift – to start to have the image in her mind of something truly positive, which made her feel energized and pulled her towards a 'lighter' life.

As we went through the module it became clear that she had a secondary gain from keeping her life difficult – if she truly enjoyed life and found living easy she felt she would lose anonymity, have nowhere to hide, and would lose her sense of safety. Before any other work was done it was imperative that we work though these beliefs and resolve them, which we did by treating them as blocks.

Go to page 57 to work through the outcome model for yourself. Pay particular attention to the final section, questions 11–16, because this will highlight any secondary gain you have. If you do have secondary gains just note them down and work through them in the next module, Blocks.

2 – Blocks

Getting rid of limiting blocks is vital to truly being able to enjoy life and involves going to the root cause of the problem. Once you are rid of your blocks – lightening a load you will have carried since you were very young – you can move forward with your life. Go to page 75 for more information or page 85 to get rid of your unconscious blocks.

Rachel had the following blocks stopping her from reaching her objective:

> - *loss of anonymity;*
> - *standing out;*
> - *having nowhere to hide; and*
> - *needing safety.*
>
> *We can see how these may fit together and affect each other: if you lose your anonymity, people notice you and can cause you pain; if you stand out you can be shot down; if you have nowhere to hide you aren't safe. These blocks all help Rachel to feel safe but safe from what? We need to know what was at the root of her drive to be safe.*
>
> *The root cause is the limiting belief 'I must be safe' and she also had the negative emotion of fear connected to it. They were so entrenched that, after getting rid of them, she felt bewildered – like she'd been carrying a heavy load and now it's gone she doesn't quite know what to do. She's happy but still needs time to get used to it to realize what new and wonderful things she can now do.*

3 – Strategy

Having an effective strategy to manage life's challenges is essential for creating a positive spiral in your life. The strategy below has been very useful for others in the past and hopefully you'll find it equally so. It's important that you adapt it over time so that it works well for you, based on your own unique motivators and preferences. But for now it will be a great start.

1. For each of the areas of your life detailed on page 11, list all the challenges you have to deal with at the moment.

2. Put them in order of priority – for each area of your life ask yourself 'What's really important to me?'. If you are short of time put them in an overall priority for your life and work through the most important first.

3   Go through the Cause or Effect module (page 15) and for each item
     note the level of control and influence you have.

4   For each, decide on an action to either deal with them appropriately
     or to approach people for advice and ideas, people you know who
     have achieved what you want to and ones whom you trust. Ensure
     each action has a time limit and that you are happy and congruent
     inside with achieving them – if not, treat it as a block and go through
     the Blocks module, page 85, until you have resolved the lack of
     congruence.

5   Take action and keep to your agreement.

6   Make alterations as necessary.

*For Rachel, just the act of writing down what she needed to deal
with helped her gain a more objective perspective She'd always
kept everything in her mind but found the process of writing and
reflecting very powerful. Equally, asking for help and advice was
something she would not have done before in such a calcu-
lated way, but she was amazed how responsive and helpful most
people were and some of the ideas put forward were far more
useful than she could have imagined or hoped for.*

Go through this strategy for yourself and see how it works for you before
moving on to the final module in this section, Feedback, to tie everything
together and ensure it works.

4 – Feedback

In this module you will learn how to use the fundamental concept of
feedback to ensure you get the outcome you desire.

For Rachel this module was useful in giving her absolute confidence that she's going to be able to get what she wants, because she's able to use it to monitor and kept to her action points.

Go to page 26 to discover the feedback-not-failure concept and how it can work for you.

Having gone through these modules you'll have uncovered and eliminated any blocks you may have had at the root-cause level, and worked through appropriate areas of your life to ensure you are *at cause* and in control. You may not have all the answers yet but you'll have an action plan and know what you are going to do about it, and a feedback method to ensure you succeed.

Health

Module	Title	Page	Exercise time (mins)
2.6.1	Losing weight naturally and keeping it off	259	275
2.6.2	Giving up smoking	269	305
2.6.3	Dealing with PMT	280	155
2.6.4	Beating the difficulties of menopause	286	370
2.6.5	Eliminating anxiety, worry and stress	292	170

2.6.1 LOSING WEIGHT NATURALLY AND KEEPING IT OFF

Sometimes it seems like everyone I know is on a diet, trying to lose weight, trying not to worry about gaining weight, trying to feel better about the way they look – it's practically the national pastime – and is it any wonder? We have more and more teenage stick insects as role models paraded on catwalks and in magazines, leaving us aspiring to something we are unlikely to achieve – the skinniness of puberty and youth!

Women from all walks of life, all over the world, struggle with their weight – constantly watching what they eat, taunting and depriving themselves. It is a soul-destroying process. Worst of all, as you get older the struggle only gets tougher. What a relief it would be to be comfortable with your body, and truly happy with the way you look.

We all know that weight loss is about what you eat and how much you exercise. Whichever of the countless possible diets you go on, if you burn more calories than you eat you are likely to get rid of fat – but the real problem isn't so much losing the weight, but keeping it off, and many of us find the constant fluctuation between thin and fat, or fat and fatter, even more difficult to cope with.

Paulette Manning is a permanent dieter. Every six months or so when she can't button up her trousers she decides enough is enough and enrolls on yet another new diet plan. Her fridge and cupboards are stripped of the 'wrong' foods and only the 'right' ones are allowed back in. Perhaps this new diet will be the one for her, maybe this time it will be different – maybe it'll work. She's tried just about every diet there is. Initially it works, but then it seems to go wrong and she gains the weight back. With each cycle she loses slightly less and puts on a little more, and that's her main concern – because at this rate, by the time she's 45 she'll not be able to see her feet when she's standing up. She doesn't want to be that person.

'For some reason,' she says, 'I can only lose weight up to a certain point and then no matter what I do I just can't seem to shift it, it's like something's stopping me. I try something new and each time after about six or eight weeks, after I've lost a lot of weight, somehow my focus shifts. For a little while I'm OK but soon enough the lost weight is back on and I am bigger than before. I can't carry on like this – it's not how I want to live my life.'

Helen Thompson has dieted since her mid teens. Now, aged 27, her weight issue is a fact of life and her love-hate relationship with food is something that cuts to her very being.

Helen adores food, especially comfort foods – there is nothing more satisfying for her than a big plate of pasta, with red wine, followed by one of her long list of comfort desserts. Food and Helen go together like a hand in glove; the problem is she hates what it does to her – she hates her rounded body. She doesn't remember being slim but she does remember, only too well, what it's like to be two stone overweight and struggling to lose each pound. The pleasure of eating is short-lived and always followed by self-loathing, anger, and a deep sense of disappointment and frustration.

Over the last year she's managed to get rid of a lot of her excess fat, so she's wearing her 'mid fat' clothes and underwear, but the fear of gaining weight is ingrained in her mind and heart and she still struggles to keep the weight off – in fact she's re-cently started to gain weight again.

'I'm really scared I'm going to bloat out again, and am not sure why this is happening now – I'm very happy, have met a really nice guy that I'm getting on well with, work's going well too. In fact, everything in my life is fine, but for some reason I'm getting bigger.'

We each have our own unique story and yet the pattern – gaining weight, losing it and gaining it back – is a way of life for many. Unfortunately, most people struggle with weight because they are working at the wrong level – at the symptom level not the cause. The root cause of a weight problem is rarely physical and nearly always psychological, and yet diets only work at the behavioural level – they just relieve the current symptom of the extra weight. For some, the root cause of over-eating is a fear of intimate relationships – they don't want to be attractive to the opposite sex and it's their way of protecting themselves; for others, food is a source of comfort because they are unhappy, and this often develops into a vicious circle (unhappiness = need for comfort/food = weight gain = unhappiness, etc.). There are an infinite number of possible root causes and everyone will have their own unique combination. Finding the root cause and working at that level is essential for effortlessly losing and maintaining a healthy weight.

TOP TIP

Your body knows what it needs and wants. Listen to your body – find the root cause of your hunger. What is it that you are really hungry for?

Getting results

The modules below are designed to help you lose weight naturally and keep it off because they will help you work at the root-cause level.

1   Outcome

2   Behaviour

3   Beliefs

4   Blocks

5   Strategy

6   Circle of Empowerment

7   Feedback

1 – Outcome

This is a simple model to highlight whether you are truly ready to be the thinner size you desire and it will flush out any secondary gains you may have from being overweight.

> *Helen found the outcome model interesting. It was clear that she wanted to lose weight and yet equally she was hiding behind her weight. If she was slim she would have to go out there and live her life and face the fear of being rejected. This is definitely a secondary gain and it was therefore important for her to deal with it straight away. For Helen this meant going to the Blocks module first and dealing with this before doing anything else.*

Go to page 57 to work through the Outcome model for yourself. Pay particular attention to the final section, questions 11–16, because this will highlight any secondary gains you have. If you do have secondary gain, go to the Blocks section to deal with them before coming back to follow the sequence of modules.

2 – Behaviour

Behavioural analysis lets you examine your eating patterns in detail. It's very important to understand what you are doing now because then you'll be able to recondition your eating habits to ones that will actually work for you later.

The behavioural exercise used previously needs to be adapted a bit for losing weight. For each time period in the exercise write down what was going on with your weight, so you are able to see the fluctuations over time. Then consider your eating patterns and answer the questions below.

1   How do you know it's time to go on a diet?
2   What has triggered you to go on a diet in the past?
3   How do you know it's time to stop dieting?
4   What has triggered you to stop dieting in the past?

Now consider the times you eat in any given day and, for each of these, consider the questions below.

1   What triggers you to eat?
2   What are your emotions before, during and after you eat?
3   What do you see, hear, smell and taste?
4   What tends to happen before, during and after you eat?
5   What do you say to yourself – before, during and after eating?

Helen discovered that her eating pattern had been problematic even before her teens. She was shocked to see that she'd spent by far the biggest part of her life unhappy with her weight and on a diet. In fact she couldn't remember a time when she wasn't larger than she should have been, always fighting the flab.
Her motivators for going on a diet have always been external – to find a man, to get ready for someone's wedding, to go on holiday – and she always stops dieting because of emotional turmoil,

when it all becomes too much for her, for example when a relationship breaks up, she changes job, or there's a death in the family. She realizes that she has a little voice in her head which screams for food, and yet when she eats, it always turns into voice of condemnation for over-eating. She has, in effect, been bullying, badgering and taunting herself throughout her life, before during and after eating. Is it any wonder she has a bad relationship with food?

3 – Beliefs

Beliefs are the foundation of behaviour – positive beliefs will help you lose weight and keep it off and limiting beliefs will hinder and sabotage you. This module helps to uncover all your beliefs around weight, both the positive and limiting ones.

It's important to highlight limiting beliefs because then we can eliminate them in the Blocks module. Equally, highlighting positive beliefs is important because you can use them to understand yourself better and they provide you with positive ammunition.

Helen's top three positive beliefs for losing and keeping the weight off are:
- *'I can do anything if I want it enough';*
- *'Once I find the right way I will be able to stick to it'; and*
- *'I can do this'.*

Her top three debilitating beliefs are:
- *'I don't deserve to be happy';*
- *'I must suffer'; and*
- *fear of being rejected.*

To do this for your own beliefs go to page 43 to get a more detailed explanation or, if you prefer, go straight to the exercise on page 45 and discover your own positive and limiting beliefs before going onto the Blocks module.

4 – Blocks

Getting rid of blocks is vital for successful, long-term weight loss. In this section we'll work on the limiting beliefs you've already uncovered in the earlier exercises, because then they'll lose their validity and you'll be able to change the structure and charge of those things that have stopped or hindered you from losing weight.

> *The blocks that Helen worked on are:*
> * *the limiting belief 'I don't deserve to be happy';*
> * *the limiting belief 'I must suffer';*
> * *fear of being rejected; and*
> * *the limiting belief 'If I am thin I will have nowhere to hide'.*
> *This is a compilation of her answers from previous modules as well as the results of going through the Blocks module. It's useful to compile your own list in the same way.*

Go to page 74 for more information on blocks or, if you prefer, go straight to the exercise on page 85 and start to get rid of the unconscious blocks stopping you from being the size you want to be, before moving on to the Strategy module.

5 – Strategy

By looking at women who are naturally slim and have a healthy relationship with food we're able to adapt this approach into our own lives. By this stage you'll have highlighted your limiting beliefs, triggers and limiting behaviours and have dealt with the blocks they present.

List each of your past eating habits as itemized in point 2 (Behaviour) above and go through each one in your mind's eye, re-living each situation one by one, using the following process. (Note: do this as many times as you need to in order to feel confident that, given the same situation again, you'll behave in the new way.)

a Listen to your body.

b Find what the hunger truly is – boredom, habit, blocks or true physical hunger?

c If it's truly hunger for food, eat what you desire and STOP when you are full.

d Only eat in the NOW. Give your full attention to what you are doing – smell the food, notice its details and its full taste in your mouth, enjoy the texture. Be 100% engrossed in the process as though you were eating for the first time.

The questions you can ask yourself are:

a 'Am I really hungry?';

b 'What is the hunger really about?';

c 'Does my body truly want/need this food?';

d 'How much do I need?' (put the amount you think you need on your plate; you can always go for more if you want); and

e 'Do I want/need more?' (ask this half-way through, about two-thirds in and again at the end).

Make sure you are listening to the right voice and give your body what it physically truly wants and needs.

Now consider times in the future when you might get distracted or lose focus and initially forget to go through this process. Imagine such a scenario and play it out in your mind's eye – feel the feelings, see what you would see, and hear what you would hear – then acknowledge that it's interesting feedback and from the time you notice that you've got yourself into such a situation, go through the steps above, with your reason for wanting to lose weight in mind. Run through each future scenario until you are 100% confident that your past and future relationship with food has changed.

> *Helen initially found this process very difficult. She thought her voice was saying 'eat more, more, MORE…' and screaming out her favourite foods. It took her over two weeks and three sessions to be able to truly listen to her body rather than her limiting blocks, which were screaming out for more and drowning out her true voice, which asked for the food her body needs to be healthy and well.*

Go through this strategy for yourself and see how it works for you before you move on to the Circle of Empowerment module.

6 – Circle of Empowerment

Confidence is crucial for losing weight. The Circle of Empowerment is a wonderful technique that utilizes the confidence you have in other areas of your life to help you build a universally confident state you can use at any time and in any situation.

> *Helen was able to tap into her other confident states very easily and was really amazed at how her perspective of her past negative eating experiences changed when she applied the Circle to them. She then went through the strategy again whilst applying her new powerful confident state – it gave her even more confidence and the steps became more of a matter a fact of the way things are – a natural progression.*

Go to page 89 to get further explanation of the Circle of Empowerment or, if you prefer, go straight to the exercise on page 90 and build your own circle of empowering emotions, and then when you've finished and are happy with how to use it, move on to the Feedback module.

7 – Feedback

In this module you will learn how to use the fundamental concept of feedback to ensure you lose weight and keep it off. You will never have to diet again because you'll simply have a different way of interacting with food.

> Helen went through three iterations before she was able to fully find her path. Each time she was able to put more information back in to the recovery strategy, and now she's comfortable with food and with her body; she eats what she wants and when she wants and is still losing weight. The loss has been slower than before and she knows it's sustainable because now its a part of her and a way of life, rather than something she has to force – it just feels natural to her.

Go to page 26 now to discover the feedback-not-failure concept and how it can work for you.

Having gone through all of these modules you will have gained a far greater understanding of yourself – you'll have got rid of any blocks, learnt new strategies for relating with food, and be confident that, over time, you'll be able to achieve and maintain the weight you want.

2.6.2 GIVING UP SMOKING

Pippa is 32 now and has already given up smoking more times than she cares to remember. It's been a consistent new year's resolution for the past seven years, along with losing weight and not biting her nails. Each year she starts with the best of intentions. She cleans up her house. Dry cleans all her smoky suits. Gets rid of all the evidence of being a smoker – the designer ashtray, the lighter, and even the collection of match boxes from her favourite restaurants. A couple of times she even changed her hair style: creating the new, non-smoking Pippa. Each time she starts anew, resolute that this time it will be different. She will crack it. She is older and wiser. She can do this.

Unfortunately, her high hopes are replaced by emotional lows as she experiences another failed attempt. Something always happens that gets her to start smoking again. Last time it was breaking up with her boyfriend. She was devastated – completely heart-broken and alone again. How could she cope with life, work and giving up smoking? The stress was so overwhelming that she couldn't keep to it, didn't want to keep to it, and just like that she was back to smoking again.

Ann Johnson is the mother of an old school friend of mine and is one of those amazing women who are larger than life itself. Her inexhaustible energy and passion for life were in stark contrast to my demure, shy, quietly loving and totally giving mother. I was both inordinately fond of her and, secretly, scared of her power. Ann was a formidable figure who oozed confidence and had smoked almost all her life – her smoking seemed as much a part of her as her arms and legs, and it was impossible to imagine her without also picturing a cigarette between her fingers. The burglar-proof windows at the top of the house were always open but their draft did little to eliminate the smell of smoke that was a permanent feature of her lively and welcoming home, and the gut wrenching, early morning coughing fit was the regular wake-up call whenever I stayed over – again very different to my quiet and peaceful home life. Sometimes the sound made me want to retch, but mostly, it just hurt to hear it.

Then suddenly at the age of 58 Ann stopped smoking. I was amazed; shocked, in fact. This was a woman who loved smoking, and loved being a smoker. And yet, overnight she decided to simply cut it out of her life and amputated her smoking habit without batting an eyelid. Ann hasn't smoked since.

How can this be? How can someone just suddenly stop after 40 years? No patches, no cutting back – just going from a 40-a-day habit to 0! For good! It's a great achievement and, although she is not unique in this, such stories are rare.

The example of Ann, and the few that are like her, doesn't seem right or fair – how can one person achieve something so easily when so many others struggle to even get close? How is it that Ann was able to give up straight away and yet Pippa has struggled so many times and failed yet again? Is it the difference between 58 and 32? What has Ann got that Pippa lacks?

Most people believe giving up smoking is to do with strength of character. If you have it then you are one of the special few who'll succeed; if you don't then you're one of the masses, and failure is sure to follow. This is a commonly held belief but it's completely untrue.

Imagine a locked door. Only the right key will unlock it and if you happen to stumble upon the right key you can pass through and never smoke again. If, however, you do not have the right key you will never get through the door, no matter how many times you might try. The difference between Ann and Pippa is that Ann stumbled on the right key first time whilst, unfortunately, Pippa is still struggling with the wrong key, each time thinking that if she is committed enough, and wants it badly enough, she will be able to quit. Sadly, every failed attempt just narrows the keyhole, and Pippa's belief in herself and in her ability is knocked. Equally, her belief in her capacity for failure and her need for cigarettes is strengthened, and giving up becomes harder and harder.

Einstein defined insanity as doing the same thing repeatedly and expecting a different result. If you are perpetually trying to give up and it's not working, it's a sign, and I highly recommend that you change your approach or stop trying – you're only making things harder. Like Ann, you can give up and know that you'll never be a smoker again. You can have the key to unlock the door and go through to the other side.

But, if it's so simple, why do so many people struggle to give up? Why doesn't everyone find the key? The answer is because it has to unlock a multi-dimensional web! 'What?' I hear you say, 'I thought it was simple?' Well, it's as simple as looking at a tree – each branch is easy enough to follow but if you try looking at the whole tree it appears to be much more difficult. Unlocking the smoker's web is exactly the same – we first need to understand its structure. My father always used to say, 'knowing you have a problem means you're half-way towards the solution'; likewise, understanding the structure of this problem will get you that much closer to solving it.

Smoking is one of those things that's deceptively complicated. It has a wide and deep root in a smoker's whole being – their psychic, physical and emotional selves. First there is the purely physical, chemical addiction to the nicotine. Then there's the habit of smoking – something you do ritually after a meal, with friends at a bar, with morning coffee, and so on.

On top of that there's the emotional satisfaction – a cigarette somehow makes it easier to deal with the stresses of life and helps you to focus better. And finally there's the association at identity level with being a smoker – 'I am a smoker!' This, unconsciously, will be fed by your associations of what it means to be a smoker – hip, maybe; belonging to a group; being sociable, etc. Your place in the world is unconsciously carved by these associations and a feeling that it's just 'what people like me do' – 'I am an artist, therefore I smoke', 'I'm social, therefore I smoke'...

All of these are bonded together into a web, creating a very powerful and highly individual driver to smoke.

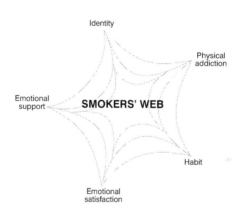

There is a generic structure to giving up smoking but, unfortunately, this is only part of the story because each smoker is unique and the solution also has to reflect this. For most of us, expecting to magically discover our solution is like expecting to win the lottery – highly unlikely! – but help is at hand. The process below is very powerful. It will provide you with the key to giving up smoking. Once you learn it you can also use it for other things you might want to achieve in your life too, because it works with the very core of how your mind and body operate.

TOP TIP

Give up smoking only when you are sure it's what you really want.

Getting results

Working through the process below, in the order given, has helped many others to give up smoking. First go through steps 1 and 2 to decide if you really do want to give up smoking. Then, if you decide you do, go through the rest. Steps 3–5 will help you to understand your own smoker's web, and step 6 will set everything in place to ensure that you *will* give up. Step 7 will build your confidence, because it really helps to collapse the negative belief structures in yourself and replace them with positive ones. The last but by no means least important step will ensure that, should the progress you made in step 6 start to wobble, you can take what you have learnt and feed it back until you get the result you want.

1   Outcome
2   Motivation
3   Behaviour
4   Belief
5   Blocks
6   Strategy
7   Circle of Empowerment
8   Feedback

1 – Outcome

This is a simple model to highlight whether you are truly ready to give up smoking. It will flush out any secondary gains you may have, and as you progress through it you'll start to collect information that will help you to understand your own smoker's web.

Pippa found the outcome model simple and straightforward; it highlighted that although she does want to have a cigarette-free life, she currently loves smoking and doesn't quite know how she's going to stop. She found some positive reasons to smoke – being trendy and getting a break from work – but when probed further it was clear that these could be defused, because she was able to be trendy and get break time through other means.

Go to page 57 to work through the outcome model for yourself. Pay particular attention to the final section, questions 11–16, because this will highlight any secondary gains you have from remaining a smoker. If you have any secondary gains just note them down and put them to one side ready for when you go through the Blocks module. For now, concentrate on progressing through the Motivation section.

2- Motivation

This is one of the most powerful tools for giving up smoking. Many locate their main driver using this technique – in fact, some feel so confident that they'll stop after going through this module because they don't see the need for carrying on with the rest of the process! Please do carry on, though, because all the steps are equally important, however they may appear or feel.

For Pippa this part was the most influential. We went through the 'What would happen if I gave up?' scenario, followed by the 'not giving up' scenario. Then towards the end of the second scenario I asked her to take out a cigarette and hold it to her lips as though she were about to smoke. Hesitantly, she did it, and the act of smoking became solidly connected with the image of all it would mean to her life. Within ten seconds the cigarette was scrunched up in the palm of her hand and thrown in the bin, closely followed by the rest of the pack and the lighter.

It all became absolutely simple – the choice between being a strong and healthy mum, playing, supporting, loving and setting a good example for her healthy kids in an environment that was clean, wholesome and pure, or, a feeble, sickly mum with yellowed teeth and prematurely wrinkled skin, tending to her not-so-healthy kids that have adopted her weakness and lack of confidence, in a smelly, negative environment, in which she'd be likely to die before her time. Pippa was still single but even so she knew she really needed to start the life she wanted and attract the right type of guy. Giving up smoking was the only true option for her and she knew it in her very core. Whatever it took, she would never be a smoker again.

Now go to the Motivation module on page 21, or straight to the exercise on page 22, to work through this for yourself. When you go through it ensure you are relaxed and just seeing what comes up for you. We each have our own unique reasons for giving up and they are the most powerful drivers. Also after you work through the second scenario (the carrying on smoking one), take out a cigarette and hold it to your lips, as Pippa did. Imagine smoking it and all the consequences of smoking for the rest of your life. Consider that even having one cigarette means that you are making a choice for your whole life – between the first scenario and the second. Once you have gone through that, move onto the next module, Behaviours.

3 — Behaviours

Just as a doctor looks at the symptoms to find the ailment, behavioural analysis looks at your smoking patterns to help you find the root cause of your behaviour. It's important that you recognize all of your patterns so that we can recondition your habit later.

The standard behavioural exercise needs to be adapted because it is not specific enough for giving up smoking. You need to focus on the number of times you tried to give up, writing down your experience of what happened for each time period. Specifically focus on:

1   what triggered you to smoke again;
2   what emotions you felt – before, during and after starting to smoke again;
3   what you saw, heard, smelled and tasted;
4   what was going on around you – before, during and after starting to smoke again; and
5   what you said to yourself.

Additionally create a log of when, where, and why you have had cigarettes in the past. When I work with clients I always ask for a log from the time the session is booked. It means the information is current, thorough, and also shows their commitment to giving up.

> *Pippa's patterns were very clear. She smoked about 15 cigarettes a day on days when she didn't go out in the evening: first thing with her morning coffee, at about one-hour intervals at work, after lunch and dinner. The rate increased if she was under any emotional stress. And, of course, when she went out with her friends, cigarettes and drinks were firm companions in her hands.*

Go to page 47 for a further explanation of behaviours or, if you prefer, go straight to the exercise on page 48 and discover your behavioural patterns for smoking, before looking at your belief structures in the next exercise.

4 – Beliefs

Beliefs are the foundation of behaviour – positive beliefs will help you stop smoking and limiting beliefs will hinder and sabotage your efforts. This section helps to uncover all your beliefs around smoking, both the positive and limiting ones. It's important to highlight limiting beliefs because then you can eliminate them in the Blocks module. Equally, highlighting positive beliefs is important because they will help you to understand yourself better and therefore provide you with positive ammunition for giving up.

> *Pippa's top three, positive giving-up smoking beliefs are:*
> - *'I can do anything if I set my mind to it';*
> - *'I want to stop smoking'; and*
> - *'Smoking will kill me'.*
>
> *Pippa's top three limiting giving-up smoking beliefs are:*
> - *'Smoking calms me down and helps me think';*
> - *'I love to smoke'; and*
> - *'I am a smoker'.*

To do this for your own beliefs go to page 43 to get a more detailed explanation or, if you prefer, go straight to the exercise on page 45 and discover your own positive and limiting beliefs around stopping smoking. Then move on to the Blocks module.

5 – Blocks

Getting rid of limiting blocks is vital to giving up smoking, and the Blocks module will help you to achieve this. Those limiting beliefs you have already uncovered from the earlier exercises will be worked on in this section so that they are invalidated.

> The blocks that Pippa worked on are:
> - 'Smoking calms me down and helps me think';
> - 'I love to smoke';
> - 'I am a smoker'; and
> - a feeling of pleasure when smoking.
>
> This is a compilation of her answers from previous modules as well as going through the Blocks module.

Go to page 57 for more information on blocks or, if you prefer, go straight to the exercise on page 85 and start to get rid of the unconscious blocks stopping you from giving up before moving on to the Strategy module.

6 – Strategy

This is like turning the key to unlock the door. Applying the strategy below to each of your existing patterns and smoking habits will ensure the conditioning that is programmed in your mind and body is changed for good.

1   Highlight each of the times you have smoked in the past – situations and circumstances – including each time you started to smoke again.

2   Knowing what you know now, and having eliminated your blocks, run through in your mind *every* key and historic scenario and ensure that, when you run through it, you break the old connection with cigarettes

and create a new connection, concentrating on what motivates you to stop.

3   Run through possible future scenarios – if the situations in the past were to repeat themselves, observe how you would behave differently.

4   Consider all possible situations where you might be tempted to smoke again – run through your new thoughts and behaviours as though you are going through the experience now, to prepare yourself for the situations, should they arise.

Ensure you are 100% confident that you will choose to stop, otherwise go back and repeat the whole process again until you are absolutely confident you have dealt with everything that might hamper you.

Go through this strategy for yourself and see how it works for you before you move on to the Circle of Empowerment module.

> *Pippa found running through different scenarios very useful; it was whilst going through these that she really became convinced she'd give up for good. This is it, there's no turning back for her now – she can take on anyone, and anything, in the full knowledge that she will never be a smoker again.*

7 – Circle of Empowerment

Confidence in yourself is crucial for giving up smoking and the Circle of Empowerment is a wonderful technique to really help build on that confidence.

> *For Pippa this was an easy and powerful experience because she was able to apply the confidence she felt in her work to the practice of not smoking.*

Go to page 89 to get further explanation of the Circle of Empowerment or, if you prefer, go straight to the exercise on page 90 and build your own personal circle of empowering emotions. Then, when you have finished, and are happy with how to use it, move on to the Feedback module.

8 – Feedback

In this module you will learn how to use the fundamental concept of feedback to ensure you give up smoking for good.

Pippa gave up smoking straight away and has not had to use this module. Even so, she feels confident knowing that if she is ever tempted to smoke again she has this as a safety net and will know what she has to do.

Go to page 26 now to discover the feedback-not-failure concept and how it can work for you.

Having gone through all of these modules you will have gained a far greater understanding of yourself. You'll have got rid of any blocks, learnt about the complexity of the addiction to smoking, found the key to unlocking the door and be firmly situated on the other side, in your new life as a non-smoker, facing a bright future you have chosen for yourself.

2.6.3 DEALING WITH PMT

The menstrual cycle is a mental, physical and emotional experience that varies throughout the month. Some women only have slight symptoms, whilst others have acute problems with it, but generally there's a point in the month when the symptoms are at their worst. All or some of the following symptoms might be felt for a day or even for about a week before the period: tearfulness, anger and frustration; feelings of being lonely, at a loss, out of control, and things being out of perspective; hot and cold flushes, stomach cramps, sore breasts, a weakened immune system, lethargy and decreased stamina. It can literally feel like you are losing your mind because your true character can be suppressed by the intensity of the symptoms.

For those with very severe symptoms it can be particularly difficult and isolating because others frequently don't necessarily understand the severity, and may even see it as an exaggeration.

Alison Meyer has suffered from PMT since she was 14, when her periods first started. Since then her life has been on a constant four-week cycle: three great weeks when she is herself, enjoying life, and getting on with things, and one week when she is insecure, extremely irritable and tearful. For that week life becomes hard and painful for her and for the people around her.

'I've tried everything that I've heard of: St John's wort, evening primrose oil, cod liver oil and some homeopathic and herbal remedies. Some have made a slight difference but I still feel awful until the second day of my period'.

Alison has got used to this cycle, but as she's getting older it's becoming less acceptable for her to fly off the handle and now it's even more imperative that she doesn't.

'Gary doesn't mind, as he's used to it now and just keeps out of my way, and if necessary he lets me rant because he knows it's not really me, but I've managed to get myself a new job, my first team-lead role, and I don't want to lose it – literally!'

She's desperate to do well and prove that she can do it, but knows she has to find a new solution very soon.

Lisa Prescott is an architect, and has learned to just get on with things no matter what. Once a month for about a day or two she finds it even more difficult managing her job and family but copes by planning around it. She'll have her husband do more of the chores at that time or get other help.

Lisa's a very practical person and has found a solution that works for her and her family, so no one has to suffer with her symptoms except her. But recently she's found it increasingly difficult to cope.

She's able to rationalize the shift in perspective but the deep negative emotions are overwhelming. She suffers with a deep sense of loss and of guilt. (She had a miscarriage seven years ago and blames herself for it because she didn't stop working when she felt discomfort – at the time she had a deadline and just assumed she had an upset stomach – she didn't even see the doctor about it.)

'I have thought of locking myself away for a couple of days a month but it seems mad in this day and age not to be able to find a solution!'

Most women who suffer from 'losing their minds' once a month know that it's no picnic; it's like something or someone has taken over the controls and determines what you pay attention to and how you perceive it, and how you feel and what you think. You are 'at effect' of the chemical reactions in your body with no apparent way out.

TOP TIP

Your mind and your emotions are the most powerful assets you have. You can use them to help you through this difficult time.

Getting results

The process below is very useful in helping you to reduce the effects of PMT, and in some cases it may get rid of the symptoms altogether. (If you use this approach you are likely to see a marked difference within 3–6 months and a substantial difference within 2–3 years.) It involves going to the root cause of your negative emotions and thoughts and then building in effective strategies to counteract them. Also, some clients like to use this phase of the month to highlight issues that may have been festering away in a dark corner of their mind – they use it as an opportunity to spring-clean their mind and emotions. You can go through this process at any stage of your cycle but generally it's most effective to go through it at the time you are feeling the symptoms of PMT, because the negative emotions and limiting beliefs are closer to the surface.

1   Outcome
2   Blocks
3   Strategy
4   Feedback

1 – Outcome

This is a simple model to highlight whether you are truly ready to let go of 'losing your mind' once a month, and it will flush out any secondary gains you may have from 'losing it'.

Alison wants to have a more balanced emotional life and yet when we went through this model it was clear that she had one very important secondary gain – she believes that 'suffering gets attention' and that 'attention is love'!

Go to page 57 to work through the outcome model for yourself. Pay particular attention to the final section, questions 11–16, because this will highlight any secondary gains you have from suffering PMT. If you do have secondary gains, just note them down so you can work through them in the next module.

2 – Blocks

Getting rid of limiting blocks is vital to letting go of 'I lose my mind once a month' and to live your life fully in balance. This means going to the root cause of the all the negative emotions and limiting beliefs that come up for you – highlighting and getting rid of them so that you can move forward with your life without the baggage:

> *The blocks Alison worked on are:*
> - *'Suffering gets attention';*
> - *'Attention is love'*
> - *fear; and*
> - *isolation/loneliness.*

Go to page 75 for more information on blocks or, if you prefer, go straight to the exercise on page 85 and start getting rid of the unconscious blocks helping you to lose your mind once a month. Then move on to the Strategy module.

3 – Strategy

Getting rid of limitations and blocks leaves you with a clean canvas to start creating an effective strategy to deal with the actual chemical reactions you have in your body. The strategy below is designed around what to do when you feel the symptoms of PMT.

1   Acknowledge what you are feeling and thinking and congratulate yourself for noticing that you are not your usual self. The suppressed

negative blocks have made themselves known to you and it's a great opportunity to get rid of them.

2   Write down a list of your thoughts and feelings then work through the Blocks module again to get rid of the ones that are holding you back – negative/limiting ones.

3   Look at your life objectively and write down all the things that are right with it (i.e. make a list of all the things you take for granted, that you love about your life, and without which you would be unhappy.)

Alison found this exercise magical and a little unnerving – being able to get rid of such bad feelings was great if a bit bewildering. She was more baffled by how she was able to get rid of her fear than she was by anything else. For the first month we worked on it together but after that she worked on it alone and other issues came up: jealousy, abandonment, anger, frustration, guilt. After about four months she noticed that there was no longer a 'charge' to her PMT. There were issues that still made themselves known to her, but they were not as easy to spot any more – she had to pay a lot more attention to notice them.

Go through this strategy for yourself and, when you have finished and are happy with how to use it, move on to the Feedback module.

4 – Feedback

In this module you will learn how to use the fundamental concept of feedback to ensure you achieve the outcome you desire.

Alison found it comforting to know that the concept had instilled confidence in her in itself. She knows that no matter what may

> *happen she'll be OK and that she's gone a long way towards resolving this – even in a worst-case scenario, if something happened she'd know how to deal with it by feeding back her knowledge and moving on.*

Go to page 26 to discover the feedback-not-failure concept and how it can work for you.

Having gone through all of these modules you will have gained a greater understanding of your emotions and beliefs, their purpose, and how to get rid of limiting ones – so you can be free of the baggage from your past. You will be happy to be you, experiencing your world in the here and now, knowing that whatever may happen, you have the knowledge and experience to feedback your knowledge and deal with it.

2.6.4 BEATING THE DIFFICULTIES OF MENOPAUSE

Menopause is something that no woman can avoid – it's one of the inevitable stages in life. It is a period of years when your body goes through 'the change' – usually starting between the ages of 45 and 55.

For some women the whole experience is pretty much a non-event – there are just slight changes, which they are able to take in their stride. However, there are women at the other end of the spectrum for whom the menopause has a major effect across the whole of their life. They have hot flushes that interrupt their daily activities and interfere with their sleep – even causing chronic sleep deprivation, mood swings, fatigue, foggy thinking, weight gain, physical and emotional stress, and possibly depression.

This chapter is designed for the latter group, to help ease this transition from a mental and emotional perspective. Please note that it doesn't address the positive things that can be done to reduce physical symptoms such as aerobic exercise and appropriate nutrition.

Heather Kepter has been going through a very strange stage in her life for the last ten years. For most of her life she's been slim, but for the last five years the weight has been piling on – 'I've ballooned out', as she puts it – and she no longer feels she has an attractive figure. She's convinced that unless something changes her husband will leave her.

Janine Rossiter is at a loss – for the past six months she's not had a single good night's sleep, and is now at the stage where she's getting desperate. If it wasn't for the fact that she hates taking pills she would have been on sleeping tablets months ago! Initially it wasn't too bad but it's gradually become worse. She's finding it harder and harder to get to sleep and the slightest noise wakes her up; then trying to get back to sleep is nearly impossible.

'I know worrying about it doesn't help but I can't help myself. I know I need to sleep, but the more I try the less I get. It's nearly always the same: I wake up at some point in the morning between 2–3, all hot and sweaty; I toss and turn until about 6; and then as I'm about to drop off the alarm goes off and I have to get up. I'm completely drained and feel like I've just gone through a spin cycle! I really don't know how much more I can take.'

The worst of it is that the lack of sleep is affecting her ability to think and respond during the day – she's ratty, irrational, and her mood swings are getting to be a part of her character. Something has to change, fast.

Menopause is a milestone in every woman's life – it highlights an important transition, and its effect can vary dramatically. Ultimately, how you choose to deal with it is a completely personal matter, but the aim of the next section is to give you more options to help you through the transition effectively.

TOP TIP

Acknowledge and accept that this is a transition you have to go through, like a caterpillar becoming a butterfly.

Getting results

Menopause is a physical change in a woman's body that can affect her whole life. Working through the process below, in the order given, has helped some women experiencing menopause to get a better perspective on what's happening, purely from a mental and emotional perspective. It's one-third of what you can do to truly help yourself, the other two-thirds involving appropriate diet and exercise – so it's highly recommended that anyone going through the menopause researches the subject and takes appropriate steps in other areas of their life too, to give themselves the best chance of making the most of the transition.

1   Outcome
2   Blocks
3   Strategy
  • Daily habit
  • Cause or Effect
  • Eliminating anxiety, worry and stress
  • Blocks
4   Feedback

1 – Outcome

This is a simple model to highlight whether you truly want and are ready to make the most of your transition. It will flush out any secondary gains you may have from struggling through it.

> *Janine's outcome is simple – to have as easy a transition as possible. But when we looked into it further we found that she has two limiting beliefs ('Life is hard' and 'I must suffer') that would sabotage her efforts unless she got rid of them.*

Go to page 57 to work through the outcome model for yourself. Pay particular attention to the final section, questions 11–16, because this will highlight any secondary gains you have. If you do have secondary gains just note them down and you can work through them in the next module.

2 – Blocks

Getting rid of limiting blocks is vital to having a healthy transition. This module goes to the root causes of your negative emotions and limiting beliefs, highlighting them and helping you tackle them so you can move forward without them.

> *The blocks Janine worked on are:*
> * *limiting belief 'Life is hard';*
> * *limiting belief 'I must suffer';*
> * *fear of the unknown; and*
> * *fear of being old.*

Go to page 75 for more information on blocks or, if you prefer, go straight to the exercise on page 85 and start getting rid of any unconscious blocks you may have before moving on to the Strategy module.

3 – Strategy

Getting rid of your limitations and blocks leaves you with a clean canvas to start creating an effective strategy for getting through this transition. The strategy below has helped other women, who have adapted it and made it their own.

1   Make two lists – one listing all the things you have done in your life that you are absolutely delighted about, and the other listing all the things you want to do in the coming years that you are very excited about.

2   Look back on your life so far and reflect upon how far you've come, how much you've learnt and grown, and acknowledge and appreciate all the things you are delighted about.

3   Research the dos and don'ts of menopause because then you'll know exactly what's best for you and what's not. Then go through the Daily habit module on page 98, and add those things into your life that will be of the most benefit.

4   Go through the Cause or Effect module on page 15, because even though going through the menopause is something you don't have control over, you do have absolute control over how you deal with it, and the exercise will help you with that.

5   If anxiety, worry or stress is a factor for you go through the module on page 292 because it'll help you to keep things in perspective

6   When appropriate, go through the blocks exercise on page 85 and eliminate negative emotions and limiting beliefs as they come up. The life change you are going through is likely to make you face things you've kept under wraps for many years – things that perhaps you would rather not face – but this is a great opportunity to spring-clean your life, get rid of past baggage, and prepare for a

lighter future – the life from the burdened caterpillar to the unfettered butterfly!

Janine initially found this a very tough process to go through – she was so tired that she could barely focus on what we were covering. Later, though, as she started to take back control of her life, things started to change for her. In the beginning life was even tougher than before, but by working through different techniques she stumbled upon a combination of exercise and meditation that worked wonders for her and enabled her to sleep. Once she was able to sleep the other steps in the strategy became far easier to go through. She now looks at this phase in her life as one of the best she has been through.

Go through this strategy for yourself and when you've finished, and are happy with how to use it, move on to the Feedback module.

3 – Feedback

In this module you will learn how to use the fundamental concept of feedback to ensure you achieve the outcome you desire.

Janine has used the feedback model for everything, including keeping to her diet and exercise regime. She's determined to be able to consistently improve her state of being. Now that she's seen the benefits of really taking care of herself she's decided to use this model to become healthier and happier all round.

Go to page 26 to discover the feedback-not-failure concept and how it can work for you.

Having gone through all of these modules you will have gained a far greater understanding of yourself, have got rid of any blocks, and have learnt powerful techniques to help you move forward in an effective way.

2.6.5 ELIMINATING ANXIETY, WORRY AND STRESS

Generally, women are considered to worry, whereas men 'stress', and both may get anxious. Although these are gender stereotypes, the emotions themselves are the same; they all have potentially catastrophic effects – physically, mentally and emotionally.

Most people tend to get on with life and belittle the effects of these emotions. They still aren't believed to be a serious issue by much of the general population, even though countless research studies have shown otherwise.

Cox's Transaction Model in psychology states:

> *'Stress depends on the interaction between an individual and his or her environment. Most specifically, stress occurs when the perceived demands of a situation exceed the individual's perceived ability to handle those demands.'*

What's interesting is that it's not the situation, but our perception of our ability to handle it, that causes the problem. That's why two people can go through exactly the same situation and one be 'OK' and the other not!

There have been countless research studies on the effects on health of stress and there is good evidence to suggest that prolonged stress can significantly increase the chances of someone becoming ill. Specifically, stress can act on our immune system and lower our resistance to disease, as well as possibly increasing the indirect effect of an unhealthy life style, e.g. smoking and drinking. (Schliefer, Keller, Camerion, Thornton and Stein, 1983.) It's important to note, however, that a small amount of stress over a short time may have a positive effect.

When we are stressed about something we are generally overcome by one of three perspectives.

1   Task oriented – where we are logically evaluating and trying to solve the problem causing the stress.

2   Emotion oriented – where we lose ourselves in the emotion of the problem and try and deal with our negative feelings (anxiety and worry).

3   Avoidance/delusion – where we go into denial and either completely refuse to acknowledge the problem or pretend it's not that serious, by suppressing stressful thoughts and replacing them with protective ones.

How we deal with stress can vary depending on our character and the context of the stress situation, and it's important to be aware of these three perspectives because it increases our ability to cope with future situations.

Charlotte Blackburn is a housewife and mum. She has a very comfortable life, having the help of a nanny, a maid and a gardener. She spends her days shopping, going to lunches, tennis lessons, taxi-ing her daughter about, and planning dinner parties and family events.

She has everything she could want – her daughter is very clever and creative and an absolute joy to be around, she loves her husband very much, and they all have a good life together. Charlotte has one problem that completely clouds her day though, and makes her life a constant challenge: she can't stop worrying about the health of her family! Initially she thought it was normal – it's what any caring wife and mother would feel – but as time's gone on she's started to realize her feelings and behaviour are quite extreme. She constantly thinks about her husband or her daughter being ill, something not being right with them and, at worst, of one or both dying. At one stage she even convinced her husband to take out extra life insurance. But it's not just monetary security – it's far more than that. It's become an obsession that the things she loves are going to be taken away from her.

Jenny Smith has been a habitual worrier for as long as she can remember. She does it so well that even when she doesn't have anything specific to worry about, she worries about that! 'It's worse then,' she says, 'because I don't know what I'm missing; worrying keeps me focused and if I don't have something to worry about it's very unnervingly worrying.'

Her life has revolved around worrying about every aspect of her life at one time or another: work (whether she's in the right career, doing a good enough job, whether her colleagues like or respect her, if she's putting in enough effort, likely to get a pay increase); personal life (whether she will ever find her soul mate and – if she ever does – if he will he want her, whether she has enough friends and do they really like her?); her identity (is she good enough, is she worthy, too needy, too greedy, too moody?); her health (does she have something seriously wrong with her, will she ever get rid of her cold, why does she always get ill?). It's like background noise chattering away in her mind, always there keeping her company, ensuring she stays focused on what's important in life.

Although she jokes about it she's incredibly tired – life's full of possible negative outcomes and the worry leaves her scared and very tired. She wants to put a stop to it if she can.

Those suffering acutely from stress, anxiety or worry know how harmful they can be, but in a way they are the lucky ones because their pain will be so great that they'll generally be forced to find a solution.

Living life free of this baggage is a skill you can learn and, as with all skills, the more you practise it the better you'll become at it, eventually living a life free of the fear of loss, and focused on the positives in situations.

TOP TIP

Regard anxiety, worry or stress as a 'temporary' loss of perspective, and focus on the skill of regaining your true perspective.

Getting results

There are many ways of achieving an empowering perspective on your life – some are more efficient and effective than others and the best solution for you will depend on your own character and the severity of the problem for you. Working through the process below, in the order given, is a great way to eliminate anxiety, worry or stress in your life. (Please note that this is a great general solution but you may wish to alter it to fit your personal situation.)

1   Outcome
2   Strategy
    • Blocks
    • Cause or Effect
3   Feedback

1 – Outcome

This is a simple model to highlight whether you are truly ready to let go of being anxious, worried and/or stressed and it will flush out any secondary gains you may have from staying that way.

> *Charlotte found this model very powerful because it made it
> alarmingly clear to her that her behaviour was hurting her family.
> She wants a healthy, happy and fun family environment and she
> know she's been sabotaging it.*

Go to page 57 to work through the outcome model for yourself. Pay particular attention to the final section, questions 11–16, because this will highlight any secondary gains you have. If you do have secondary gains just note them down and we'll work through them in the next section.

2 – Strategy

Whenever you catch yourself being anxious, worried and/or stressed about anything, follow the steps below – either just before, during or after you had the thoughts/feelings.

1   Acknowledge what you are feeling and thinking and congratulate yourself for noticing that you are not 'on form', and that this is a disempowering state for you to be in.

2   Commit to change your state whatever it takes.

3   Focus inside yourself and write down a list of:

    a your emotions;

    b the main facts about the situation and how you may solve it; and

    c your limiting beliefs.

4   Using the list above, deal with your negative emotions and limiting beliefs as blocks and go to the Blocks module on page 85 to work through them.

5   Focus on the main facts from point 3b above and consider if they are really important to you. If they are, go through the Cause or Effect module on page 15 and note the level of control and influence you have over them.

6   Decide on an action plan to deal with the challenge appropriately, i.e. to the level of control and influence you feel you have. So you may want to provide the solution yourself or you may prefer to approach others for advice and ideas – people you know who have achieved what you want to, and ones that you trust. Ensure each action has a time limit and that you're happy/congruent inside with achieving them. If not, treat the incongruence as a block and go through the module on page 85, until you have resolved the lack of congruence.

7   Run through your solution in your mind three times so it's really embedded in your psyche. Then take action and keep to your agreement.

8   Make alterations as necessary and repeat this strategy *every* time you catch yourself being anxious, worried or stressed.
    (NB some people find that if they make a plan to deal with the worst-case scenario it gives them confidence to just get on with things, because they know what to do if the worst happens.)

The root cause of Charlotte's problem is the loss of her mother at a very young age – it has unconsciously embedded itself in her mind that when all is going well it will be taken away from her, resulting in the limiting belief 'I lose the one I love the most' and the associated feelings of sadness and of loss. Once she was able to deal with that, by treating it as a block and getting rid of it, the new strategy was fairly straightforward to implement. Initially she did find herself falling into old patterns and it took her about two months before she was able to fully let go of her old behaviours, but this is very unusual – usually it only takes about a month.

Go through this strategy for yourself and see how it works for you before moving on to the final module in this section, Feedback, to tie everything together and ensure it works.

3 – Feedback

In this module you will learn how to use the fundamental concept of feedback to ensure you achieve the outcome you desire.

Charlotte found the whole process useful and is using the feedback process to help her stay focused on her outcome of having a happy and light-hearted life, free of stress, worry and anxiety.

Go to page 26 now to discover the feedback-not-failure concept and how it can work for you.

Whilst going through the entire process for eliminating anxiety, worry and stress you'll probably have found some of the steps easier to follow than others. That's fine – with practice they'll be like second nature and you'll be doing them all unconsciously. It's wonderful when you notice that you no longer worry, that when you come across a situation that makes you feel uncomfortable the new you just looks at it objectively, acknowledges what is going on externally and internally, takes appropriate action, and just gets on with life's fun journey.

Coping with Life Changes

Module	Title	Page	Exercise time (mins)
2.7.1	Making the most of a big birthday	301	165
2.7.2	Coping with the kids leaving home	305	265
2.7.3	Retiring with flair	311	265
2.7.4	Coping with losing a loved one	317	215

2.7.1 MAKING THE MOST OF A BIG BIRTHDAY

When we're young we tend to look forward to our birthday. It's a day that's full of all the things we love: lots of presents, love and attention, and lovely things to eat and do. Birthdays are a time of fun, laughter and parties.

At one stage or another in our lives, though, this perspective can shift and we start to dread our big day. Usually it starts when the birthday is a large milestone – 30, 40, 50… – sometimes it can also include the '5s' – 25, 35, 45, etc. Commonly it's related to our expectations of where we thought we would be and where we actually are on our milestone birthdays. The birthday is a neon sign, often highlighting that we've not got what we've wanted. It's a highlighter that we've somehow *failed* or let ourselves down.

Sometimes we don't want to be reminded that we are ageing. A big milestone birthday highlights that even more than a standard one – we focus on more sagging, more wrinkles, believing that the best days are gone and it's only going to get worse and worse.

As with many things, we deal with this in our own unique way, some wanting to tactfully forget about it and pretend it's not happening, busily getting on with life; others forcing themselves to have a big do because that's what they think they *should* do or what others want; and some hiding themselves away and feeling sorry for themselves. However we may behave, if we're not looking forward to a birthday it's because there is something within ourselves that we need to pay attention to and deal with – after which we can look forward to our life, with full joy and happiness.

> *Jessica Stevens has just had a big birthday – up until a week before she had decided that she wasn't going to celebrate it much and would just have a small dinner with her family. Her life hasn't*

turned out as she'd planned and she didn't feel like celebrating: she was still single; still renting, and on top of that she'd been ill and was feeling rather sorry for herself and her ageing body.

How could she face her friends knowing she'd failed in every big goal she'd set herself? It would be dishonest to celebrate something that was so obviously negative. She'd failed to achieve her goals and there was no getting around it.

Helen Clarke is a 49-year-old mother of three and is relatively happy with her life except she just doesn't like getting older. She hates what's happening to her body, and the thought of her 50th birthday is truly abhorrent to her – why celebrate the build-up of all these wrinkles and the sagging? And there's no doubt it's going to get worse.

On the face of it one birthday is like any other and yet the way we react to them and their importance can vary greatly. There's always a deeply-rooted cause to our behaviour – the trick is to discover and eliminate it and to move on and fully enjoy life and its every milestone.

TOP TIP
Expand your perspective and look at your life as a whole.

Getting results

Working through the process listed below, in the order given, is an incredibly powerful way of getting to truly appreciate your life and enjoy every birthday that you have.

1   Outcome
2   Strategy
    • Blocks
    • Goals
3   Feedback

1 – Outcome

This is a simple model to highlight whether you are truly ready to look forward to a birthday and enjoy your life. It will flush out any secondary gains you may have from not doing so.

> *Jessica thought celebrating her birthday was a joke until we started working together on this. Her outcome was to enjoy her big birthday and all the subsequent ones – there was no secondary gain stopping her.*

Go to page 57 to work through the Outcome model for yourself. Pay particular attention to the final section, questions 11–16, because this will highlight any secondary gains you have. If you do have secondary gains just note them down and we'll work through them within the next module.

2 – Strategy

There are many ways of enhancing your perspective. The process below is one that has worked for many people.

1   Acknowledge what you are feeling and thinking and congratulate yourself for noticing that this is not what you want in your life and that you want it to change – for you to be happy about your up coming birthday and other future birthdays.
2   Focus within yourself and write down a list of:

a your emotions around the forthcoming birthday;

b the main logical points and facts about the situation and how you may solve the situation; and

c your limiting beliefs (go to page 43 for an explanation of limiting beliefs if you haven't covered these already).

3 Using the list above, deal with your negative emotions and limiting beliefs as blocks by going to the Blocks module on page 85 to work through them.

4 Focus on the main facts from point 2b above and how you may solve the situation. Consider what it is that you are overlooking.

5 Look back on your life so far and make a list of all the things that you like about it that you are taking for granted. Make sure these are things that you really value, the loss of which would detract from your current happiness.

6 Consider all the things you have learned up until now – things that have shaped you, the people that you love, and the things you value.

7 Take as much time as you need to fully appreciate yourself and your life so far.

8 Consider what you want from your future and go through the Goals module on page 65 for each of the things you wish to achieve.

9 Reflect on your past, present and future.

Jessica's whole perspective shifted when she realized the truth about her life: yes she's not yet achieved all the things she wanted to but there is so much more that she's achieved that she has taken for granted – so much that she had to do some of the exercise as a homework. Ultimately what she realized was that she's ambitious, she does want more, and the quality of her life is all about a peaceful and happy frame of mind – being happy effortlessly, just by being!

Go through this strategy for yourself and see how it works for you before moving on to the final module in this section, Feedback, to tie everything together and ensure it works.

3 – Feedback

In this module you will learn how to use the fundamental concept of feedback to ensure you achieve the outcome you desire.

> *Jessica found the feedback concept useful and has also applied it to other areas of her life to help feed the feeling of being effortlessly happy.*

Go to page 26 to discover the feedback-not-failure concept and how it can work for you.

Having gone through all of these modules you will have gained a far greater understanding of what's really important to you, highlighted and got rid of any blocks, and learnt a strategy to help you to truly look forward to all your future birthdays.

2.7.2 COPING WITH THE KIDS LEAVING HOME

Mothers instinctively know that their kids leaving home will be a very important phase in their own lives. They may rationalize it but most have a deep feeling that it'll be a difficult and substantial change. As with most things, depending on your character, your relationship with your partner, and the overall situation you are in, the effect of your children leaving home can vary from a mild sense of loss and of excitement for the future, to one of deep loss and crisis, where the empty-nest syndrome is felt to the very core. For many it's somewhere in the middle, but it generally tends to be more difficult than they expect.

It *is* a big change, however long you've had your children at home. Almost everything about your home life will have revolved around your family – running the day-to-day household, cooking, communicating with and relating to them as a group. When the kids leave there is a void left in their place and the 'unknown' of what happens next. There can also be pressure because of the increased attention on your relationship with your partner.

Audrey Templeton has two daughters, Cynthia and Clara. Audrey has been a housewife and mum for the last 20 years and has fulfilled the role lovingly and in full confidence that she's doing the best thing for her family. But now that Clara, her youngest, has left the house is empty and life feels hollow.

She stays in touch with the girls but that hardly takes any time as they tend to be very brief communications and her days are long and dull. Harry, her husband, works harder than he did when the kids were at home and always seems to be too tired to do anything, so she's getting more and more frustrated.

'I feel so alone. My life feels like its turned upside down. I don't feel like doing anything. I don't want it to be like this!'

Whenever we go through a permanent change we go through substantial stress. Children leaving home is definitely an example of a permanent change and will leave you and your partner, as well as your children, feeling the strain. One way or another you'll get through it – everybody does – but this chapter is designed to ensure you go through it in the best possible way for you.

TOP TIP

Acknowledge that this is a substantial change you are going through – that things will change. With that alteration aim to create the life you want.

Getting results

The process below has helped mothers as well as families make the most of their transition and ensure they do the things that are important to them.

1   Outcome
2   Blocks
3   Strategy
    • Life Purpose
    • Values
    • Circle of Life
    • Goals
4   Feedback

1 – Outcome

This is a simple model to highlight what you truly want and whether you are ready to get it. It will flush out any secondary gains you may have from having an average or bad time after your kids have left home.

Audrey wants to have a focus to her life, as she had when the kids were around. She has no secondary gain but has a lot of fear about the future.

Go to page 57 to work through the outcome model for yourself. Pay particular attention to the final section, questions 11–16, because this will highlight any secondary gains you may have. If you do have secondary gains just note them down and work through them in the next module.

2 – Blocks

Getting rid of limiting blocks is vital to experiencing change in a positive way. This means going to the root cause of all the negative emotions and limiting beliefs that come up for you at this time – highlighting and getting rid of them so that you can move forward without them.

The blocks Audrey worked on are:
- *fear of the unknown;*
- *guilt over what she 'should' have done;*
- *anger with herself about not having done anything before;*
- *sadness about her kids leaving; and*
- *feelings of abandonment.*

Go to page 75 for more information on blocks or, if you prefer, go straight to the exercise on page 85 and start getting rid of the unconscious blocks hindering you from enjoying this phase in your life before moving on to the Strategy module.

3 – Strategy

Getting rid of limitations and blocks leaves you with a clean canvas to start creating an effective strategy for moving forward.

1   Acknowledge what you have done, achieved, and lived, up until now – make a list of all the major things that you have done so far that you're really delighted about/proud of.

2   Celebrate the change with your whole family to mark the occasion for all of you, and perhaps have another celebration just for you and your partner – something symbolic to you that you all think and feel will be good to do.

3   Having a Life Purpose is important at any stage of life and at this stage it's wonderful that you have the time to truly discover yourself and what you really want from your life. Go through the Life Purpose module on page 59 to gain a better understanding of yourself and your life's true meaning.

4   Go through the Values module on page 39 and find out what your life values are for this new phase you are entering into, because then you will have the blue print of what's really important to all of you now.

5   Go through the Circle of Life module on page 11, and the Goals module on page 65, and set yourself short-, medium- and long-term goals that you wish to achieve for all the different areas of your life.

6   If stress, or your relationship with your partner or your children are major challenges then also go through appropriate modules: Keeping your man, or not! (page 122), Maximizing your relationship with your kids (page 190), Eliminating anxiety, worry and stress (page 292).

Audrey loved working together on this because from the start she didn't feel so isolated and alone. She was able to discover what she really wanted and also to understand Harry a lot more – it's obvious to her now that busying himself with work is his way of dealing with the kids leaving. She decided to let him be for a while and focus on herself because when she initially tried to face the subject he just got 'busier'! Audrey had always been rather creative at school and had dreamed of being an artist, so when we worked though the Life Purpose exercise it was very clear that she had taken every opportunity to be creative and was recognized for her talent. She's now choosing between sculpting and water-colour classes at the local college and generally feels far more positive about her life. Even though Harry still works far too much, Audrey's relaxed attitude is starting to rub off on him and he's starting to open up a lot more when he's at home. They're even planning to go away to Seville for a week for a celebratory trip.

Go through this strategy for yourself and see how it works for you before moving on to the final module in this section, Feedback, to tie everything together and ensure it works.

3 – Feedback

In this module you will learn how to use the fundamental concept of feedback to ensure you achieve the outcome you desire.

Audrey found the whole process useful and has decided to use this feedback process to help her fine-tune what she really wants to do.

Go to page 26 now to discover the feedback-not-failure concept and how it can work for you.

Having gone through all of these modules you'll have got rid of any blocks hindering you from making the most of this life change, gained a far greater understanding of what's really important to you (your values), discovered your Life Purpose, and set some goals for your future. You will have also acknowledged and celebrated this life change.

2.7.3 RETIRING WITH FLAIR

Many people look forward to retirement and some even fantasize about it, creating dreams and expectations of what it'll be like to have all the time in the world and the freedom to do anything you want. How far your fantasies have gone and how entrenched they are in your expectations will depend on the problems you've faced throughout your working life and on your character.

Retiring is a big step, whether you are looking forward to it or not. It marks a new phase in your life where there'll be major change in the way you do things. Because it's a permanent change and affects your whole life it's likely to be stressful, and all the more so if the stress is unexpected; retirement is supposed to be so positive that many retirees are surprised when it isn't all they had hoped for.

As with all unknowns there can be a lot of anxiety about what your life will mean once you have retired – what you'll do and who you will be without a job to identify you. And of course you may worry that it's a beacon highlighting that you are in the autumn of your life. If you have a partner he may also be retiring and behaving very differently. Men generally find retirement harder to deal with because they tend to associate who they are with what they do for a living whereas women's identities are more strongly linked to their role within the family. This can all create additional stress at an already challenging time.

Nicola Irving retired a year ago, joining her husband Peter, who had decided to take early retirement. She thought that retiring together would be great because they could start to enjoy all those things they didn't have time for before. She'd planned to travel to warm places off-season, when it was cheaper and less

> busy, so they could really explore and rediscover each other and new places, but Peter doesn't seem to want to do anything.
>
> 'I've never seen him like this,' she says. 'He used to be quite an energetic person, always busy, but now he just wants to play golf or watch TV. I even thought we could do a golfing holiday and I would learn, but he wasn't even keen on that!'

> Carol Peterson decided to retire because she could, and because it felt like the right thing to do. She'd been suffering increasing problems with her health and knew that unless she changed her lifestyle she wouldn't get a retirement at all. Money would be tight but these days flights and holidays are so cheap that she didn't think it was really such an issue.
>
> It's been six months since she quit her job and Carol says 'I don't know where all the time goes but I seem to fritter it away!' She is working more now than she has ever worked before. She is always doing something for someone and what started off as an idea for a good rest has ended up as unpaid work helping everyone else. Surely that's not what retirement is about!

There are two big challenges when you retire. The first is maintaining your sense of identity and self-worth. Work generally gives us a lot of confidence, makes us feel useful and important and, to varying extents, defines us – without a job we no longer 'know' who we are, and we can be at risk of feeling we're not valuable.

The other big challenge is time. Work usually takes up a lot of our time and once we retire we have all that time to do as we please and of course when you're not answerable to anyone it can be very easy to let the days drift into one another, without focus. Most people find that once they've done everything they wanted to do, they get into the 'now what?' stage. Managing your time and getting the most of your retirement is as challenging as it is rewarding.

TOP TIP

Consider what you really want – what's really important to you?

This module is designed to help you get the most from retirement, which gives you the most precious of resources – time.

Getting results

Getting the most from your retirement can be as easy as it is difficult – it's easy because you have the greatest freedom and least responsibility, but it's difficult for exactly the same reason, because its easy to let yourself go and then discover that you aren't very happy with your life. The process below has helped others to achieve what they want to in retirement. (Please note that two people can go through this process and end up doing completely different things.)

1 Outcome
2 Blocks
4 Strategy
   • Life Purpose
   • Values
   • Circle of Life
   • Goals
4 Feedback

1 – Outcome

This is a simple model to highlight what you truly want and whether you are ready to get it – it will flush out any secondary gains you may have from having an average or bad retirement.

> *Nicola wants her retirement to be an exploration – she wants to go to places she's never been to before, try things she's never tried, and in between spend time with her grandchildren. One block came out of this exercise – a belief that 'retirement is a stepping stone to death', which is something her mother used to say all the time.*

Go to page 57 to work through the outcome model for yourself. Pay particular attention to the final section, questions 11–16, because this will highlight any secondary gains you have. If you do have secondary gains just note them down and we'll work through them in the next module.

2 – Blocks

Getting rid of limiting blocks is vital to having a good retirement. This means going to the root cause of all the negative emotions and the limiting beliefs that come up for you at this time – highlighting and getting rid of them so that you can move forward without these blocks.

> *The blocks Nicola worked on are:*
> * *fear of being unwell;*
> * *fear of being alone;*
> * *limiting belief 'I don't deserve much'; and*
> * *limiting belief 'retirement is a stepping stone to death'.*

Go to page 75 for more information on blocks or, if you prefer, go straight to the exercise on page 85 and start getting rid of the unconscious blocks hindering you from having a successful retirement before moving on to the Strategy module.

3 – Strategy

Getting rid of limitations and blocks leaves you with a clean canvas to start creating an effective strategy for having a wonderful retirement:

1   Acknowledge how you have lived and what you have achieved up until now – make a list of all the major things that you have done so far that you're really delighted about/proud of.

2   Celebrate your retirement in whatever way you wish – some like to have a big party, others a quiet holiday, and some want to do both and more. Do what ever you think is the right thing for you as a symbol of saying goodbye to your working life and hello to your life of retirement.

3   Having a Life Purpose is important at any stage of life and at this stage it's wonderful that you have the time to truly discover yourself and what you really want from your life. Go through the Life Purpose module on page 59 to gain a better understanding of yourself and your life's true meaning.

4   Go through the Values module on page 39, and find out what your retirement and life values are, because then you'll have the blue print of what's really important to you now.

5   Go through the Circle of Life and Goals modules on pages 11 and 65, and set yourself short-, medium- and long-term goals that you wish to achieve during your retirement for all the different areas of your life.

6   If stress or your relationship with your partner are major challenges in your retirement also go through the modules Keeping your man, or not! (page 122) and Eliminating anxiety, worry and stress (page 292).

> *Nicola was completely excited and energized about her new life. Before, she wanted to travel and be there for her children and grandchildren, but now she also has a deep respect for herself, for what she has achieved, and has clarity and focus about her aspirations for the future. Going through the 'past' in the Life Purpose exercise really brought it home to her – she knows that her environment is very important to her (so has decided to redecorate her home) and that her children and grandchildren are of the utmost importance to her. She has also let go of the idea that Peter has to go on holiday with her and decided to either find a friend to go with or go on her own. Making plans in line with her Life Purpose (to raise a healthy extended family) and values for the future was invigorating for her – for example, one of her goals is to spend quality time together with each of the people she loves the most, doing what they both fancy doing together. This goal seemed so simple and she would gone some way towards it, but if the past was anything to go by, other 'things' would have got in the way. Now it has pride of place and is an important goal for her to focus on.*

Go through this strategy for yourself and see how it works for you before moving on to the final module in this section, Feedback, to tie everything together and ensure it works.

3 – Feedback

In this module you will learn how to use the fundamental concept of feedback to ensure you achieve the outcome you desire.

> *Nicola found the whole process useful and has decided to use this feedback process to help her to fine-tune what she really wants to do.*

Go to page 26 now to discover the feedback-not-failure concept and how it can work for you.

Having gone through all of these modules you'll have got rid of any blocks hindering you from enjoying your retirement, gained far greater understanding of what's really important to you about retiring (your values) and your Life Purpose, and set some goals for your future. You will also have acknowledged and celebrated the change in your life, ensuring that you are really ready to start your retirement with flare.

2.7.4 COPING WITH LOSING A LOVED ONE

Losing someone you love can be very difficult to deal with, whether it's the dearest of friends or a beloved relative. When we love someone and he or she is no longer there we are at a loss. How can we cope without them? What do we do now? The loss cuts to the very heart of us and we are left alone with the pain, the memories, and the screaming awareness of our own mortality.

How we deal with bereavement depends on our character, the situation we are in, and our relationship with the the person who has died. Even so, there are some similarities between all experiences of bereavement.

Sheila lost her husband at 70, after 50 years of marriage. The last few years had been incredibly difficult for her – after his first stroke he was unable to walk, talk or feed himself, which was difficult enough, but he also kept her up most of the night with his needs and wants, so for five years she's only slept 30 minutes at a time. Despite the difficulties, though, she still longs for him. She can't believe that he has finally, truly gone. Feelings of hurt and anger manifest themselves at the strangest of times. 'Why

is it that others have their husbands, alive and well, and mine had to die early? Why couldn't we have had a few more years together? Why is it that we couldn't have travelled a bit more?'
The reality that he's gone has not fully sunk in, and night-time, when everyone else has gone, is the toughest time of all. Even though Sheila has the time to sleep now, she can't – a few hours' sleep is all she can manage and the rest of the time she sits and stews in her unhappy loneliness. Feelings of guilt about the things she had and hadn't done are her only companions.
The thought of her husband's body being buried in the earth horrifies and torments her. When it's all too much she starts to clean and tidy the house – anything to keep her distracted, to keep the torment away.

Sarah lost a dear friend when she was 35. She had loved him like a brother and although she mourned his death she was also happy to rejoice in his life rather than focus on her loss as other people seemed to be doing. She'd known an incredibly wonderful person and the world was a richer place for his having been there. Despite it all, though, she still felt incredibly guilty because she hadn't seen him before he died. If only she'd made that visit, if only …

When we lose a loved one it can have the most devastating effect on our life. We go through so much emotionally: grief, a huge sense of loss, loneliness, anger, guilt, frustration with life and the unfairness of it all, and fear of our own mortality. It can turn our world upside-down. Equally it can also be the chaos before clarity. There is nothing that focuses the mind more about life than death. When we lose a loved one it brings home the reality of our own mortality, and that in turn can help us to focus on what's really important in our lives. It's a powerful positive outcome to what is an inherently painful situation.

Many people find that they behave out of character after a bereavement, that they're not themselves. Some want to wallow in the hurt, loss and misery; others may go into denial and focus on something completely different; others choose to go out and celebrate life, making the most of it before their time comes; and there are those that just want to be, to let it wash all over them. Whatever your response is, be assured that it's OK – we all handle things in different ways.

TOP TIP

Give yourself, and others, the time and space to grieve in your own unique way.

Getting results

There is no single 'right' way to deal with bereavement. It's highly individual and determined by the character of the griever, the situation around the loss, and the relationship with the deceased. Nothing can take back your loss but the process below has helped others through their grief.

Before you start the process itself, try to follow the points below.

1   Accept that we all show our grief in different ways and that it's a time of stress.
2   Let the wounds breathe – when wounds are fresh they need to breathe and rest. Give yourself and others time.
3   Take care of yourself physically, even when you really don't feel like it or want to.

When you have had enough grieving time and are ready to move forward, go through the following modules at your own pace:

1   Outcome
2   Blocks
3   Perception Enhancer
4   Circle of Empowerment
5   Feedback

1 – Outcome

This model will help you to move forward with your life and/or uncover any hidden secondary gains from staying in a bereaved state.

> *Sheila wants to move on but is scared. After 50 years of marriage the fear of being alone is overwhelming. If she's a vulnerable victim her son and others will take pity on her and she won't be alone – anything is better than being alone. Realizing and vocalizing her fear made it somehow easier to deal with. It was no longer an intangible feeling but a concept she could work with.*

Go to page 57 to work through the outcome model for yourself. Pay particular attention to the final section, questions 11–16, because this will highlight any secondary gains you have. If you do have secondary gains just note them down and work through them in the next module.

2 – Blocks

Getting rid of limiting blocks is vital to helping you to move on with your life. This means going to the root cause of all the negative emotions and the limiting beliefs that come up for you at this time – highlighting and getting rid of them so that you can move forward.

The blocks Sheila worked on are:
- *sadness;*
- *hurt; and*
- *fear of being alone.*

Go to page 75 for more information on blocks or, if you prefer, go straight to the exercise on page 85 and start getting rid of the unconscious blocks hindering you. Then move on to the Perception Enhancer module.

3 — Perception Enhancer

This module helps you to connect to and communicate with the part of you that knows and understands the deceased best. It enables you to say those things that you may not have said whilst they were alive, and helps you to achieve closure and move on with your life.

When Sheila went through this model she found it very difficult to focus, and when she did she burst into tears. His advice to her was 'Don't hurt yourself, dear Sheila. Get on with your life.' She could barely get the words out but she knew it was true – he had loved her dearly and could never bear it when she was upset.

Go to page 93 for more information on perception enhancement or, if you prefer, go straight to the exercise on page 94 and work through it before moving on to the Circle of Empowerment module.

3 — Circle of Empowerment

Circle of Empowerment is a model that helps to build confidence and resources at a time when everything may seem unstable. It's very useful to be able to draw upon your inner strength to help you at this very difficult time.

> *Sheila loved this model because she discovered she had far more experiences of being confident than she'd thought. It gave her hope that she might be all right on her own after all, and if not, she would change her environment so she was.*

Go to page 89 for more information on the Circle of Empowerment or, if you prefer, go straight to the exercise on page 90 and work through it before moving onto the final module in this section, Feedback, to tie everything together and ensure it works.

4 – Feedback

In this module you will learn how to use the fundamental concept of feedback to ensure you achieve the outcome you desire. Use the principles of this module to do what's best for you, and those you love, until you are feeling comfortable.

> *Sheila found it useful to know that there was more to the work we were doing together and that it would carry on. She decided to do a little review every week to remember Peter and to check on herself, to ensure she was OK and on the right path.*

Go to page 26 now to discover the feedback-not-failure concept and how it can work for you.

Bereavement is a difficult stage to go through and having given yourself time and space to grieve, and having gone through these modules, you will be in as good a place as can be for moving forward and making the most of your life, whilst appreciating and celebrating the unique life and love of the deceased.

Conclusion to Part 2

The solutions offered in Part 2 are useful for getting quick and effective results with the challenges you face in your life. Even though the solutions are general, and you may have to tailor them a little for your own specific needs, they are still a long way from the basic techniques in Part 1, and I very much hope they have helped you get to the heart of the issues you face. The great thing about the Part 2 modules is that you only need to go through the ones that are valid for you at any given time, and can refer to them just when you need them.

If there were just one thing that I'd wish you to take away with you as a result of using this book, it would be the overarching theories for achieving whatever you want in life:

- Have a clear and positive outcome in mind.
- Be true to yourself.
- Take 100% responsibility.
- Go to the root cause.
- Feed back your insights and adapt your behaviour until you achieve your outcome.

More than Men and Make-up
– Conclusion

The aim of this book has been to share with you the concepts and techniques that I've seen work for others in the past, whilst ensuring that you remain your own expert on your life, and that you maximize your uniqueness. I hope it has helped you to realize that only *you* are the true expert. Yes, there are techniques you can use that tend to work across the board, but ultimately you are unique and only one person can know that uniqueness inside out – and that's you.

People sometimes ask me whether I use these techniques myself and, if I do, do I have the perfect life? The truth is that I love these techniques because they have given me a structure to work within that's effective and powerful. Life is no more perfect than it was before but I've witnessed a shift in my perception that makes me see it as more perfect – I'm a more flexible and positive person and I've got choices about what I do and when I do it. Even now, if I have a negative emotion (which is rare these days but does happen sometimes) but I don't want to deal with it straight away, I can choose to experience it with the knowledge that I can get rid of it whenever I want to. Knowing that you have choice, that you can control your thoughts and feelings if you wish to, that in fact you are in control of your life, is an incredibly powerful thing.

As I mentioned in the introduction to this book, this is the first time that these techniques have been put together in this way, so it's really important to me that I take the feedback from your experiences to make it even better next time. Therefore, when you use this book for specific challenges in your life, I would truly appreciate it if you could take a few minutes to send your feedback to me at mmmu@odyssey-solutions. com. I'd most like to know:

- the things you really liked and that worked well for you;
- what perhaps didn't work so well and what you'd like to see changed – ideally with specific suggestions, to ensure I fully understand what you mean; and
- overall, what you thought about the book.

I wish you all the very best for the rest of your unique journey and I hope that you will continue to find this book useful as you progress through your life, gaining clarity and focus at times when there appears to be none, and benefiting from your increased choice and flexibility about the way you interpret and live your life.

Appendices

APPENDIX A – GUIDANCE CHART

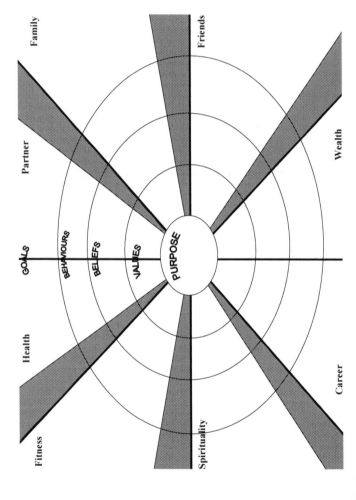

APPENDIX B – ONE AREA CHART

Area of Life : _____

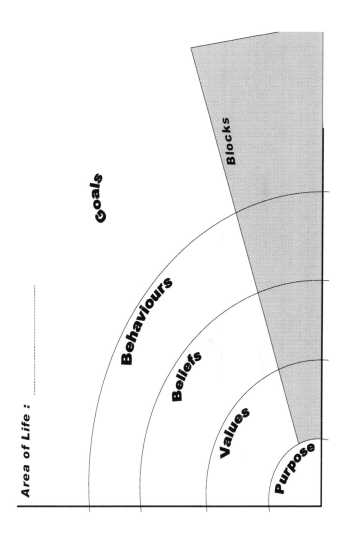

APPENDIX C – DISCOVERING YOUR BEHAVIOURS

	0–7	7–13	13–18	18–21…
What significant thing happened?				
How did you behave?				

	21–26	26–30	30–35	35–40…
What significant thing happened?				
How did you behave?				

APPENDIX D – PAST PURPOSEFUL BEHAVIOURS

	0–7	7–13	13–18	18–21…
What was the accomplishment?				
How did you behave?				
What did you actually do?				
What skills were demonstrated?				
What feelings were associated with it?				
What was it about the environment you liked?				
What was it about the people you liked?				
What does this accomplishment do for you?				

APPENDIX D – PAST PURPOSEFUL BEHAVIOURS (CONT.)

	21–26	26–30	30–35	35–40…	
What was the accomplishment?					
How did you behave?					
What did you actually do?					
What skills were demonstrated?					
What feelings were associated with it?					
What was it about the environment you liked?					
What was it about the people you liked?					
What does this accomplishment do for you?					

APPENDIX E – OUTCOME MODEL ANSWERS FOR SARAH

1 What is it you really want? (Be specific and state it in a positive way.)

To be in a loving, fulfilling relationship with one man for the rest of my life. He will be loving, loyal, honest, fun and take care of me.

2 Consider where you are now – really *connect* with it. What's your current situation? What do you see, hear and feel around you right now in relation to the outcome you want?

I am single, feel alone, as if something in my life is missing, see others in relationships and it hurts to be alone. I hear my friends saying I will find someone but I don't believe them – I don't think I am good enough to be in a loving relationship.

3 When you get your outcome, what will you see, hear and feel around you? Imagine you have it now and visualize yourself living that life; see yourself in the picture of what it would be like.

I will see him and things around me that indicate I am with him. I will hear his voice and others talking about us – saying what a great couple we make. I will feel happy and be smiling. He will also be smiling. I can't quite imagine seeing him as I don't know what he would look like but I can sense him.

4 Consider your outcome. How will you know when you have it? What will you need to see, hear, feel and do to know you have it?

I will be in a relationship and have a 100% feeling that it is absolutely right, be more relaxed about things and more carefree.

5 What will this outcome enable you to do?

To be happy and get on with my life, have a family with a 'Daddy'.

6   Is the outcome only for you? If not, who else is it for? Where, when, how and with whom do you want it?
He will also be delighted about it. My parents will also be happy. But ultimately it's for me.

7   Consider your outcome. What resources do you need to be able to achieve it (e.g. skills, empowering emotions, strategies/processes)?
To be confident, to be clear on what I want and have faith that I shall get it.

8   Of these resources, which do you already have and which do you need in order to achieve your outcome? (Consider if you have done something like this before? Do you know someone else who has that you can learn from?)
I am confident in my career but not my personal life. I have a couple of friends who are very good in this area.

9   Act as if you have achieved your outcome. (As they say in business, 'Perform/dress to the level above and you will get promoted'.)
I can act confident and carefree.

[10 **Relax** even more – be aware of your body. Feel each muscle relaxing, and your body becoming heavier with each exhalation.]

11 Consider your outcome. What will you gain if you get it?
I will gain my partner for life and be able to get on with my life – get a new home, etc.

12 Consider your outcome. What will you lose if you get it?
I'll lose the excitement of being single.

13   Consider your outcome. What will happen if you get it?
I'll be happy, settled. But something inside me dies.

14   Consider your outcome. What will happen if you don't get it?
I'll need to explore further – the excitement of the struggle and chase. Opportunities are endless – I could have so many different lives! When you're attached you know what you have got.

15   Consider your outcome. What won't happen if you get it?
Excitement.

16   Consider your outcome. What won't happen if you don't get it?
Happiness.

APPENDIX F – THE GLIDE METHOD

The Glide Method is a shorthand process of getting rid of blocks. It's what I generally use myself and with clients and it's the kind of shorthand you may want to create for yourself so that you have the best possible solution for you.

Appropriate setting

- Have an attitude of curiosity and fun.
- Be honest and true to yourself.
- Have the beliefs that:
  - life is a journey;
  - you can do it;
  - whatever comes up is OK; and
  - this process will be effortless, interesting and quick.
- This will only work if your conscious and unconscious minds work together in a fully integrated partnership.
- Be open to feedback.
- **Relax** – if at any stage you are finding the process difficult then relax even further, because it will make it easier.

Getting rid of blocks

1 Confirm it is OK, safe and good to let go of the block.

2 Fire up the problem by going back to past experiences where the block has been an issue; also consider possible future situations where it may be a problem.

3 Get a plain sheet of paper and, in the centre of the sheet, write a description of the block. Ask yourself the following questions:

   a 'What is it that I need to know, the knowing of which will allow me to let go of the problem?'

   As the answers (these are also blocks) pop into your mind, write them down on the paper around the block. Just intuitively follow which location is right for each.

b 'Is there anything else I need to know, the knowing of which will allow me to get rid of this block?'

  If you get a 'yes', write down what it is; if not move on to the next question.

c 'If I get rid of these blocks will my main block go away?'

  Unless you have a 'yes' then you need to find out what's stopping you and deal with it directly.

4 Thank your unconscious mind for assisting you in this process.

5 Prioritize the things that actively have to be worked on by asking the following questions:

a 'What are the 1–3 key things that, if I got rid of them, would allow me to let go of the problem?'

  Allow your mind to highlight them – they will just pop into your mind.

b 'What is the most effective one to work with first?'

  One will pop out as the answer.

6 Get rid of them in order of priority. Be respectful of what comes up and go with the flow.

7 Ensure the block has gone by asking directly: 'Has the block gone, yes or no?' Unless you get an unequivocal 'yes' then you still need to work on it.

8 Thank your unconscious mind for assisting you in this process.

Confirming and creating positive empowering strategies

1 Consider times in the past when the block has been an issue and see how those experiences would be different now.

2 Consider times in the future that, if you still had the block, would be a problem and see how the situation differs now.

NB You want to be 100% confident that your block has gone and you have a new way of behaving for the future.

APPENDIX G – HABIT 1: POSITIVE THOUGHT HABIT

Aim: To help you increase the control you have over your mind and to empower you.

Duration: 10 minutes

What you need:

- an open mind
- an attitude of curiosity and fun
- a safe, quiet environment, free of distractions and disruptions

Important point: Be relaxed to get the most from the exercise.

If I said to you 'Don't think of a pink Christmas tree – no really, don't think of a pink Christmas tree' you can't help but go to your mind's eye and visualize the image of a pink tree. Some of you may even turn it into a different colour tree because you have processed it just that little bit more literally and thoroughly. Either way you thought of a tree, and probably a pink one! This is because our minds can only hold positive representations (pictures/images). It's impossible to *not* think of something because attempting to do so will always conjure up the very thought we're avoiding. This is why, when you say to a child 'Don't touch that hot stove', you're actually giving a suggestion to touch the stove. As we get older we tend to adapt this to our own advantage for some things by learning to translate what is being said, so a statement like 'Don't forget your keys' is unconsciously translated into 'Remember your keys'.

The Positive Thought Habit is designed specifically so that you can start to master your negative thoughts and create positive ones out of them. The challenge is to notice negative thoughts and deal with them as you go through your daily activity. What's likely to happen initially is that you'll only realize that you've been dwelling on negative thoughts *after* the event. Then as you become more practised you'll notice them *at* the event, then finally, just *before* the event. Whenever you realize it's happening, just follow the steps below.

1   Congratulate yourself for noticing it.

2   Note it down as a block and get rid of it at the appropriate time.

3   Dwell on a positive thought twice as long as you did the negative thought.

4   Dwell on your Life Purpose and goals for a few minutes.

This may initially seem like a lot of effort, but it only takes a minute or two and what's interesting is that, by doing it consistently, there will come a point when you'll do it automatically, and only realize it afterwards, in the same way that you drove unconsciously for the first time and realized that you had no recollection of how you got from one location to the other.

Positive thinking is fundamental to utilizing the power of your mind, because it's essential to have clear communication between your conscious and unconscious minds. Remember you've had your habits for a long time, some that go back to your early youth, so be gentle with yourself and persevere. It *will* make a big difference to you and the people around you.

APPENDIX H – HABIT 2: VISUALIZING YOUR GOALS

Aim: To help you stay focused. To motivate you and allow you to reflect on, and appreciate, how much you've achieved.

Duration: 10 minutes

What you need:

- an open mind
- an attitude of curiosity and fun
- a safe, quiet environment, free of distractions and disruptions
- your One Area Charts

Important point: Be relaxed to get the most from the exercise.

This is a very powerful way to increase the 'pull' towards your objectives on a daily basis, because it ensures that you're reminded of the goals you've set for yourself. For a small investment of a few minutes of effort every day you can really stack up your 'pull' energy.

Every morning (and/or evening) go through the steps below.

1 Put all your One Area Charts together so that you can see all your goals easily.

2 Sit comfortably, and be aware of your body relaxing – feel each muscle relaxing and your body becoming heavier with each exhalation.

3 When you're totally relaxed think about each of your goals one by one.

4 Taking the first goal, imagine you have achieved it. Consider you have it now – dwell on how it feels, the sounds you hear, what you see, and the impact it has had on your life. Have the feeling flow through you.

5 Consider your past in relation to this goal – the personal journey you have completed, the discoveries you've made, and the things you've learned. Go back as far as you need to go, to see the progress you have made.

6 Come back to now with the satisfaction and knowledge of how far you've come, how wonderful it feels to be making progress, and how great it feels to have your goal.

7 Repeat this process for all your goals.

Sometimes you'll be able to focus completely, and at other times it'll be disrupted with other unrelated thoughts, or you may have additional insights. Just relax and focus, see what happens and enjoy it – it's a great experience.

Equally, every so often (once a month, once a quarter or annually) it's very powerful to just look back to where you were a while ago and take time to appreciate how much progress you've made and the discoveries you've had. Doing so will help you to stay motivated and stick with your goal by increasing the 'pull' towards it, and encourage you to take consistent, persistent action until you get it.

Bibliography

Brody, L.R. & Hall, J.A. (1993) Gender and Emotion. In M. Lewis & J.M. Haviland (Eds), *Handbook of Emotions*. New York: Guilford Press.

Chopra, Deepak (1990) *Quantam Healing: Exploring the Frontiers of Mind/Body Medicine*, p. 44. New York: Bantam New Age Books.

Cox, T. (1978) *Stress*. London: Macmillan Education.

Davison, G. & Neale, J. (1994) *Abnormal Psychology*, 6th edn. New York: Wiley.

Gross, Richard (2005) *Psychology: The Science of Mind and Behaviour*, 2nd edn, p. 347. London: Hodder & Stoughton.

Hill, Napoleon (1960) *Think and Grow Rich*. New York: Fawcett Books.

Lerner, M. J. (1980) *The Belief in a Just World: A Fundamental Delusion*. New York: Plenum.

Litvinoff, Sarah (1994) *The Relate Guide to Better Relationships: Practical Ways to Make Your Love Last from the Experts in Marriage*, p. 155. London: Vermilion.

Massey, Morris (1979) *The People Puzzle*. Reston, VA: Reston Publishing Company.

Mehrabian, Albert. (1980) Silent Messages: Implicit Communication of Emotions and Attitudes, 2nd edn. London: Wadsworth.

Pavlov, I.P. (1927) *Conditioned Reflexes*. Oxford: Oxford University Press.

Rogers, C.R .(1961) *On Becoming a Person*. Boston: Houghton Mifflin.

Schliefer, S.J., Keller, S.E., Camerion, M., Thornton, J.C., and Stein, M. (1983). Suppression of lymphocyte stimulation following bereavement. *Journal of the American Medical Association*, **250**, 374–377.

Printed in the United States
By Bookmasters